The Grenada Invasion

The Grenada Invasion

Politics, Law, and
Foreign Policy Decisionmaking

Robert J. Beck

Westview Press

BOULDER • SAN FRANCISCO • OXFORD

E
183.8
G84
B43
1993

Copyright © 1993 by Westview Press, Inc.

Published in 1993 in the United States of America by Westview Press, Inc., 5500 Central Avenue, Boulder, Colorado 80301-2877, and in the United Kingdom by Westview Press, 36 Lonsdale Road, Summertown, Oxford OX2 7EW

Library of Congress Cataloging-in-Publication Data
The Grenada invasion : politics, law, and foreign policy decisionmaking
    / by Robert J. Beck
    p.   cm.
  Includes bibliographical references and index.
  ISBN 0-8133-8709-4
  1. United States—Foreign relations—Grenada.
2. Grenada—Foreign relations—United States.
3. Grenada—History—American invasion, 1983.   I. Title.
183.8.G84B43   1993
327.730729845—dc20   93-6432
                                                                                  CIP

Printed and bound in the United States of America

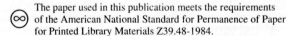 The paper used in this publication meets the requirements
of the American National Standard for Permanence of Paper
for Printed Library Materials Z39.48-1984.

10   9   8   7   6   5   4   3   2   1

CONIUGI
DILECTISSIMAE

Contents

Acknowledgments

This work could never have been concluded without the invaluable assistance of many individuals and institutions. First, I would like to thank all those former Reagan administration officials who agreed to answer my questions about the "Urgent Fury" decisionmaking process. I am particularly indebted here to Francis McNeil, Langhorne "Tony" Motley, and Milan Bish. Second, I must acknowledge the consistent support of Georgetown University and my Government Department mentors: William V. O'Brien, Robert J. Lieber, and Anthony Clark Arend. Professor O'Brien instilled in me a love of international law, Professor Lieber convinced me that "mere mortals" could write books, and Professor Arend ensured that this mere mortal did write one. Professor Abi Williams of Georgetown's School of Foreign Service graciously agreed to serve as a reader of my study, and Georgetown's Graduate School provided financial support for my preliminary research. Third, I must thank the University of Virginia for helping to fund the completion of my project, and my colleagues in the Woodrow Wilson Department of Government and Foreign Affairs for their constructive editorial suggestions, especially Timothy Prinz and John Duffield. Fourth, I wish to recognize a number of other scholars whose advice has informed my work: Christopher Joyner; Alfred Rubin; Richard Ullman; and Abram Chayes. Next, I am grateful to Jennifer Knerr, Eric Wright, Thomas Kennedy, Todd Wiedemann, Lynn Arts, and Laurie Milford for their technical and production assistance. Finally, I must express my profound gratitude to my family for their unfailing love and encouragement. My parents, Mr. and Mrs. Robert C. Beck, Jr., provided an environment extremely well-suited to my initial research and writing. My brother and his wife, Mr. and Mrs. William J. Beck, somehow managed always to sound enthusiastic about my rather arcane endeavors. And Bernadette N. Beck never doubted that her husband would complete this study, even when he had grown weary or disheartened.

Robert J. Beck

Preface

This book examines the influence of international law on foreign policy decisionmaking. It is motivated by two principal concerns. First, this study embraces Roger Fisher's premise that "if we want law and legal institutions to play larger and more effective roles in coping with international conflict, we shall need to understand more clearly the roles they now play."[1] Professor Fisher's argument, made in 1974, is perhaps even more compelling today when the twin notions of "New World Order" and "the rule of law" are routinely invoked by pundits, diplomats, and presidents. Second, this study seeks to help bridge the gap between the fields of international law and political science which emerged in the post-World War II period and which continues to plague the contemporary study of international relations.[2] For too long, political scientists have insufficiently appreciated the significance of the law's impact upon international politics, assuming with Dean Acheson that "law simply does not deal with ... questions of ultimate power — power that comes close to the sources of sovereignty."[3] Similarly, legal scholars have too often neglected the political underpinnings of international law, preferring to concentrate instead on the more familiar question of the law's substance.[4] But, as this study will show, law cannot fully be comprehended without reference to politics, nor politics without reference to law.

This book focuses specifically on the Reagan administration's decision to invade Grenada. Why examine the Grenada episode? After all, in the years since the American intervention, Grenada has returned to relative obscurity and Reagan to private life. The Soviet Union has ceased to exist, and democracy has come to numerous formerly communist states. Despite the advent of a post-Cold War era, the Grenada case offers several conspicuous advantages to students of international law's policy-relevance. First, President Reagan's 1983 policy choice involved the recourse to armed force. Such "use of force" decisions constitute the most challenging test of international law's efficacy. Second, the decision to launch Operation "Urgent Fury" was made within a brief, bounded time frame and was prompted by distinct, relatively straight-forward circumstances. Hence, its reconstruction is far simpler than are reconstructions of other foreign policy decisions made incrementally over longer periods in response to more complicated events. Moreover, given the brevity of the Grenada deliberations, it is less difficult to isolate law's role in the policy process. Finally, until very recently one could not reconstruct with any balance, scope, or nuance the Grenada decision-making process. Now, however, the departure of Reagan administration officials from government service has made personal, detailed reports of the Grenada episode more readily available, and thus, has greatly facilitated the scholar's task.[5] Memoir accounts, for example, have been written by President Reagan's National Security Assistant for Latin America, by his special emissary to the Caribbean, by his Secretaries of Defense and State, by his White House Counsellor, and even by Ronald Reagan himself. Meanwhile, formerly tight-lipped officials have become increasingly willing to discuss candidly an event that has faded from popular consciousness, but not yet from their own. Only in such a congenial environment can a proper study of law's policy-relevance be undertaken.

Three primary methodological propositions inform this book. First, this study accepts Hedley Bull's definition of "international law" as "a body of rules which binds states and other agents in world politics in their relations with one another and is considered to have the status of law."[6] The specific "rules" upon which this work will concentrate are the *jus ad bellum* provisions of the United Nations Charter. Second, this study assumes that the motives underlying foreign policy decisions are best found not by focusing on a monolithic "state" or its "government," but rather by examining very closely the actual process of decision-making.[7] This inquiry begins, therefore, with the presumption that individual persons can significantly influence policy outcomes. Third, like a number of prior analyses of international law's policy-relevance,[8] this one assumes that precise measurement of law's role in the decision-making process is virtually impossible. It allows that the persuasive force of legal arguments and their ultimate efficacy "will depend on infinitely complex moral, psychological, and interpersonal processes of group decisionmaking," and hence, that "quantification must always elude us."[9] This limitation need not deter the scholar, however, for as Professor Fisher has cogently observed: "What one needs to know is not *how much* did law affect a given decision, but *how*."[10]

R.J.B.

Notes

1.   Roger Fisher's "Foreword" to Abram Chayes, *The Cuban Missile Crisis: International Crises and the Role of Law* (New York: Oxford University Press, 1974), p. v.

2.   See David Bederman's review of Friedrich Kratochwil's *Rules, Norms, and Decisions* in *American Journal of International Law* 84 (July 1990): 775-777; Francis A. Boyle, *World Politics and International Law* (Durham, NC: Duke University Press, 1985); Anne-Marie Slaughter Burley, "International Law and International Relations Theory," *American Journal of International Law* 87 (April 1993): 205-239; and Richard Falk, "Foreword," in David P. Forsythe, *The Politics of International Law: U.S. Foreign Policy Reconsidered* (Boulder, Colo.: Lynne Rienner Publishers, 1990), pp. xiii-xvi.

3.   Dean Acheson, *Proceedings of the American Society of International Law* 57 (1963): 14. See also Stanley Hoffmann, "International Law and the Control of Force," in Karl Deutsch and Stanley Hoffmann, eds. *The Relevance of International Law* (Garden City, NY: Anchor Books, 1971), pp. 34-66.

4.   According to Professor Boyle, "too often public international law has been taught as if it were just another black-letter law course whose subject matter was about as straight-forward as the federal tax code." Francis A. Boyle, *American Journal of International Law* 83 (April 1989): 403.

5.   See Chapter One for complete citation of memoir accounts and interviews by the author.

6.   Hedley Bull, *The Anarchical Society: A Study of Order in World Politics* (New York: Columbia University Press, 1977). This study rejects the notion that law should be defined in terms of "the probable perceptions of participants [in decisionmaking]" or of "the normative expectations of those who are politically effective in the world community." See Thomas Ehrlich, *Cyprus 1958-1967* (New York: Oxford University Press, 1974), p. 4; and W. Michael Reisman and Andrew Willard, eds., *International Incidents: The Law That Counts in World Politics* (Princeton: Princeton University Press, 1988).

7.   My study's approach will depart, for example, from that taken by Professor Henkin. See Louis Henkin, *How Nations Behave: Law and Foreign Policy* (New York: Columbia University Press, 1979).

8.   See Georges Abi-Saab, *The United Nations Operation in the Congo 1960-1964* (New York: Oxford University Press, 1978); Robert R. Bowie, *Suez 1956* (New York: Oxford University Press, 1974); Chayes, *The Cuban Missile Crisis*; Scott Davidson, *Grenada: A Study in Politics and the Limits of International Law* (Aldershot: Avebury, 1987); Ehrlich, *Cyprus*; Roger Fisher, *Points of Choice* (New York: Oxford University Press, 1978); Forsythe, *The Politics of International Law*; and Louis Henkin, "Comment," in Ehrlich, *Cyprus*, pp. 128-133. The works of Abi-Saab, Bowie, Chayes, Ehrlich, and

Fisher comprise a series on "International Crises and the Role of Law" sponsored by the American Society of International Law.

The "international incidents" approach advocated by Professor Reisman would appear at least implicitly to reject the possibility of quantifying law's influence. See Reisman and Willard, eds., *International Incidents*.

9.   Abram Chayes, *The Cuban Missile Crisis*, p. 103.

10.   Fisher, "Foreword," p. v.

1

International Legality and Use of Force Decisionmaking

Grenada, we were told, was a friendly island paradise for tourism. Well, it wasn't. It was a Soviet-Cuban colony, being readied as a major military bastion to export terror and undermine democracy. We got there just in time.[1]
— Ronald Reagan, October 1983

If you are going to pronounce a new law that "wherever there is communism imposed against the will of the people then the U.S. shall enter," then we are going to have really terrible wars in the world.[2]
— Margaret Thatcher, October 1983

At 9:07 A.M. on October 25, 1983, Ronald Reagan walked into the White House briefing room accompanied by Eugenia Charles, the Prime Minister of Dominica. As the current chair of the Organization of Eastern Caribbean States (OECS) stood beside him, the President made a startling announcement: "Early this morning, forces from six Caribbean democracies and the United States began a landing or landings on the island of Grenada in the eastern Caribbean." The United States had taken this decisive step, Reagan explained, for three reasons: to protect innocent lives, including those of almost a thousand Americans; to forestall further chaos; and to assist in the restoration of conditions of law and order and of government institutions to the island. Ultimately, he concluded, the U.S./OECS "collective action" had been "forced" on the United States by events that had "no precedent in the eastern Caribbean and no place in any civilized society."[3]

Of the many persons listening to President Reagan that early Tuesday morning, few had ever heard of Grenada, a sovereign state of 133 square miles and approximately 110,000 inhabitants.[4] Perhaps even fewer had heard of Dominica and its hard-boiled Prime Minister, Eugenia Charles. And certainly, only a handful of experts at the time could correctly identify the OECS, the regional grouping that had formally requested American military assistance on October 23.[5] Hence, Reagan's brief remarks left many questions, both grave and trivial, to be answered. From the outset, however, one fact was apparent to virtually everyone: the United States had sent its troops into combat for the first time since the Vietnam War.[6]

Reaction on the island of Grenada to the American "rescue mission" was overwhelmingly positive.[7] A CBS poll of Grenadian public opinion, for example, found that ninety-one percent of those contacted were "glad the United States troops [had come] to Grenada."[8] Similarly, by early November, Reagan's decision to employ American armed force had won broad support in the United States: an ABC-*Washington Post* survey showed seventy-one percent in favor and only twenty-two percent opposed.[9] Outside Grenada and the United States, however, the story was quite different.[10]

Within a week of the invasion, seventy-nine governments had condemned, repudiated or in some way expressed disapproval of the operation.[11] As one might expect, the Soviet Union was among the first to voice a scathing denunciation. TASS, the official Soviet news agency, called Reagan "a modern Napoleon," devoid of conscience and simple-minded; it characterized the American action as "an act of open international banditry."[12] Shortly thereafter, the United Nations General Assembly joined in the attack, voting 108 to 9 to condemn the American action as a "violation of international law." The November 2 resolution was approved by an even larger majority than that which had earlier condemned the Soviet invasion of Afghanistan.[13] More surprising, however, was the reaction of British Prime Minister Margaret Thatcher, Reagan's most staunch supporter in Europe and a strident anti-communist. In a Sunday phone-in radio program on the BBC World Service, the Tory leader remarked, "If you are going to pronounce a new law that 'wherever there is communism imposed against the will of the people then the U.S. shall enter,' then we are going to have really terrible wars in the world."[14]

For two reasons, the General Assembly resolution and Prime Minister Thatcher's terse assessment are especially provocative. First, they illustrate well the depth and breadth of international disapproval that the Grenada intervention engendered. Second, and more importantly, they draw attention to two fundamental questions raised by the American use of force in Grenada. Was the American action legal? And what was the relationship between international law and the Reagan administration decisionmaking process?

Since October of 1983, the question of the Grenada invasion's permissibility under the *jus ad bellum*, the international law relating to the state's recourse to armed force, has been the subject of no little controversy.[15] Not surprisingly, a wide array of scholars has entered the fray, armed with an equally wide array of legal arguments. Over the years, the American action has been condemned as illegal on a host of grounds, *inter alia*: (1) as a violation of the U.N. Charter's prescriptions on the use of force; (2) as a violation of the OAS Charter; and (3) as inconsistent with the OECS Charter. Likewise, the U.S. operation has been defended on a number of grounds: (1) as an intervention in response to an "invitation by lawful authority," the Grenadian Governor-General; (2) as "regional peace-keeping" authorized by competent regional treaties and grounded in Article 52 of the U.N. Charter; (3) as a "protection of nationals abroad"; and (4) as a "humanitarian intervention."[16] Such diversity of legal interpretation reflects general disagreement over the proper understanding of the contemporary *jus ad bellum*,[17] and specific disagreement over the facts surrounding the Grenada invasion.[18]

While the question of the international legality of Operation "Urgent Fury" is a worthwhile one, it is far from novel and therefore will not be considered in any great detail here. However, the question of the role played by international law in the Reagan administration's decision to launch "Urgent Fury" has thus far received inadequate scholarly attention.[19] Indeed, only Scott Davidson, a Lecturer in Law at the University of Hull, has yet attempted in a systematic way to divine how law influenced Reagan's Grenada decision. Although his 1987 work, *Grenada: A Study in Politics and the Limits of International Law*, is admirable in many other respects, Davidson's analysis of "the role which law played" is based on "interpolation,"[20] and hence, is of very limited utility. As Davidson himself concedes:

> Unfortunately, there is, at present, very little direct information on the actual decisionmaking processes of the intervening states other than relatively exiguous references in post-intervention statements and it is therefore necessary to attempt to infer from references to legal norms within those statements the importance which was attached to the law in reaching decisions. Reconstruction is thus likely to be a hazardous process.[21]

Because "the evidence is clearly incomplete and the full details of the decisionmaking process with all its variable inputs will not emerge for some time," his is admittedly only "an interim assessment."[22]

The goal of this study is to provide more than an interim assessment. Drawing upon the memoir accounts of those who participated in[23] or witnessed the Reagan administration's decisionmaking process,[24] and upon interviews and correspondence with key participants,[25] it will reconstruct as accurately as possible the thirteen-day period during which the decision to invade Grenada was made. Without such a reconstruction, a reasonably accurate assessment of law's role in decisionmaking can probably not be made.

In order best to evaluate the relationship between international law and the Reagan administration's invasion decision, the remainder of this study will be divided into six chapters. Chapter Two, "In Search of Motives," will tell the story of the Grenada invasion in order to establish the factual record and to draw tentative conclusions about Reagan administration motives. It will examine first the antecedents and course of the American action, recounting both the triumphs and tragedies of Grenada's New Jewel Movement (NJM), as well as those of America's armed forces. Then, it will set out the foreign policy context within which President Reagan's invasion decision was made, considering formative events in both the Carter and Reagan administrations. Chapter Three, "The Public Rationale," will trace the evolution of the Reagan administration's public rationale for its action, as articulated first by the President himself and then by a succession of government officials. As in Chapter Two, tentative conclusions will be drawn about Reagan administration motives. In addition, Chapter Three will offer provisional conclusions about the Reagan administration's general attitude toward international law, the role played by law in the Grenada decision, and the conformity of the administration's legal justification with the *jus ad bellum* as it has been commonly rendered.

Chapter Four, "The Stage is Set," will begin a careful reconstruction of the administration's invasion decision. Specifically, it will relate the events of Thursday, October 13, through the early morning of Saturday, October 22. Chapter Five, "The Decision is Made," will complete the story of the invasion decision by recounting the events of Saturday, October 22 through Tuesday, October 25. Here, the decision to invade Grenada was tentatively reached, reconsidered, confirmed, and ultimately implemented. Chapter Six, "Law After the Invasion Announcement," will explore international law's influence upon the post-invasion justification of American policy, focusing particularly on the discussions between the State Department Legal Adviser's Office and the U.S. Mission to the United Nations. Chapter Seven, "Thirteen Days in October, Again," will answer specifically the central question of this study: What role did law play in the Reagan administration's decision to use military force? In so doing, it will first set out the three legal principles cited by the State Department Legal Adviser's Office to justify Operation "Urgent Fury." Next, it will determine how these principles actually influenced the administration's decisionmaking process. Finally, it will assess whether the principles cited did in fact justify the American invasion. The chapter will conclude with a discussion of the Grenada episode's broader "lessons" for international law and foreign policy decisionmaking.

Notes

1.   "Address to the Nation, October 27, 1983," *Weekly Compilation of Presidential Documents* 19 (October 24, 1983): 1501.

2.   "Remarks of Prime Minister Thatcher," *Documents on the Invasion of Grenada, Caribbean Monthly Bulletin,* October 1983, Supplement No. 1, item XX, pp. 87-88 (hereafter cited as *Documents on the Invasion*).

3.   "President's Remarks, October 25, 1983," *Department of State Bulletin* 83 (December 1983): 67.

4.   Grenada is about twice the size of Washington, D.C. United States Department of State, Bureau of Public Affairs, "Background Notes: Grenada," March 1980, p. 23. Indicative of the island's obscurity in October of 1983, there was some doubt then over how properly to pronounce its name.

5.   The OECS was established June 4, 1981, as a successor to the West Indies Associated States Council of Ministers, set up in September 1966. The group includes seven member states: Antigua/Barbuda, Dominica, Grenada, Montserrat, St. Kitts/Nevis, St. Lucia, and St. Vincent and the Grenadines. The governing treaty of the OECS is the OECS Treaty of Establishment, June 18, 1981. Reprinted in *International Legal Materials* 20 (1981): 1166.

6.   This does not include Operation "Rice Bowl," the failed Iran hostage rescue mission launched by President Carter on April 24, 1980. See Richard A. Gabriel, *Military Incompetence* (New York: Hill & Wang, 1985), pp. 85-116; David C. Martin and John Walcott, *Best Laid Plans: The Inside Story of America's War Against Terrorism* (New York: Harper & Row, 1988), pp. 1-42; and Gary Sick, *All Fall Down* (New York: Viking Penguin, 1985), pp. 327-356.

7.   Even years after the American action, local Grenadians continued to call it a "rescue mission." See Cristina Garcia, "One U.S. Invasion Later ...," *Time*, November 23, 1987, p. 43; and Don A. Schanche, "Grenada struggles to shake off recent past," *Los Angeles Times*, October 23, 1988, sect. 1, p. 16. See also, William C. Adams, "The Public's Attitudes," *Public Opinion* 7 (February/March 1984): 53-55.

8.   Eighty-five percent believed they had been in danger under the Revolutionary Military Council. Seventy-six percent thought Cuba had wanted to take control of the Grenadian government. See Gregory Sandford and Richard Vigilante, *Grenada: The Untold Story* (New York: Madison Books, 1984), p. 16; and "Grenadians Welcomed Invasion, A Poll Finds," *New York Times*, November 6, 1983, p. 21.

9.   Cited by Kai Schoenhals and Richard A. Melanson, *Revolution and Intervention in Grenada: The New Jewel Movement, the United States, and the Caribbean* (Boulder, Colo.: Westview Press, 1985), p. 141. See also Michael Jay Robinson and Maura Clancey, "Student Attitudes," *Public Opinion* 7 (February/March 1984): 52-53; and David P. Forsythe, *The Politics of International Law: U.S. Foreign Policy Reconsidered* (Boulder, Colo.: Lynne Rienner, 1990), pp. 77-80.

Initially, Congress was rather critical of the administration's action. However, opinion on Capitol Hill did an abrupt about-face in response to several factors: the massive public support of the action; the apparent evidence of danger in Grenada provided by the returning students; the discovery of Cuban and Soviet weapons; and the popularity of Reagan's October 27 speech. See Schoenhals and Melanson, *Revolution and Intervention in Grenada*, pp. 154-158.

Larry Speakes recalled later: "When that first planeload [of medical students] returned ... and the first student off the plane knelt and kissed the ground and they all cheered their country and thanked the U.S. military for rescuing them from a dangerous and chaotic situation, the public relations problem was solved right there." Larry Speakes, *Speaking Out* (New York: Charles Scribner's Sons, 1988), pp. 159-160.

10. On the international reaction, see especially Scott Davidson, *Grenada: A Study in Politics and the Limits of International Law* (Aldershot: Avebury, 1987), pp. 138-149; Hugh O'Shaughnessy, *Grenada: Revolution, Invasion and Aftermath* (London: Hamilton Hamish, 1984); pp. 173-216; Anthony Payne et al., *Grenada: Revolution and Invasion* (New York: St. Martin's Press, 1984), p. 168; Schoenhals and Melanson, *Revolution and Intervention in Grenada*, pp. 162-163; and Forsythe, *The Politics of International Law*, pp. 80-81.

11. Anthony Payne et al., *Grenada: Revolution and Invasion*, p. 168.

12. Cited by Walter Isaacson, "Weighing the Proper Role," *Time*, November 7, 1983, p. 42; and Payne et al., *Revolution and Invasion*, p. 168.

13. John Norton Moore, "Grenada and the International Double Standard," *American Journal of International Law* 78 (January 1984): 153.

14. "Remarks of Prime Minister Thatcher," *Documents on the Invasion*, pp. 87-88. The Grenada episode engendered "the sharpest and most public dispute between Thatcher and Reagan throughout the whole of their time in politics together." Geoffrey Smith, *Reagan and Thatcher* (London: The Bodley Head, 1990), p. 125.

15. Three book-length legal analyses have been done: Davidson, *A Study in Politics*; William C. Gilmore, *The Grenada Intervention: Analysis and Documentation* (London: Mansell, 1984); and John Norton Moore, *Law and the Grenada Mission* (Charlottesville, VA: Center for Law and National Security, 1984).

A large number of shorter analyses have also been done: Francis A. Boyle et al., "International Lawlessness in Grenada," *American Journal of International Law* 78 (January 1984): 172-175; Richard P. Dieguez, "The Grenada Invasion: 'Illegal' in Form, Sound as Policy," *New York University Journal of International Law and Politics* 16 (Summer 1984): 1167-1203; Isaak I. Dore, "The US Invasion of Grenada: Resurrection of the 'Johnson Doctrine?'" *Stanford Journal of International Law* 20 (Spring 1984): 173-189; L. Doswald-Beck, "The Legality of the U.S. Intervention in Grenada," *Netherlands International Law Review* 31 (1984): 362-366; H. Aubrey Fraser, "Grenada: The Sovereignty of the People," *West Indian Law Journal* 7 (October 1983): 205-291; Edward Gordon et al., "International Law and the United States Action in Grenada," *International Law* 18 (1984): 331; Christopher Joyner, "Reflections on the Lawfulness of Invasion," *American Journal of International Law* 78 (January 1984): 131-144; Jon M. Karas and Jerald M. Goodman, "The United States Action in Grenada: An Exercise in Realpolitik," *University of Miami Inter-American Law Review* 16 (Spring 1984): 53-108; Michael J. Levitin, "The Law of Force and the Force of Law: Grenada, the Falklands, and Humanitarian Intervention," *Harvard Journal of International Law* 27 (Spring 1984): 621-657;

John Norton Moore, "Grenada and the International Double Standard," pp. 145-168; Ved P. Nanda, "The United States Intervention in Grenada — Impact on World Order," *California Western International Law Journal* 14 (Summer 1984): 395-424; Mackubin Thomas Owens, "Grenada, Nicaragua and International Law," *This World*, no. 9 (Fall 1984), pp. 3-14; John Quigley, "The United States Invasion of Grenada: Stranger than Fiction," *The University of Miami Inter-American Law Review* 18 (Winter 1986-1987): 271-352; Ronald M. Riggs, "The Grenada Intervention: A Legal Analysis," *Military Law Review* 1 (Summer 1985): 1-81; P. St. J. Smart, "Revolutions, Constitutions and the Commonwealth: Grenada," *International and Comparative Law Quarterly* 35 (October, 1986): 950-960; Fernando R. Tesón, *Humanitarian Intervention: An Inquiry into Law and Morality* (Dobbs Ferry, NY: Transnational Publishers, 1988), pp. 188-200; Detlev Vagts, "International Law Under Time Pressure: Grading the Grenada Take-Home Examination," *American Journal of International Law* 79 (January 1984): 169-172; Maurice Waters, "The Invasion of Grenada, 1983, and the Collapse of Legal Norms," *Journal of Peace Research* 23 (September 1986): 229-246; Maurice Waters, "The Law and Politics of a U.S. Intervention: The Case of Grenada," *Peace & Change* 14 (January 1989): 65-105; and Laura K. Wheeler, "The Grenada Invasion: Expanding the Scope of Humanitarian Intervention, *Boston College International and Comparative Law Review* 8 (Summer 1985): 413-430.

16. For a recent, thorough discussion of the various legal analyses of the Grenada invasion that have been advanced, see Davidson, *A Study in Politics*, pp. 79-137; and Tesón, *Humanitarian Intervention*, pp. 188-189.

17. See Anthony Clark Arend and Robert J. Beck, *International Law and the Use of Force: Beyond the U.N. Charter Paradigm* (London: Routledge, 1993).

18. Among the material facts that have been disputed: (1) the degree to which American students were in danger; (2) the degree to which the United States attempted to solve the crisis by peaceful means; (3) whether the Grenadian Governor-General, Sir Paul Scoon, actually invited American intervention; (4) whether the United States stimulated a request from the OECS; (5) whether the Reagan administration had been planning an American invasion of Grenada for a long period prior to October, 1983; and (6) whether the Revolutionary Military Council was a "government" whose assurances were trustworthy or a band of "brutal thugs."

19. For a good though abbreviated account, see Forsythe, *The Politics of International Law*, pp. 63-87.

20. Davidson, *A Study in Politics*, p. 159.

21. Davidson, *A Study in Politics*, p. 159.

22. Davidson, *A Study in Politics*, p. 151.

23. Michael K. Deaver, *Behind the Scenes* (New York: William Morrow, 1987); Edwin Meese III, *With Reagan: The Inside Story* (Washington, D.C.: Regnery Gateway, 1992); Constantine C. Menges, *Inside the National Security Council: The True Story of the Making and Unmaking of Reagan's Foreign Policy* (New York: Simon and Schuster, 1988); Frank McNeil, *War and Peace in Central America: Reality and Illusion* (New York: Charles Scribner's Sons, 1988); Ronald W. Reagan, *An American Life: The Autobiography* (New York: Simon and Schuster, 1990); George P. Shultz, *Turmoil and Triumph: My Years as Secretary of State* (New York: Charles Scribner's Sons, 1993), and Caspar W. Weinberger, *Fighting for Peace: Seven Critical Years in the Pentagon* (New York: Warner Books, 1990).

24. Allan Gerson, *The Kirkpatrick Mission: Diplomacy Without Apology* (New York: The Free Press, 1991); John F. Lehman, Jr., *Command of the Seas* (New York: Charles Scribner's Sons, 1988); H. Norman Schwarzkopf with Peter Petre, *General H. Norman Schwarzkopf: The Autobiography: It Doesn't Take A Hero* (New York: Linda Grey Bantam Books, 1992); Thomas P. O'Neill, *Man of the House* (New York: Random House, 1987); and Speakes, *Speaking Out*.

25. The following individuals provided useful information, either as background or for the record: Milan D. Bish, former U.S. Ambassador to Barbados; Lawrence S. Eagleburger, former Undersecretary of State for Political Affairs; Ludlow Flower, former Deputy Chief of Mission, U.S. Embassy - Barbados; K. Scott Gudgeon, former State Department Assistant Legal Adviser for Inter-American Affairs; Fred C. Ikle, former Undersecretary of Defense for Policy; L. Craig Johnstone, former Principal Deputy Assistant Secretary of State for Inter-American Affairs; Michael G. Kozak, former State Department Deputy Legal Adviser; Kenneth A. Kurze, former Foreign Service Officer, U.S. Embassy - Barbados; Robert C. McFarlane, former National Security Adviser; Francis McNeil, former Special Emissary of the President; Constantine Menges, former Latin America Adviser, NSC; Langhorne A. Motley, former Assistant Secretary of State for Inter-American Affairs; Davis R. Robinson, former State Department Legal Adviser; and Lawrence G. Rossin, Foreign Service Officer.

2

The Invasion Decision:
In Search of Motives

Grenada is a small island. It's eight by eighteen miles; it's less than a hundred thousand people. It's not something people dwelled on, but it could be considered a minor irritant.[1]
— Assistant Secretary Langhorne Motley

In the White House, ... there was obsession with Grenada.[2]
— Ambassador Francis McNeil

Success seems to shine on us and I thank the Lord for it. He has really held me in the hollow of His hand.[3]
— President Ronald Reagan's diary,
shortly after the Grenada invasion

As with any major foreign policy decision, the Reagan administration decision in October of 1983 to launch Operation "Urgent Fury" poses a variety of intriguing questions. This chapter will limit its focus to two. First, what general motives underlay the administration's determination to use military force? And second, what specific impact if any did regard for international legality have upon the decisionmaking process? To facilitate answering these related questions, three critical factors will be considered in turn: (1) the situation on Grenada from the time of Maurice Bishop's successful coup on March 13, 1979 until his murder on October 19, 1983; (2) the conduct of Operation "Urgent Fury" by U.S. forces; and (3) the evolution of relations between Washington and the People's Revolutionary Government (PRG) of Grenada from 1979 to 1983. These factors, it will be shown, provide a partial though ultimately incomplete picture of the Reagan administration decision to use force.

Grenada and the Bishop Regime

On Thursday evening, October 13, 1983, Grenadian Prime Minister Maurice Bishop was placed under house arrest by a dissident faction within his People's Revolutionary Government (PRG). Bishop's forced confinement, followed only six days later by his murder on "Bloody Wednesday," would set the stage for President Reagan's decision to launch the invasion of Grenada.

Maurice (pronounced "Morris") Bishop had been no stranger to political intrigue. At 34, the handsome and charismatic leader of the New Jewel Movement (NJM) became Prime Minister of Grenada following a coup that ousted Sir Eric Gairy from the Premiership.[4] The Gairy regime, though pro-western, had been "corrupt, repressive and sustained only by rigged elections."[5] Gairy himself, whose reign has often been likened to that of Haiti's "Papa Doc" Duvalier, was an eccentric figure who "combined flamboyant populism and strong-arm tactics with interest in unidentified flying objects and unconventional religion."[6] Thus, when "Uncle Gairy" and his ruthless "Mongoose Gang" were removed on March 13, 1979, the Grenadian people embraced the "NJM, its revolution, and particularly Maurice Bishop who, to Grenadians and foreigners alike, became the symbol of the revolution."[7] Yet, as the distinguished Grenadian journalist Alistair Hughes would later be careful to emphasize, the Grenadian people had gone "Bishop, not socialist."[8]

Between March of 1979 and October of 1983, the precise character of Bishop's New Jewel Movement was the subject of no little controversy.[9] In those four and a half years before "the revo went lunatic," many observers contended that the NJM was merely a typical Third World radical regime; others, including some within the Reagan administration, sharply disagreed and emphasized the movement's Marxist-Leninist aspect.[10] Today, however, the essential nature of the NJM seems clear. Following the post-invasion discovery and publication of the Grenadian government's voluminous secret files,[11] "it is difficult to deny either the

NJM's inclinations towards Leninism or its extensive political, ideological, and above all military ties with the Soviet Union and Cuba."[12]

The NJM's revolution certainly had its *opera bouffe* aspects: Bishop and his Central Committee colleagues were at times naive, confused, or even inept; and the Marxist-Leninist vocabulary they assiduously employed probably reflected more formulaic acquaintance than ideological sophistication.[13] Nevertheless, the path embarked upon by the NJM gained the Grenadian movement classification by Soviet authorities as a "fraternal party," the most elevated step in the Soviet ideological hierarchy.[14] Moreover, given its explicitly Marxist-Leninist objectives, Bishop's 1982 "Line of March" would surely have merited Lenin's imprimatur.[15] The PRG would pursue three basic objectives: the building of a vanguard party based on democratic centralism; the establishment of a socialist society; and adherence to "proletarian internationalism."[16]

At first, the NJM's efforts to improve the living conditions and the general lot of the masses enjoyed a certain measure of success: unemployment was reduced from 40 percent to 33 percent; the public sector was substantially expanded, primarily in the service area; and illiteracy declined. The Bishop regime built an agro-industrial plant, subsidized the creation of at least twelve agricultural cooperatives, and instituted a variety of significant social reforms. These reforms included free milk and hot lunches for primary school children, the reduction and then elimination of secondary school fees, the creation of the nation's first eye clinic, the expansion of dental clinics to all seven parishes (there had only been one on the island), an increase in medical doctors from eight to thirty-nine, and a boost in university scholarships from three in 1978 to 209 in 1981.[17] Perhaps most visibly, the PRG began in January of 1980 the construction of an international airport with the help of Cuba, the EEC and a number of other states.[18] Given the apparent successes of Bishop's first several years, morale was high both in and out of government.[19]

Trouble in the NJM

In 1983, however, as the "revo" moved into its fifth year, economic conditions on Grenada stagnated or worsened. Grenadians by then were "no better off than they had been under Gairy." The economy had been stretched thin and kept afloat by public spending on construction projects. The current account deficit was one-third of the total gross domestic product, and unemployment approached 40 percent.[20] Given these ominous circumstances, dissension began seriously to threaten the New Jewel Movement's future.

Apparently, no single cause had precipitated the party's factional strife; rather, the personal ambition of Deputy Prime Minister Bernard Coard, coupled with a common recognition within the Politburo that the revolution was failing, seem to have triggered a power struggle.[21] That struggle became increasingly apparent during a series of Central Committee meetings in July and August. Then, a number of Politburo members expressed fears about the general "state of demoralization," about the "slow pace of party development along Leninist lines," and even about the "threat of [party] disintegration."[22]

Fundamentally, the People's Revolutionary Government of Grenada was "split in its perception of how best to remain in power."[23] One faction, lead by Prime Minister Bishop, remained essentially Leninist in its assumptions and strategic goals but advocated a flexible, pragmatic approach.[24] Against this "moderate" faction was a hard-line one led by Bernard Coard, a Brandeis-trained economist and the NJM's chief theoretician. Comrade Coard demanded that the PRG, its policies, and leadership reflect clearly the tenets of Leninist thought. Although the contrast between the two men and their tactical views was marked, it should not be exaggerated, however:

> It would be a misinterpretation to see in Bishop the accommodating tactician and in Coard the inflexible doctrinaire. Both men shared many ideas and ideological positions as well as the same strategic objectives. But their temperament, character, and exposure to realities from two different executive positions endowed with different responsibilities led them to see things in different ways, to conceive the discharging of their duties in a distinctive manner and to act in a dissimilar fashion.[25]

On September 25, 1983, after a series of emotionally-charged Central Committee meetings earlier in the month, Maurice Bishop agreed tentatively to a power-sharing arrangement with his rival.[26] By early October, however, while Bishop was away visiting Czechoslovakia and Hungary, the Coard faction began to fear with some justification that the Prime Minister would renege on his pledge.[27] They even became concerned that he might be preparing to have them eliminated.[28] Hence, when Bishop arrived on October 8 from Cuba, the final stop on his brief trip abroad, he was curtly greeted at Pearls Airport by only one Central Committee member, Selwyn Strachan.[29]

Less than a week after Maurice Bishop's unheralded return to Grenada, the pro-Coard majority of the Central Committee launched a coup against him. Very early Wednesday morning, October 12, the group clandestinely assembled trusted security personnel and party members within the People's Revolutionary Army (PRA), told them of the dire party crisis, and obtained from them their pledge of loyalty. Late that Wednesday evening, they purged from the party George Louison, the former Agriculture Minister and Bishop's strongest ally. Meanwhile, recognizing that his position was rapidly deteriorating and hoping that he might enlist popular support, Bishop began that same day to circulate a rumor that the Coard faction was planning to kill him.[30]

At 10:00 P.M. Thursday, October 13, Bishop was summoned to an NJM party members' meeting to account for the "assassination plot" rumor. There, the Prime Minister, a London-educated attorney, at first denied that he had initiated the story. After one of his own security guards confirmed that Bishop had done so, however, Bishop refused to deny the man's testimony. The Prime Minister's silence was commonly taken as his admission of responsibility, and party members immediately denounced him: Maurice Bishop had "disgraced the party" and was "without redemption." Calls were made for his arrest and court-martial. Ultimately, the Central Committee resisted demands that Bishop be expelled from the NJM; instead, they decided that he would be placed under house arrest and his telephone disconnected.[31]

After the October 13 meeting ended, "life on Grenada moved rapidly toward disintegration and anarchy."[32] The masses, with whom Maurice Bishop had remained quite popular, were shocked at the news of his detainment. Hence, almost immediately "a furious cussing-out of the Central Committee began to heat up the streets."[33] On Saturday, October 15, demonstrators in St. George's, the Grenadian capital, at Pearls Airport near Grenville, and on the nearby island of Carriacou, demanded Bishop's release chanting, "No Bishop, no revo." By Monday, October 17, the popular mood had turned overwhelmingly against Coard and his faction, although torrential rains prevented its active expression.

On the next day, however, large protests were led throughout Grenada by groups of high school students. For a time, a student sit-down strike even closed Pearls airport. Also on Tuesday, October 18, the five remaining Ministers loyal to Bishop — Jacqueline Creft, Norris Bain, George Louison, Lynden Ramdhanny, and Unison Whiteman — resigned from the PRG, claiming that Bernard Coard had refused to seek a peaceful solution to the crisis engulfing the regime.[34]   Bernard Coard's intransigence, George Louison would recall, "had reached a point of fanaticism."   Bishop's rival "by this time had tasted the power he [had] always wanted and was relishing it.   Both he and [Selwyn] Strachan were in good moods, puffing cigars.   Coard thought that with the party and the army on his side there was no way he could lose power."[35]

"Bloody Wednesday"

Early on the morning of October 19, a crowd of at least ten thousand people — about one-tenth of the entire Grenadian population — assembled in the Central Market Square of St. George's to protest Bishop's arrest.[36]   All restaurants, schools, stores, and offices had been closed by strikes and the people had poured in from around the countryside.   "We want Maurice," they chanted.   "C for corruption, C for Coard!"   They carried signs reading "Give us Maurice or the masses will blast!" "America, we love you!" and "Free Maurice - No Coard - No Communism!"[37]

Around 9:00 A.M., about 3,000 people broke away from the throng. The band, led by former Foreign Minister Unison Whiteman and composed mainly of uniformed schoolchildren, marched up the steep streets of St. George's to Bishop's house on Mount Royal.   As they stood in front of the Prime Minister's residence, some of the crowd were scattered when a reinforced PRA guard of approximately one hundred men fired shots over their heads.   The majority who remained, however, merely pushed the government soldiers aside and released the thirty-nine year old Prime Minister and Jacqueline Creft, his pregnant mistress.[38] Bishop, extremely weak and clad only in dark green undershorts, was lent a jersey and assisted with Creft into a waiting vehicle.   It was now 10:35 A.M.

Instead of traveling to the Market Square and addressing the crowd, as some had expected, Bishop proceeded up the precipitous hill to Fort Rupert with his entourage of perhaps two thousand.[39]   Upon their arrival, the group was confronted by PRA guards standing at the entrance.   At Bishop's orders, however, the Grenadian soldiers set down their arms.   Then, the commander of the fort, Major Christopher

Stroude, ordered his men to hand over their weapons.[40] Once inside Fort Rupert, Bishop and his closest colleagues freed Major Einstein Louison, the former PRA chief of staff, and occupied the operations room. At length, Major Louison and Vincent Noel, another Bishop loyalist, went to the arsenal and began arming the crowd.

Meanwhile, the pro-Coard faction of the New Jewel Movement's Central Committee — at first from Bernard Coard's house and then from the safety of Fort Frederick, an eighteenth-century gun emplacement surmounting Richmond Hill — had been anxiously observing Bishop's rescue and his subsequent seizure of Fort Rupert. With the acquiescence of General Hudson Austin, Lieutenant Colonel Ewart "Headache" Layne assumed direction of a counter-Bishop operation.[41] Immediately, the zealous officer dispatched three Soviet-built BTR-60P armored cars and an armored troop carrier to Fort Rupert. These PRA vehicles, filled with troops loyal to the Central Committee, arrived around 1:00 P.M. Shortly thereafter, the shooting began.[42] Some of the crowd of Bishop supporters panicked, jumping to their deaths from Fort Rupert's limestone battlements ninety feet above the rocky shoreline. Others were killed by shells and machine-gun bullets fired from the armored cars. To end the carnage, Bishop decided to surrender.[43]

Iman Abdullah, a Coard loyalist and PRA officer, promptly took charge. First, he ordered the surviving civilians out of Fort Rupert. Next, he directed Maurice Bishop, Jackie Creft, and six of Bishop's chief allies to march up through a tunnel that opened to the uppermost courtyard of the fortress.[44] Finally, the eight victims were told to line up against a wall upon which, ironically, "Toward Higher Discipline in the PRA" had been written. "Is execution time," gloated Lester "Goat" Redhead.[45] After a few brutal moments, Lieutenant Colonel Layne could report, "Central Committee orders given, Central Committee orders obeyed."[46] It was 2:00 P.M.

Seven hours after the gruesome murder of Bishop and his colleagues, around 9:00 P.M., General Hudson Austin addressed the people on Radio Free Grenada. After recounting his version of the day's events, the PRA chief and boyhood friend of Bishop announced the formation of a sixteen-member Revolutionary Military Council (RMC) which would rule Grenada until order could be restored.[47] General Austin then proclaimed a round-the-clock curfew that would last until Monday, October 24. All workplaces and schools were to remain closed during this four-day period. "Anyone who seeks to demonstrate or disturb the peace," he warned, "will be shot."[48]

After the bloody events at Fort Rupert, Leslie Manigat has observed, "only terror could rule Grenada."[49] Terror became a method of government to launch the new regime and to control the situation, the *raison d'etre* of the strict curfew and the stringent security measures adopted by the RMC. To comprehend the full impact of the curfew, one must recognize that the Grenadian populace had not stocked any foodstuffs, that less than forty percent of their homes had running water, and that less than twenty-five percent of their dwellings had internal toilets. "Under such conditions, terror went hand in hand with hardship to build up individual and collective fear."[50]

By their imposition of a "draconian 96-hour curfew," Austin and the RMC had unwittingly sealed their own fates as well as that of Marxist-Leninist rule on Grenada. Within four days, their neighbors in the eastern Caribbean would formally request American military assistance "to remove [a] dangerous threat to peace and security in their subregion and to establish a situation of normalcy on Grenada."[51] Two days later, on October 25, U.S. forces would officially begin landing on the island.

The Conduct of Operation "Urgent Fury"

It is axiomatic that "the best battles are those that you cannot lose." For the United States, Grenada was surely such a battle.[52] Indeed, it is probably not much of an exaggeration to suggest that even "the New York Police Department could have won on Grenada," for by any reasonable standard the Grenadian-Cuban force defending the island was marginal in terms not only of its strength but also of its firepower.[53] Outnumbered approximately ten to one, it had no air support or heavy weapons, and very little popular support.[54] Despite the manifest inferiority of its opposition, however, the American invasion of Grenada was fraught with difficulties from the very beginning.[55]

The overall military goal of Operation "Urgent Fury" was to overwhelm the defenders of Grenada in a quick, massive "surgical" action that would minimize loss of life and material damage.[56] The operation sought specifically to "protect and evacuate U.S. and designated foreign nationals, neutralize Grenadian forces, stabilize the internal situation to maintain peace and order, and in conjunction with OECS friendly participants, assist in the restoration of democratic government on Grenada."[57]   Achievement of these official military objectives implied, in turn, the completion of a number of particular missions.[58] First, U.S. forces would have to secure a variety of facilities deemed strategically or politically significant, including the nearly-completed airfield at Point Salines, the Pearls Airport, the Radio Free Grenada (RFG) station, and the island's main diesel generating plant near Grand Mal Bay. Second, perhaps as many as a thousand individuals had to be rescued: the American citizens on the island, including approximately six hundred students at St. George's Medical School; Sir Paul Scoon, the British-appointed Governor-General of Grenada who was being held under virtual house arrest; and a number of Grenadian political prisoners who had been incarcerated at Richmond Hill Prison.[59]   Finally, those NJM members who had undertaken the coup against Bishop had to be captured.

Complete control of "Urgent Fury" was entrusted to the office of the Joint Chiefs of Staff (JCS), chaired by General John W. "Jack" Vessey, Jr., which approved plans for a "combined service" operation[60] seventy-two hours before the actual invasion.[61] A Joint Task Force, designated "JTF 120," was created under the command of Vice Admiral Joseph Metcalf III and his deputy, Army Major General H. Norman Schwarz-kopf.[62]   According to CINCLANT-developed plans, the island of Grenada would be divided approximately in half, with the Army responsible for the southern half and the Marines for the northern. First, Marines from the I-84 Amphibious Readiness Group and two battalions of Army Rangers would seize the Grenadian airheads and other key objectives.[63]   These troops would then be reinforced by the Army's 82nd Airborne Division, airlifted from Fort Bragg, North Carolina. Even before the formal start of the operation, Delta Force and Navy SEAL commandos would undertake a variety of "special operations."[64]

Problems of the operation

Despite Admiral Metcalf's post-operation contention that U.S. forces had "blown away" the defenders of Grenada, and President Reagan's later characterization of "Urgent Fury" as "a brilliant campaign," virtually none of the American missions went particularly well.[65] Efforts to seize strategic positions on the island, for example, were marred by bad luck and by errors in planning and execution. Pearls airport ("LZ Buzzard") was secured by 7:30 A.M. on October 25, only two hours after its heliborne assault by Marines. Nevertheless, a SEAL reconnaissance team dispatched there late Monday night only narrowly escaped discovery by PRA forces. Stormy weather had driven SEAL Team 4 hundreds of yards off its intended course; as a consequence, the group landed within only ten feet of a Grenadian militia group.[66]

The attempt to secure Point Salines airfield was less fortunate. On Sunday evening, October 23, four members of SEAL Team 6 drowned during an ill-fated bid to reconnoiter the runway and to place infrared guidance beacons there.[67] The next night, rough weather again thwarted a SEAL scouting mission to Point Salines. "That meant," recalled General Schwarzkopf, that "the Ranger battalions now en route from Savannah still did not know what they'd find."[68] When 500 Army Rangers finally arrived at Point Salines at 5:54 A.M. Tuesday, they were compelled to parachute into unexpectedly heavy antiaircraft fire from a perilous height of five hundred feet, instead of the usual 1,100 feet. Not until four hours later was the runway at Point Salines declared "safe and secure,"[69] and this pronouncement proved premature. The 82nd Airborne's landing there at 2:05 P.M. was greeted by heavy fire.[70]

Even an early-morning attempt by SEAL Team 6 to seize the transmitter building of Radio Free Grenada ultimately failed.[71] Though the SEALs at first captured the facility, they were compelled to withdraw when confronted by a numerically superior force.[72] Accordingly, the radio station was not silenced until midmorning of October 25, when an AC-130 Spectre gunship reduced the RFG building to ruins.[73]

The various "rescue missions" undertaken by U.S. forces fared scarcely better. The "high priority" mission to rescue Sir Paul Scoon, for example, nearly proved disastrous. Before dawn on October 25, twenty-two SEALs, a CIA agent, and one courageous Foreign Service Officer flew toward Government House in two Blackhawk armored helicopters. SEAL Team 6 forces had been dispatched to free Scoon, who was inside his residence guarded by a small contingent of PRA soldiers. Lawrence G. Rossin, the State Department's Peru Desk Officer, had come along to identify the Governor-General, thereby preventing his accidental injury or death. During his 1980-1982 tour as a political officer in Bridgetown, Rossin had visited Grenada several times and could therefore recognize Scoon.[74]

As the clandestine heliborne rescue party was arriving at Government House, it came under intense AK-47 fire. Undeterred, the first helicopter flew in close and dropped its complement of SEALs. Shortly thereafter, the second UH-60 with Larry Rossin aboard followed. While SEALs rappeled into the Governor-General's front yard, the helicopter came under more intense groundfire. Once all the "special ops" forces had cleared, the helicopter's pilot maneuvered to get out of harm's way while waiting to see how the battle below developed. Immediately, however, the Blackhawk began taking anti-aircraft and 50-caliber machine gun fire from Fort Frederick and Fort Rupert. Accordingly, Rossin and the CIA official were flown back to the *Guam*, and the lightly-armed American commandos left behind with Sir Paul. Before reaching the aircraft carrier at 7:15 A.M., Rossin's helicopter would absorb forty-eight rounds and nearly crash into the ocean.[75]

At first, the SEAL team remaining at Scoon's residence received support from two AH-1T Cobras of Marine Medium Helicopter Squadron 261, until both attack helicopters were shot down.[76] Then, an Air Force AC-130 Spectre gunship was called in to keep Grenadian forces at bay.[77] With justification, Admiral Metcalf became "mad as hell" about the continuing vulnerability of Scoon and of the SEALs. Thus, with General Schwarzkopf's agreement, he decided at 11:45 A.M. to order an airstrike upon Fort Frederick, the enemy's major command post which seemed to have been coordinating the assault.[78] An A-7 fighter from the USS *Independence* promptly silenced the fortress, but in the process, mistakenly destroyed nearby Richmond Hill Mental Hospital and killed a significant number of its patients.[79]

Around 2:00 P.M. that afternoon, General Schwarzkopf suggested that the best way to secure St. George's and to relieve the besieged Government House would be to transport part of the heavily-armed Marine unit at Pearls airport to the southeastern part of the island.[80] After Metcalf's approval of the plan, the redeployed armor landed at Grand Mal Bay, "LZ Fuel," between 7:00 and 8:00 P.M. that evening. Moving inland from the sandy beach one mile north of St. George's, the Marine force took up temporary positions for the evening.

Very early Wednesday morning, perhaps around 3:00 A.M., Larry Rossin managed to contact Scoon by radio from the *Guam*. According to Rossin, the two discussed then Sir Paul's "invitation to U.S. and Caribbean forces to restore order in Grenada, which [Scoon] confirmed, and possible later use by him of an AM radio facility which I had learned would be installed on Grenada shortly. The conversation was quite brief as dictated by multiple use of the radio net."[81]

About 7:30 A.M., after Company G had been reinforced by F, thirteen "amtracs" (LVTPs) and five M-60 tanks rolled toward Scoon's mansion. The Cuban-Grenadian force scattered quickly and their twenty-six-hour siege ended. Finally, a helicopter could evacuate Sir Paul Scoon, his wife, and twenty-two SEALs to the USS *Guam*.[82] Later that same morning, Scoon was flown to Point Salines, where he was greeted by Rossin and Barbadian Brigadier General Rudyard Lewis, the Commander of the Caribbean Forces.[83] Probably then, but certainly at some point on the morning of October 26, the two men received Sir Paul's written request for intervention.[84]

Another rescue mission was much less fortunate: a Delta Force assault on Richmond Hill Prison. According to Joint Special Operations Command (JSOC) plans, nine Blackhawk UH-60 helicopters flown by Task Force 160 were to arrive at the prison shortly after dawn of October 25 and to free the political detainees held there.[85] Of the seven helicopters that actually reached Richmond Hill at 6:30 A.M., however, at least one was downed by intense machine-gun and heavy small-arms fire from the prison and from nearby Fort Frederick. The rescue plans had therefore to be aborted.[86] It was not until D plus 2 that the former British army barracks was "taken," but only after those Marines previously deployed to rescue Governor-General Scoon had found the prison abandoned and then occupied it.[87]

Shortly after their occupation of Richmond Hill prison, the Marines moved to seize "Fort Adolphus." After considering the use of TOW missile and heavy machine gun fire to "prep" the fort, Lieutenant Colonel Smith, the Marine commander, decided not to employ such measures unless resistance was encountered:

I'm not sure what stopped us from doing it. The only thing that stopped us from going in and prepping it, is that we had been so successful without shooting that I recall consciously making a decision: "It's working, let's just keep doing it the way we're doing it." And I said, "Just scout it out. If you take any fire, back off and we'll blow the hell out of it."[88]

With these instructions, the Marines cautiously closed in on Fort Adolphus, until they came upon the Venezuelan ambassador. The unfamiliar flag which they had seen flying above the fort was the flag of Venezuela; Fort Adolphus was, in fact, the Venezuelan Embassy. U.S. forces had only narrowly missed attacking the embassy and likely killing

Venezuelan diplomats. In the event that Lieutenant Colonel Smith had chosen to "prep" Fort Adolphus, Admiral Metcalf had even put naval gunfire and air support at his disposal.[89]

Of all the rescue missions undertaken by U.S. forces, perhaps the most poorly executed was that of the American students at St. George's Medical School. Despite President Reagan's assertion on October 25 that the "personal safety" of Americans on Grenada had been his "paramount concern," the U.S. forces sent there "had almost no idea where the students were."[90] Thus, when Army Rangers secured True Blue Campus at 8:50 A.M. on October 25, they discovered to their chagrin that another still larger campus existed.[91] Although the Rangers were unable to pinpoint that other campus, Grand Anse, until maps were captured from the enemy, they managed to contact it by telephone and found that its 224 students, while safe, were nearly surrounded.[92] Not until late on the afternoon of D-Day did Metcalf and Schwarzkopf learn of St. George's second campus.[93]

At 9:45 A.M. Wednesday, October 26, the first group of American medical students, the 138 from St. George's True Blue campus, were evacuated from Grenada in a C-141 Galaxy transport plane. Meanwhile, their colleagues at Grand Anse campus, four miles north of Point Salines, still awaited rescue.[94] Standing on the bridge of the *Guam*, General Schwarzkopf had a brainstorm:

> I looked straight across [the water] at the students' building, which was fronted by a long stretch of white, sandy beach. Then I looked directly down onto the flight deck and focused on the dozens of Marine helicopters just sitting there. *Why are we fixated on attacking over land?*[95]

Schwarzkopf promptly suggested to Metcalf that U.S. forces launch a seaborne rescue operation. With the Admiral's enthusiastic assent, Schwarzkopf directed a force of nine Marine CH-46 helicopters to fly from their command post on the *Guam*, pick up Ranger forces still at Point Salines, and lift them over the Cuban positions to Grand Anse. Beforehand, Navy A-6 and A-7 jet fighters, along with an Air Force AC-130 Spectre gunship, would move in to strafe emplacements around the campus while Army paratroopers kept the Cuban defenders occupied.

In a scene "right out of 'Apocalypse Now,'" the nine helicopter force began a vertical assault on Grand Anse beach at 4:19 P.M. on October 26, arriving there in three waves.[96] After the Rangers had disembarked and reached the medical school annex, four CH-53 helicopters were called in, and the medical students quickly evacuated in these to Point Salines. The operation cost the Marine squadron one CH-46, and another one damaged, but all the students at Grand Anse were evacuated without injury and without loss of any Rangers or Marine airmen.[97] Once they reached Point Salines, the students were given fruit juice and captured K rations and then boarded a C-141 jet bound ultimately for Charleston, South Carolina. At last, it then seemed, all the American students had been evacuated.

By Thursday evening, October 27, President Reagan could tell a national television audience that U.S. forces on Grenada were "in the mopping-up phase."[98] While true, the words of the Commander-in-Chief were misleading: over two hundred American students on the island had yet to been rescued. This anxious group would not be discovered until the following day when elements of the 82nd Airborne stumbled upon them while the Army was conducting routine clearing operations. By that point, the 202 men and women had been waiting for four days in their housing complex at Lance aux Epines, several miles east of the Point Salines airstrip. In those ninety-six hours, enemy forces had been in control of the area and could easily have killed the Americans or taken them hostage. Fortunately, none of the students had been harmed.

The costs of "Urgent Fury"
Although hostilities on Grenada officially ceased on November 2, 1983, it would take some time before an accurate accounting of the American use of force there could be made.[99] Predictably, post-invasion assessments of the Grenada "rescue mission" by the Reagan administration were consistently positive. In his September 22, 1986, letter to the *New York Times*, for example, Caspar W. Weinberger argued that in "both military and political terms, the operation on Grenada was a success." Indeed, the Defense Secretary concluded, "Urgent Fury" had been a success "by any definition."[100] Similarly, on February 20, 1986, Ronald Reagan told an enthusiastic Grenadian audience at St. George's, "I will never be sorry that I made the decision to help you."[101] In his 1990 memoir, he called the American operation "[m]ilitarily, ... a textbook success."[102] And Constantine Menges, President Reagan's Special Assistant for National Security Affairs during the Grenada mission, exulted in 1988: "[O]ur citizens were rescued, the

people of Grenada were liberated, and today they are citizens of a functioning democracy."[103]

Such favorable administration evaluations notwithstanding, observers in the United States and abroad have come to recognize that despite its benefits, the Grenada mission was not without its attendant costs. First, the operation exacted a significant human price. According to official casualty figures, nineteen Americans died on Grenada while 115 were wounded. In addition, twenty-five Cubans were killed and another fifty-nine wounded. Moreover, a disturbingly high number of Grenadian civilians, forty-five, were inadvertently killed and 358 wounded.[104] Second, and of far less significance, "Urgent Fury" required a substantial monetary expenditure. According to figures compiled by the Defense Department, the mission cost the United States $134.4 million, not including the salaries of the soldiers who participated. This figure corresponds to $1 million per square mile of Grenadian territory or $224,000 per rescued American student.[105] Finally, the American invasion of Grenada took a significant toll on the reputation of the United States and on that of its armed forces. General Schwarzkopf offered this remarkably candid assessment of "Urgent Fury" in his 1992 memoir: "[W]e lost more lives than we needed to," and the operation revealed numerous shortcomings including "an abysmal lack of accurate intelligence, major deficiencies in communications, flareups of interservice rivalry, interference by higher headquarters in battlefield decisions, [and] our alienation of the press."[106]

The Foreign Policy Context

Like that of many American foreign policy decisions, the story of the "Urgent Fury" decision begins many months before the President's formal signature of a National Security Decision Directive (NSDD). Indeed, in order properly to understand Ronald Reagan's rationale for the Grenada invasion, one must look four and a half years earlier, to the latter days of the Carter Presidency.

Sir Eric Gairy, Prime Minister of Grenada since its independence from Britain in 1974, had never been especially popular in Washington; although pro-Western, Gairy had seemed increasingly eccentric and repressive with the passage of time. Hence, by 1979, the Carter administration harbored serious reservations about the Grenadian premier: he seemed "a blemish not only on the face of Grenada, but also on the Caribbean."[107] Accordingly, when Gairy was removed from power by the New Jewel Movement, the Carter administration's reaction was initially ambivalent. Although technically Sir Eric had been the democratically-elected leader of a Westminster-style regime, his departure on March 13, 1979, appeared perhaps "a blessing for Grenada."[108]

While the Carter administration did not miss Gairy, it soon became anxious about his replacement, Maurice Bishop, about Bishop's People's Revolutionary Government, and about the PRG's relationship with Cuba. Within three weeks of Bishop's assumption of the premiership, a Cuban ship carrying weapons and ammunition arrived in Grenada.[109] In the months that followed, the PRG undertook a number of actions troubling to the administration.

Seeking to consolidate its position and to forestall opposition, the Bishop regime suspended the Grenadian constitution and the parliament, while detaining perhaps a hundred political prisoners. In addition, it closed Grenada's only independent newspaper, suspended *habeas corpus*, and refused to schedule elections.[110] At the same time, Bishop and his colleagues frequently and vociferously denounced the United States in various international fora. Even more disturbing was Bishop's announcement in November of 1979 that Fidel Castro would help Grenada build a new international airport with a 10,000-foot runway. While the Prime Minister spoke of tourist-laden jumbo-jets landing at Point Salines, American strategists feared the airport's use by Cuban and Soviet long-range military aircraft.[111] The *coup de grace* was finally delivered in January, 1980 when Grenada refused to condemn the Soviet invasion of Afghanistan at the United Nations: Michael Manley's Jamaica and Sandinist Nicaragua had abstained in the vote; the majority of the nonaligned Third World states had either voted for the resolution or had abstained; and in the entire western hemisphere, only Cuba had cast a similar vote.[112] How near had Grenada moved to the Soviet/Cuban orbit?

Back in 1979, only three weeks after the NJM had seized power, U.S. Ambassador Frank Ortiz had written to Bishop that the United States "would view with displeasure any tendency on the part of Grenada to develop closer ties with Cuba." This American diplomatic missive drew a stinging rebuke from the Grenadian Prime Minister: "No country has the right to tell us what to do or how to run our country, or who to be friendly with. We are not in anybody's backyard, and we are definitely not for sale."[113] From this point on, relations between Washington and St. George's deteriorated rapidly.

At first, the Carter administration considered covert action to remove Bishop.[114] Ultimately, however, it decided to distance itself from Grenada, to treat the Prime Minister with hands-off hostility. Thus, it refused to accept the credentials of Grenadian ambassador-designate Dessima Williams, sought to block aid for Grenadian flood relief from the OAS Emergency Fund, and denied AID assistance to Grenada after Hurricane Allen had damaged its banana crop.[115] Although the Carter administration was certainly concerned about the leftist path embarked upon by Bishop and the PRG, it never viewed Grenada as a major foreign policy issue. By late 1980, the administration was preoccupied with much more pressing matters: Iran, Afghanistan, and Ronald Reagan.[116]

The Reagan administration and Grenada

In the presidential election of 1980, Ronald Reagan campaigned effectively on foreign policy issues, particularly on those related to such "crisis" areas as Central America and the Caribbean. Not surprisingly, Reagan carried this perspective into his post-inaugural policy-making, elevating the Caribbean Basin to an area of foremost concern for American policy. Since the Carter administration had already assumed a relatively antagonistic posture toward Grenada, the new administration seemed only to intensify American antagonism, rather than to change the basic trajectory of U.S. policy.[117] Accordingly, from January of 1981 until October of 1983, it pursued a policy of diplomatic isolation, economic hostility, and military intimidation — reinforced by harsh Presidential rhetoric.[118] Despite tough actions by the administration and even tougher words, however, Grenada was never as great a concern to Washington as many outside observers judged it then to be.

Although the United States maintained formal diplomatic relations with Grenada in the first three years of Reagan's presidency, the administration was noticeably cool to the Bishop regime. In 1982, Representative Michael Barnes would tersely describe the mindset which seemed then to prevail: "If the United States has a policy toward Grenada, it appears to consist of not answering mail and avoiding being seen in the same room with officials from Grenada."[119] Typical of the new administration's diplomatic approach, when Milan D. Bish was appointed Ambassador to Barbados and the Eastern Caribbean, the Nebraska banker was pointedly not accredited to Grenada.[120] Moreover, like the Carter administration had done, the Reagan administration chose not to accredit a Grenadian ambassador to the United States. Hence, Dessima Williams would serve as Ambassador to the OAS only, not concurrently as Ambassador to the United States.

In 1982, Ambassador Williams lamented, "[I]n March and again in August, 1981, our Prime Minister wrote President Reagan, expressing a desire for better relations between our two countries. To this date, no reply from President Reagan has been received to these letters."[121] In fact, Ronald Reagan would never meet personally with Maurice Bishop to discuss the Grenadian's missives, although his administration did have at least one brief diplomatic encounter with the charismatic leader. Less than half a year before his murder and three months after Reagan's alarming "Star Wars" speech,[122] Bishop made in June of 1983 an unofficial visit to Washington. There, he spoke for about forty minutes with Deputy Secretary of State Kenneth Dam and National Security Adviser William Clark.[123] Reportedly, the two American officials gave the Prime Minister an anticommunist lecture and issued a warning: if he truly wanted improved relations, he must first ease his repressive rule and hold free elections.[124] Although Bishop would call the meeting "a useful first step," some scholars would later attribute the Premier's political demise, at least in part, to his apparent attempt at conciliation with the United States.[125]

If the Reagan administration's diplomatic relations with Grenada seemed cool, its economic relations with the People's Revolutionary Government were downright frigid. Indeed, virtually from the beginning, the administration sought to exert economic pressure upon the Bishop regime. Upon his taking office as Secretary of State, for example, Alexander Haig directed the Bureau of Inter-American Affairs to ensure that Grenada would not receive "one penny" from any international financial institution (IFI). Hence, Grenada was added to the State Department's informal "hit list"[126] and suffered reduced or withheld loans from international lenders such as the International Monetary Fund (IMF) and the World Bank.[127] Similarly, on at least three occasions the administration pressed European Economic Community (EEC) members not to co-finance Grenada's Point Salines International Airport project.[128] In June 1981, moreover, the United States offered the Caribbean Development Bank a $4 million grant for basic human needs projects on the condition that none of the funds go to Grenada; the Bank refused. Perhaps the most visible sign of American disfavor toward the Bishop regime, Reagan specifically excluded Grenada from participation in his vaunted Caribbean Basin Initiative (CBI), a program designed to serve as a "Mini-Marshall Plan" for the Caribbean region.[129]

While the PRG could do without an accredited Ambassador to the United States and some sources of international capital, it obviously could not survive an American invasion. Yet, the Reagan administration did little to discourage Bishop's fears of just such a prospect.[130]

Between August 1 and October 15 of 1981, the United States coordinated the largest naval maneuvers since World War II.[131] The Caribbean exercises, dubbed "Ocean Venture '81," involved over 120,000 troops, 250 warships, and 1,000 aircraft. During part of the exercises, Operation "Amber and the Amberdines," American troops liberated the Puerto Rican Island of Vieques. According to the fictional scenario of the military operation, the island to be invaded was "our enemy in the eastern Caribbean where U.S. hostages were in need of rescue." After rescuing American hostages, troops were to "install a regime favorable to the way of life we espouse."[132] Prime Minister Bishop charged in a subsequent statement that the exercise was "a practice run for direct invasion of Grenada by U.S. troops." Given the many striking coincidences between Grenada and the mythical island attacked by the U.S. forces, Bishop's conclusion was not altogether implausible.[133]

In 1982, a second set of Ocean Venture exercises was held by the United States. Although these were less overtly political, Maurice Bishop continued to emphasize his theme of American aggression: "Such huge military maneuvers, so perilously close to our shores, only demonstrate one more time the proximity of war and the blasé, imperial and Monroe doctrine-like attitude of the United States to our region and waters."[134] In May 1983, a third set of American exercises, code-named "Universal Trek," showed "how U.S. forces could land in a small Caribbean nation where a civil war [was] taking place."[135] These came a scant three months after the *Washington Post* had reported a proposed CIA covert action plan against Grenada. Although it was apparently never implemented, the July 1981 scheme of "economic destabilization affecting the political viability of the [Grenadian] government" seemed to some even more suggestive of the Reagan administration's desire to topple the PRG.[136]

At a minimum, President Reagan's rhetoric indicated his personal dissatisfaction with the Marxist regime in Grenada.[137] Indeed, on a number of important occasions, the President offered sharp and vivid denunciations of Grenadian policies. On February 24, 1982, for example, Reagan issued an implicit call for Grenada to return to the fold while introducing his "Caribbean Basin Initiative" (CBI). In an address to the Permanent Council of the Organization of American States (OAS), the President maintained:

> Nowhere in its whole sordid history have the promises of communism been redeemed. Everywhere it has exploited and aggravated temporary economic suffering to seize power and then to institutionalize economic deprivation and suppress human rights ....
>
> In the Caribbean we above all seek to protect those values and principles that shape the proud heritage of this hemisphere. Some, however, have turned from their American neighbors and their heritage. Let them return to the traditions and common values of this hemisphere and we all will welcome them. The choice is theirs.[138]

Only two months later, while in Bridgetown, Barbados, Reagan observed:

> El Salvador isn't the only country that's being threatened with Marxism, and I think all of us are concerned with the overturn of Westminster parliamentary democracy in Grenada. That country now bears the Soviet and Cuban trademark, which means that it will attempt to spread the virus among its neighbors.[139]

And less than a year later, on March 10, 1983, the President painted a menacing picture of Grenada using predominantly red hues:

> Grenada, that tiny little island — with Cuba at the west end of the Caribbean, Grenada at the east end — that tiny little island is building now, or having built for it, on its soil and shores, a naval base, a superior air base, storage bases and facilities for the storage of munitions, barracks, and training ground for the military. I'm sure all of that is simply to encourage the export of nutmeg.

> People who make these arguments haven't taken a good look at a
> map lately or followed the extraordinary buildup of Soviet and Cuban
> military power in the region or read the Soviet's discussions about why
> the region is important to them and how they intend to use it.
>   It isn't nutmeg that's at stake in the Caribbean and Central
> America; it is the United States' national security.[140]

Maurice Bishop, who had been in India when Reagan delivered these
words, cut short his visit, returned to Grenada, and declared a full-scale
alert. Dismissing Ronald Reagan's claims of Cuban and Soviet military
installations as "a pack of lies," he reported that Grenadian intelligence
knew of an impending attack organized by CIA-supported exiles using
a neighboring island as a base.[141]

The President delivered his rhetorical *coup de grace* to Grenada on
March 23, 1983. In his "National Security Address to the Nation,"
Reagan unveiled aerial reconnaissance photographs of Grenada.[142]
Here, he dramatically revealed to the American television audience what
had been no secret to students of Caribbean politics or even to those
American medical students who had been jogging around it: Grenada
was building a lengthy runway at Point Salines. Reagan explained:

> On the small island of Grenada, at the southern end of the Caribbean
> chain, the Cubans with Soviet financing and backing, are in the process
> of building an airfield with a 10,000-foot runway. Grenada doesn't even
> have an air force. Who is it intended for?
>   The Caribbean is a very important passageway for our international
> commerce and military lines of communication. More than half of all
> American oil imports now pass through the Caribbean. The rapid
> buildup of Grenada's military potential is unrelated to any conceivable
> threat to this country of under 110,000 people and totally at odds with
> the pattern of other eastern Caribbean states, most of which are unarmed.
>   The Soviet-Cuban militarization of Grenada, in short, can only be
> seen as power projection into the region.[143]

What Reagan neglected to observe was that British, European and
American companies had been involved in the Grenadian airfield's
construction,[144] that Grenada had received direct financial backing from
the EEC but *not* from the Soviet Union,[145] and that a variety of
Caribbean states had built similarly lengthy runways to support their
tourist economies.[146] What Bishop felt compelled to observe was that

Reagan was "a true to life fascist ... about to promote invasion of the island."[147]

By the Autumn of 1983, the Reagan administration would have shed few tears if the Maurice Bishop regime had been replaced by a democratic government on Grenada. That it would have taken overt military steps to remove the People's Revolutionary Government seems unlikely, however, despite the fears that were being voiced regularly by Bishop. According to Ambassador Francis McNeil, a career diplomat and the President's Special Emissary during the Grenada deliberations:

> The behavior of the United States belied the President's harsh rhetoric about the danger from Grenada. For most of the U.S. government, there were *more important things to worry about*, notwithstanding genuine concern that the airstrip at Point Salines which the Cuban engineers were slowly building might eventually be used by Soviet reconnaissance aircraft. The U.S. military practiced a mock invasion in 1982, but stored the plans in the limbo of lost contingencies.
>
> The Department of State, which thought of Grenada as *an irritant*, paid as little attention as possible, except insofar as Grenada provided another reason for giving economic and security assistance to other poor but certifiably democratic nations of the Caribbean.[148]

Admittedly, in the White House, "there was an obsession with Grenada," but the "rhetoric was huff and puff." Before the Prime Minister's murder, McNeil maintains, there was "no possibility the United States would take military action against the Maurice Bishop regime, though the sulphurous language from the White House scared Grenada's Caribbean neighbors."[149] The Ambassador's conclusion may be overstated, but if so, only slightly. This will become clear in this study's examination of the policy process that preceded Reagan's decision to invade.

Conclusions

In search of the motives that informed the Reagan administration's decision to launch "Urgent Fury," as well as the specific role played by international law in the decisionmaking process, this chapter has examined three factors: (1) the situation on Grenada from the time of Bishop's coup until his murder; (2) the conduct of the military action; and (3) the evolution of US-Grenadian relations from 1979 to 1983.

Each factor imparts a different hue to the multicolored canvas of American objectives. However, only when all three are considered simultaneously does anything resembling an accurate portrait emerge.

Even a cursory examination of the pre-invasion conditions on the island of Grenada yields one safe conclusion about Reagan administration aims: given the nature of the Maurice Bishop regime's political objectives and of its foreign support, the administration had substantial grounds for wishing the PRG's demise, if not for taking active steps to remove it. As we have seen, the People's Revolutionary Government of Grenada was a genuine Leninist regime. It was not, as has sometimes been asserted, merely a misunderstood third world leftist regime: during its brief tenure, the Bishop government suspended elections, ended freedom of the press and other freedoms, and embarked on an intensive militarization of Grenada — all in support of its self-consciously Leninist ends. Moreover, although sometimes exaggerated, the influence upon Grenada of a number of Communist states was of no little consequence. The Bishop regime's strongest ties by far were to Fidel Castro's Cuba. Indeed, as one Caribbean scholar has observed, "in St. George's, there was a kind of 'Cuban fixation.'"[150] Nevertheless, the Soviet Union, Czechoslovakia, East Germany, Bulgaria, and North Korea all provided the PRG with valuable assistance. The Soviet Union in particular could well have exacted long-term geopolitical benefits from its second Caribbean ally.

If one considers only the conduct *per se* of Operation "Urgent Fury," three tentative conclusions about Washington's motives emerge. First, in view of the many manifest problems of the military action, it would seem certain that American planning for the Grenada invasion did in fact take place within the short 72-hour period before D-Day, as the Reagan administration would later publicly contend. If the operation had long been on the Pentagon's "drawing board," as some critics have charged, then its planning and execution by the American military were pitiful at best. Given the very limited capabilities of the "defenders" of Grenada, American and foreign casualties were very high. Army Rangers were compelled to use Grenadian tourist maps. The Venezuelan Embassy, "Fort Adolphus," was nearly attacked by mistake. None of the various "rescue operations" fared particularly well. And the effort to liberate Richmond Hill Prison proved disastrous.

A second conclusion is sustained by an examination solely of the conduct of "Urgent Fury": the Reagan administration would seem to have accorded a very high priority to the rescue of Sir Paul Scoon. As we have seen, extraordinary measures were employed in order to liberate him. At first a special SEAL force, supported by an FSO who could identify the Governor-General, was dispatched in armored helicopters for this purpose. When that special operation failed, a diverted Marine force was called in by Admiral Metcalf, himself. Such unusual effort could indicate several things. It could signal Sir Paul's perceived political significance. Certainly, in establishing an interim post-invasion government on Grenada, the Governor-General would play an essential role. Alternatively, it could indicate the international legal significance attached by Washington to the Governor-General. As the Grenadian Head of State, the Reagan administration would later maintain, Scoon had invited American action. Should he be killed, the American legal justification for its action would be significantly undermined. Most likely, the unusual effort reflected both the political and legal calculations of the administration.

Third, when considering *only* the rather pathetic way in which they were rescued, the safety of the American students on Grenada would seem to have been a lesser priority of Washington. The first group of St. George's medical students, those of the True Blue campus, were not rescued until the second day of the invasion. The existence of a second university campus at Grand Anse was unknown to American military forces until after "Urgent Fury" had begun. And the last two hundred and two students were not evacuated from the island until "D plus three," after ninety-six hours of vulnerability to seizure by hostile forces.

A review of US-Grenadian relations from 1979-83 suggests two conclusions. First, even before Reagan's inauguration, there were real fears in Washington about the character of the new airport being built on Grenada. Clearly, the facility was perceived by the Reagan administration as a cause for geostrategic concern. Whether the Point Salines International Airport would eventually have become a Soviet or Cuban base is debatable; indeed, given the unfortified nature of the facility's design, it appears the airport had actually been intended for nonmilitary purposes — at least, principally so. It is enough, though, to conclude that the administration was genuinely anxious about the 10,000-foot runway at Point Salines.

Second, in view of its rhetoric, the Reagan administration had even greater geostrategic apprehensions about Grenada than had its predecessor. As Reagan concluded in March, 1983, only seven months before

Urgent Fury, "the Soviet-Cuban militarization of Grenada ... [could] only be seen as power projection into the [Caribbean] region." Hostile presidential rhetoric and administration actions notwithstanding, Grenada was never as significant an issue as many outside observers had believed it then to be. Accordingly, it seems doubtful that without the unusual circumstances of mid-October 1983, the United States would have taken military action.

Notes

1.   Langhorne A. Motley, interviewed by Seymour Hersh in "Operation Urgent Fury," a PBS "Front-line" report originally broadcast on February 2, 1988.

2.   McNeil, *War and Peace In Central America*, p. 172.

3.   Reagan, *An American Life*, p. 455.

4.   Three people lost their lives in the twelve hour operation. Latin American Bureau, *Grenada: Whose Freedom?* (London: Latin American Bureau, 1984), p. 30.

For more on the New Jewel Movement, the 1979 revolution and its aftermath, see Davidson, *A Study in Politics*, pp. 12-13, 17-46; EPICA Task Force, *Grenada: The Peaceful Revolution* (Washington, D.C: EPICA Task Force, 1982); Latin America Bureau, *Whose Freedom?*, pp. 31-88; Gordon K. Lewis, *Grenada: The Jewel Despoiled* (Baltimore: Johns Hopkins, 1987); O'Shaughnessy, *Revolution, Invasion and Aftermath*, pp. 77-172; Payne et al., *Revolution and Invasion*, pp. 18-147; Gregory Sandford, *The New Jewel Movement: Grenada's Revolution 1979-1983* (Washington, D.C.: Foreign Service Institute, 1985); Chris Searle, *Grenada: The Struggle Against Destabilization* (London: Writers and Readers Publishing, 1983), pp. 23-120; Schoenhals and Melanson, *Revolution and Intervention*, pp. 32-84; and Jiri Valenta and Virginia Valenta, "Leninism in Grenada," in *Grenada and Soviet/Cuban Policy: Internal Crisis and U.S./OECS Intervention*, eds. Jiri Valenta and Herbert J. Ellison (Boulder, Colo.: Westview Press, 1986), pp. 3-37.

5.   Great Britain, Parliament, House of Commons, Foreign Affairs Committee, Fifth Report, *Caribbean and Central America*, session 1981-1982, p. xlv.

6.   United States Information Agency, "Grenada: Background and Facts," 1983, p. 3.

7. Courtney Glass, "The Setting," in *American Intervention in Grenada: The Implications of Operation Urgent Fury*, eds. Peter M. Dunn and Bruce W. Watson (Boulder, Colo.: Westview Press, 1985), p. 7.

The New Jewel Movement came into being in 1973 when two radical groups, the Joint Endeavor for Welfare, Education and Liberation (JEWEL) and the Movement for the Assemblies of People (MAP), merged and adopted a socialist manifesto. The manifesto, infused with large doses of Tanzanian Christian socialism, was an interesting amalgam of various socialist theories. See Anthony P. Maingot, "Options for Grenada: The Need to be Cautious," *Caribbean Review* 12 (Fall 1983): 25-26; and V.S. Naipaul, "An Island Betrayed," *Harper's*, March 1984, pp. 61-72.

8. Interview with Alistair Hughes in St. George's, February 24, 1984, cited by Valenta and Valenta, "Leninism in Grenada," in *Grenada and Soviet/Cuban Policy*, eds. Valenta and Ellison, p. 5.

9. For an excellent summary of the PRG and the events leading up to the U.S. invasion, see Great Britain, Parliament, House of Commons, Foreign Affairs Committee, Second Report, *Grenada*, Session 1983-1984, pp. vi-ix (hereafter cited as "Second Report").

10. On Grenada, the 1979 revolution was commonly referred to as the "revo." The phrase itself is drawn from Bob Shacochis, "Yesterday's Revolution: Grenada, Mr. Reagan, and the Hangman," *Harper's*, October 1987, p. 44.

11. A preliminary evaluation of some of the twelve and a half tons of Grenada documents was published by the U.S. Department of State and Department of Defense on December 16, 1983 under the title, "Grenada: A Preliminary Report."

In September, 1984, the State and Defense Departments published the three-volume *Grenada Documents: An Overview and Selection*, edited by Michael Ledeen and Herbert Romerstein. See also Paul Seabury and Walter A. McDougall, eds., *The Grenada Papers* (San Francisco, Cal.: Institute for Contemporary Studies, 1984); and Nicholas Dujmovic, *The Grenada Documents: Window on Totalitarianism* (Washington, D.C.: Pergammon-Brassey's, 1988).

12. Valenta and Valenta, "Leninism in Grenada," in *Grenada and Soviet/Cuban Policy*, eds. Valenta and Ellison, p. 3.

The Foreign Affairs Committee of the British House of Commons drew a similar conclusion in 1984: "The NJM appears to have become, essentially, a classic revolutionary movement in the Bolshevik mould, dependent on a small number of party members and sustained in power by its control of the media and the armed services." See "Second Report," p. viii.

13. V. S. Naipaul, an eminent scholar from Trinidad, has captured well the PRG's essence: "The apparatus was absurd. But the power was real." Naipaul, "An Island Betrayed," p. 63.

14. Howard Wiarda, "The Impact of Grenada in Central America," in *Grenada and Soviet Cuban Policy*, eds. Valenta and Ellison, p. 108.

15. For a clear articulation of Maurice Bishop's goals, see his "Line of March for the Party," presented by Maurice Bishop, Central Committee Chairman, General Meeting of the Party, September 13, 1982. Reprinted in Seabury and McDougall, eds., *The Grenada Papers*, pp. 59-88.

16. As early as 1975, the NJM's political bureau had opted for Marxism. See Leslie Manigat, "Grenada: Revolutionary Shockwave, Crisis, and Intervention," in *The Caribbean and World Politics: Cross Currents and Cleavages*, eds. Jorge Jeine and Leslie Manigat (New York: Holmes & Meier, 1988), p. 183. For a detailed discussion of the Leninist character of the NJM, see Valenta and Valenta, "Leninism and Grenada," pp. 6-19.

17. See U.S. Congress, House of Representatives, Committee on Foreign Affairs, Subcommittee on Inter-American Affairs, *United States Policy toward Grenada*, 97th Congress, 2nd session, 1982, pp. 82-83 (hereafter cited as *United States Policy toward Grenada*); and Latin American Bureau, *Whose Freedom?*, p. 45.

18. On the early activities of the PRG, see Valenta and Valenta, "Leninism in Grenada," p. 8; Payne et al., *Revolution and Invasion*, pp. 18-41; and Schoenhals and Melanson, *Revolution and Intervention*, pp. 43-56. For more on the airport, see below.

19. To increase the productivity of the Grenadian people and to bolster their "social consciousness," the NJM used various means of mass mobilization were used including slogans, "productivity poems," marches and rallies. See especially EPICA Task Force, *The Peaceful Revolution*; and Searle, *The Struggle Against Destabilization*.

A selection of Bishop's most important speeches is reprinted in Bruce Marcus and Michael Taber, eds., *Maurice Bishop Speaks: The Grenada Revolution, 1979-83* (New York: Pathfinder Press, 1983).

20. Margaret Daly Hayes, "Girding for the Long Run," in *Grenada and Soviet/Cuban Policy*, eds. Valenta and Ellison, p. 212.

21. For a more detailed account, see Major Mark Adkin, *Urgent Fury: The Battle for Grenada* (Lexington, Mass.: D.C. Heath and Company, 1989), pp. 27-45 (hereafter cited as Adkin, *The Battle for Grenada*); Glass, "The Setting," pp. 9-11; Payne et al., *Revolution and Invasion*, pp. 105-117; Schoenhals and Melanson, *Revolution and Intervention*, pp. 64-71; Valenta and Valenta, "Leninism in Grenada," pp. 19-20; and Manigat, "Grenada: Revolutionary Shockwave, Crisis, and Intervention," pp. 191-204.

22. See the "Central Committee Report on First Plenary Session, July 13-19, 1983," *Grenada Documents*, Log. No. 100243; and "Minutes of Emergency Meeting of NJM Central Committee, August 26, 1983," *Grenada Documents*, Log. No. 100319. Cited by Valenta and Valenta, "Leninism in Grenada," p. 20.

23. Shacochis, "Yesterday's Revolution," p. 44.

24. According to Kai Schoenhals, the "record shows that Maurice Bishop believed as much as Coard in democratic centralism and the eventual evolution of Grenada into a Communist state. It was after all Bishop who named one of his sons Vladimir in honor of Lenin and who, ... urged his comrades ... to study the history of the Communist Party of the Soviet Union in order to solve the crisis facing the New Jewel Movement." Schoenhals and Melanson, *Revolution and Intervention*, pp. 81-82.

25. Manigat, "Grenada: Revolutionary Shockwave, Crisis, and Intervention," p. 193.

26. See "Extraordinary General Meeting, 9/25/83," reprinted in Seabury and McDougall, eds., *The Grenada Papers*, pp. 300-315.

27. While Bishop was traveling with George Louison and Unison Whiteman, his trusted supporters, the Prime Minister began to doubt the feasibility of shared power. Louison then told a group of Grenadian students in Hungary that neither he, Bishop, nor Whiteman had accepted the notion of joint leadership. When word of Louison's meeting traveled back to Grenada, many Central Committee members were infuriated. Schoenhals and Melanson, *Revolution and Intervention*, p. 71.

28. On October 6, Cletus St. Paul called a member of the Central Committee from Cuba. Bishop's trusted bodyguard said that the Prime Minister had not accepted joint leadership and hinted that "blood will flow." This was reported and taken to mean that Bishop was plotting the deaths of the leaders of the radicals. Payne et al., *Revolution and Invasion*, pp. 128-129.

29. Davidson, *A Study in Politics*, p. 68; Payne et al., *Revolution and Invasion*, pp. 128-129; and Schoenhals and Melanson, *Revolution and Intervention*, pp. 71-72.

30. O'Shaughnessy tersely summarizes the day's events: "Bishop had been stripped of much of his personal protection, had had the PRA manipulated against him, its Commander-in-Chief, and had had one of his principal supporters stripped of power in the party." *Revolution, Invasion, and Aftermath*, p. 125.

31. Payne et al., *Revolution and Invasion*, p. 81.

32. Schoenhals and Melanson, *Revolution and Intervention*, p. 74. The news of Bishop's arrest, O'Shaughnessy relates, "went round Grenada with the force of a hurricane." *Revolution, Invasion and Aftermath*, p. 126.

33. Shacochis, "Yesterday's Revolution," p. 44.

34.   "Second Report," p. ix.

35.   Bernard Diederich, "Interviewing George Louison: A PRG Minister Discusses the Killings," *Caribbean Review* 12 (Fall 1983): 18.

36.   A number of accounts of the brutal day have been written. Sometimes graphic in their detail, they are often contradictory. For my necessarily abbreviated version, I have drawn upon the following sources: Adkin, *The Battle for Grenada*, pp. 47-81; Davidson, *A Study in Politics*, pp. 71-74; Latin American Bureau, *Whose Freedom?*, pp. 74-76; Lewis, *Jewel Despoiled*, pp. 53-61; O'Shaughnessy, *Revolution, Invasion and Aftermath*, pp. 131-139; Payne et al., *Revolution and Invasion*, pp. 133-136; Shacochis, Yesterday's Revolution," pp. 45-47; Schoenhals and Melanson, *Revolution and Intervention*, pp. 75-78; Valenta and Valenta, "Leninism in Grenada," pp. 24-25; and Geoffrey Wagner, "End of a Revo: Some Fell Slow and Some Fell Fast," *National Review*, June 5, 1987, pp. 32-33.

37.   The ironic juxtaposition of "Free Maurice" and "No Communism" was indicative of the public's ignorance of Bishop's Leninist objectives.

38.   Creft, formerly the Minister of Education, Youth, and Social Affairs, had voluntarily joined Bishop in his detention. She had borne Bishop a son, Vladimir, and was now pregnant with another of his children.

39.   Bishop had rechristened Fort George after his own father, Rupert Bishop, who had been killed in 1974 in an anti-Gairy demonstration. O'Shaughnessy, *Revolution, Invasion, and Aftermath*, p. 2.

40.   Davidson, *A Study in Politics*, p. 71.

41.   M. S. Thompson, "The day Grenada's leader went to the wall," *The Guardian*, May 24, 1985, p. 12; Diederich, "Interviewing George Louison" p. 19; and Shacochis, "Yesterday's Revolution," p. 46.

42.   Who fired the first shot will probably never be known, but there are neutral and even pro-Bishop eyewitnesses who later testified that the first shots were fired from the pro-Bishop crowd. The firing may have been started by provocateurs; nevertheless, during the ensuing melee, both sides suffered casualties. See Schoenhals and Melanson, *Revolution and Intervention*, p. 77; and Payne et al., *Revolution and Invasion*, p. 135.

43.   The precise number of deaths that took place around the fort is not known. "[T]he general consensus among observers was that it was over 100." Payne et al., *Revolution and Invasion*, p. 136.

44.   The other six to be killed were: Keith "Pumphead" Hailing from the Market and Import Board; Evelyn "Brat" Bullen, a business supporter of Bishop; Evelyn Maitland of Maitland's Garage; Unison Whiteman, creator of the original JEWEL movement; Norris Bain, former Minister of Housing; and Fitzroy Bain, the President of the Agricultural and General Workers Union. O'Shaughnessy, *Revolution, Invasion, and Aftermath*, p. 138.

45. The details of Bishop's murder are provided by Shacochis, "Yesterday's Revolution," pp. 46-47; and Wagner, "End of a Revo," pp. 32-33.

46. Interview with George Louison, conducted by International Press correspondent Mohammed Oliver, International Press, April 14, 1984, p. 214.

47. General Austin headed the RMC, which included fifteen other PRA officers. Joint Chairmen were Lieutenant Colonels Leon James and Ewart Layne who, together with Majors Leon Cornwall, Tan Bartholomew, and St. Bernard, made up the former Central Committee faction. Then came the key officer of the political department, Major Chris Stroude; the security service, Keith "Chicken" Roberts; and the operational staff officer of the army, Major Basil "Akee" Gahagan. The remaining seven — Captains Lester Redhead and Huey Romain, Lieutenants Cecil "Dumpy" Prime, Rudolph Ogilvey, and Iman Abdullah, and Second Lieutenants Kenrick Fraser, and Raeburn Nelson — held senior executive or administrative posts in the PRA. Coard, Selwyn Strachan and John Ventour served as advisers. Adkin, *The Battle for Urgent Fury*, p. 83.

48. Cited in Mary Grieves et al., "The Grenada Document: The Bitter, Epic Struggle for the Isle of Spice," *Nation*, special edition, Barbados, February 1984, p. 25; and "Broadcast by General Hudson Austin," in *Documents on the Invasion*, p. 11.

49. Manigat, "Grenada: Revolutionary Shockwave, Crisis, and Intervention," p. 203.

50. Manigat, "Grenada: Revolutionary Shockwave, Crisis, and Intervention," p. 203.

51. "OECS Statement, October 25, 1983," *Department of State Bulletin* 83 (December 1983): 67-68.

52. Early reports of the American mission in Grenada were provided in: Richard Harwood, "Tidy U.S. War Ends: 'We Blew Them Away,'" *Washington Post*, November 6, 1983, pp. A1-A20; Ed Magnuson, "D-Day in Grenada," *Time*, November 7, 1983, pp. 22-28; and Mark Whitaker et al., "The Battle for Grenada," *Newsweek*, November 7, 1983, pp. 66-76.

More recent accounts include: Adkin, *The Battle for Grenada*; Dorothea Cypher, "Urgent Fury: The U.S. Army in Grenada," in *American Intervention in Grenada*, eds. Peter M. Dunn and Bruce W. Watson (Boulder, Colo.: Westview Press, 1985), pp. 99-108; William S. Lind, *Report to the Congressional Military Reform Caucus* (Washington, D.C.: Military Reform Institute, 1984); James Berry Motley, "Grenada: Low Intensity Conflict and the Use of U.S. Military Power," *World Affairs* 16 (Winter 1983-1984): 221-238; Schwarzkopf, *It Doesn't Take A Hero*, pp. 244-258; Ronald H. Spector, *U.S. Marines in Grenada* (Washington, D.C.: History and Museums Division Headquarters, 1987); and Frank Uhlig, Jr., "Amphibious Aspects of the Grenada Episode," in *American Intervention in Grenada*, pp. 89-97.

53. William S. Lind, former Senate aide and President of the Military Reform Institute. Interviewed by Seymour Hersh in "Operation Urgent Fury," a PBS "Frontline" report broadcast on February 2, 1988.

54. The force defending Grenada consisted of Cubans, the People's Revolutionary Army (PRA), and the territorial militia. The 784-strong Cuban contingent was mainly composed of construction workers; no more than 43 were military. The 1,000 PRA members were the best equipped, with AK-17 and AK-47 automatic rifles, light anti-aircraft weapons, rocket launchers, military trucks, and a number of armored personnel carriers. While there were between 2,000 and 5,000 in the Grenadian militia, these had been disarmed for fear that they would be disloyal to the RMC. See Gabriel, *Military Incompetence*, pp. 154-155; and Lewis, *The Jewel Despoiled*, pp. 101-102.

55. For a brief discussion of the problems of Operation Urgent Fury, see John H. Cushman, Jr., "Pentagon Study Faults Planning on Grenada," *New York Times*, July 12, 1986, pp. A1, A4; Steven Emerson, "What went wrong on Grenada?" *U.S. News & World Report*, November 3, 1986, p. 42; Benjamin F. Schemmer, "Grenada Highlights One of DoD's C3 Problems But Increased Funding is Bringing Solutions," *Armed Forces Journal*, February, 1984, pp. 50-52; and George C. Wilson and Michael Weisskopf, "Pentagon, Congress Seek Cure to Shortcomings Exposed in Grenada Invasion," *Washington Post*, February 20, 1986, p. A24.

For a lengthier critique, see Richard A. Gabriel, *Military Incompetence*, pp. 149-186; Arthur T. Hadley, "Inside America's Broken War Machine," *New Republic*, May 7, 1984; William S. Lind, *Report to the Congressional Military Reform Caucus: The Grenada Operation* (Washington, D.C.: Military Reform Institute, April 4, 1984); and Edward Luttwak, *The Pentagon and the Art of War* (New York: Simon and Schuster, 1985). Perhaps the most balanced recent assessment is Adkin, *The Battle for Grenada*.

56. U.S. Joint Chiefs of Staff, "Urgent Fury Chronology of Events," Working Paper, undated, p. 2, cited by Dorothea Cypher, "Urgent Fury: The U.S. Army in Grenada," p. 101.

57. JCS, "Urgent Fury Chronology of Events," p. 2, cited by Dorothea Cypher, "Urgent Fury: The U.S. Army in Grenada," p. 101. See also Tom Burgess, "Grenada Report Critical of Tactical Communications," *Air Force Times*, February 4, 1985, p. 4.

58. In his testimony before the House Armed Service Committee, the Assistant Secretary of State listed the significant military objectives of the U.S. action. See Langhorne A. Motley, "The Decision to Assist Grenada," *Department of State Bulletin* 84 (March 1984): 70-73. See also Weinberger, *Fighting for Peace*, p. 110.

59. Among those imprisoned at Richmond Hill were Alistair Hughes, Leslie Pierre, Winston Whyte and Lloyd Noel. O'Shaughnessy, *Revolution, Invasion and Aftermath*, p. 25. Ultimately, 740 U.S. citizens would be evacuated from Grenada; of these, 595 were medical students. U.S. Army, Public Affairs Office, Consolidated List, Grenada casualties, June 1984.

60. A trenchant critique of the "jointness obsession" is offered in Lehman, *Command of the Seas*, pp. 291-305.

61. The invasion plans were drafted at the headquarters of the U.S. Atlantic Command, with all four services represented. Admiral Wesley McDonald, the Commander-in-Chief Atlantic (CINCLANT), at first proposed a unilateral Navy-Marine effort. This plan was withdrawn after its rejection by the Joint Chiefs, and another using a "combined service organization" was suggested. This second plan were then reviewed and approved by the JCS. When the JCS recommended the number of troops needed to invade Grenada, Weinberger arbitrarily ordered them to double the size of the force.

On the invasion planning, see especially Adkin, *The Battle for Grenada*, pp. 125-144; Caspar Weinberger, "Letter to the Editor: Grenada Invasion was a Military, Political Success," *New York Times*, September 30, 1986, p. 34; Gabriel, *Military Incompetence*, pp. 151-156; and Cypher, "Urgent Fury," pp. 101-102.

62. Perhaps ironically, Vice Admiral Metcalf was chosen to command "Urgent Fury," an operation which would later be cited as evidence of American recovery from "Vietnam syndrome." Earlier, Metcalf had helped manage the evacuation of Saigon. For the "Vietnam syndrome" argument, see Dov Zakheim, "The Grenada Operation and Superpower Relations: A Perspective from the Pentagon," in *Grenada and Soviet/Cuban Policy*, eds. Valenta and Ellison, p. 179.

63. Although the plan had called for committing two Ranger battalions of about eight hundred men each, only about five hundred ever made it to Grenada. Because of early reports of heavy fighting at Point Salines, C-130 transport aircraft en route to Fort Stewart to pick up the remaining Rangers were diverted to Fort Bragg instead. Gabriel, *Military Incompetence*, pp. 161-163.

64. On Grenada "special ops," see especially Adkin, *The Battle for Grenada*, pp. 167-192. Of some use are Gabriel, *Military Incompetence*; Lehman, *Command of the Seas*, pp. 298-299; and John J. Fialka, "In Battle for Grenada, Commando Missions Didn't Go as Planned," *Wall Street Journal*, November 15, 1983, pp. 1, 21.

65. Harwood, "Tidy U.S. War Ends," p. A1; "Address to the Nation, October 27, 1983," p. 1501. General Schwarzkopf, for example, conceded in his memoir: "measured against our objectives, the first day's results were pretty dismal .... the coup de main had failed utterly." Schwarzkopf, *It Doesn't Take A Hero*, p. 252.

66. Though they eventually were able to escape undetected, the SEALS were compelled to bury themselves in the sand and to listen while the Grenadians complained and smoked marijuana. Commander Richard Butler interview, November 4, 1983 (Oral History Collection, MCHC, Washington, D.C.), cited in Spector, *U.S. Marines in Grenada.* On Pearls reconnaissance efforts by the SEAL forces, see also Spector, *U.S. Marines in Grenada,* p. 6; Ralph Kinney Bennett, "Grenada: Anatomy of a 'Go' Decision," *Reader's Digest,* February, 1984, p. 76; and Frank Uhlig, Jr., "Amphibious Aspects of the Grenada Mission," pp. 91-92.

67. Donn-Erik Marshall's interview with Robert P. Hilton, September 9, 1988, cited in Donn-Erik Marshall, "Urgent Fury: The U.S. Military Intervention in Grenada," University of Virginia, Department of History, Master's Thesis, 1989, p. 11. The deaths of the four SEALs were confirmed by Langhorne Motley. Author's interview with Ambassador Motley, March 7, 1989. See also Weinberger, *Fighting for Peace,* p. 118.

68. Schwarzkopf, *It Doesn't Take A Hero,* p. 249.

69. The arrival of the Rangers had been delayed for at least a half hour because of bad weather and a failure of a transport aircraft's inertial guidance system. See Fialka, "Commando Missions Didn't Go as Planned," p. 1; and Cypher, "Urgent Fury," p. 102.

70. "JCS Replies to Criticism of Grenada Operation," *Army* August 1984, p. 32.

71. According to John Lehman, the SEAL team assigned to capture the Radio Free Grenada station "attacked the wrong building" because of a lack of proper intelligence information. Lehman, *Command of the Seas,* p. 298. Numerous contradictory accounts of this mission have been offered. See Fialka, "Commando Missions Didn't Go as Planned," p. 21; Sandford and Vigilante, *Grenada: The Untold Story,* p. 10; Gabriel, Military Incompetence, p. 159, 161-162; and Lind, *Report to the Congressional Military Reform Caucus,* p. 1.

72. Donn-Erik Marshall's interview with Richard Scholtes, January 12, 1989, cited in Marshall, "Urgent Fury," p. 112.

73. Of the many "black" (secret) operations conducted on Grenada, only the seizure of the power plant appears to have been successfully accomplished. Here, on the morning of the invasion, a sixteen-man SEAL team captured six civilian employees of the local power company. Gabriel, *Military Incompetence,* p. 162.

74. Author's interviews of Ambassador Francis McNeil, September 20, 1988; and with Michael Kozak, November 3, 1988. See also "Under Fire in Grenada," in *Duty & Danger: The American Foreign Service In Action* (Washington, D.C.: American Foreign Service Association, 1988), pp. 1-3. According to Rossin, his stint at the U.S. Embassy in Bridgetown lasted from December 1980 to August 1982. Rossin's letter to author, March 20, 1989.

75. "Under Fire in Grenada," *Duty & Danger*, p. 2. Author's interview with Ambassador McNeil, September 20, 1988.

76. See Spector, *U. S. Marines in Grenada*, pp. 10-12.

77. When the Cobras were shot down by PRA anti-aircraft weapons, three pilots were killed and a fourth wounded. Cypher, "Urgent Fury," pp. 103-104.

78. Fialka, "Commando Missions Didn't Go as Planned," p. 1; Schwarzkopf, *It Doesn't Take A Hero*, pp. 250-252. Fire from the fort had also complicated a raid on nearby Richmond Hill Prison. See below.

79. Davidson and Lewis report that thirty patients were killed. Davidson, *A Study in Politics*, p. 85; and Lewis, *Jewel Despoiled*, p. 101. According to Cypher and other sources, however, eighteen were killed in the unfortunate incident. Cypher, "Urgent Fury," p. 104.

80. Schwarzkopf, *It Doesn't Take A Hero*, p. 250.

81. Lawrence G. Rossin's letter to the author, June 12, 1989.

82. For more on the Scoon rescue, see Adkin, *The Battle for Grenada*, pp. 167-191; Cypher, "Urgent Fury," pp. 103-104; Fialka, "Commando Missions Didn't Go as Planned," pp. 1, 21; Gabriel, *Military Incompetence*, pp. 158-161; and Spector, *U.S. Marines in Grenada*, pp. 10-16. Gabriel implies that the airstrike on Fort Frederick was ordered in support of the Richmond Hill prison rescue operation. The strike may in fact have supported both rescue attempts.

83. See "Under Fire in Grenada," *Duty & Danger*, p. 3; Sandford and Vigilante, *The Untold Story*, p. 13; and Lawrence G. Rossin's letter to the author, June 12, 1989.

84. According to Larry Rossin, "On the morning of October 26, I together with ... Rudyard Lewis received a written request from Sir Paul Scoon for intervention." Rossin's letter to the author, June 12, 1989.

85. Task Force 160, the "Nightstalkers," is a secret helicopter battalion stationed at Fort Campbell, Kentucky, responsible for airlifting Delta on its missions. On an October 24, 1984 ABC "Nightline" episode, Pentagon spokesman Michael Burch admitted that Delta Force had assaulted the prison in nine Blackhawk helicopters. For more on TF 160, see Adkin, *The Battle for Grenada*, pp. 174-180; and Steven Emerson, *Secret Warriors: Inside the Covert Military Operations of the Reagan Era* (New York: G.P. Putnam's Sons, 1988), pp. 45, 47-48.

86. Gabriel argues that perhaps as many as five helicopters were downed. See Gabriel, *Military Incompetence*, pp. 157-159. According to Lehman, the "Delta commandos were assigned to capture Richmond Hill Prison, but their daylight assault was repelled, with the loss of a helicopter." Lehman, *Command of the Seas*, p. 299.

87. See O'Shaughnessy, *Revolution, Invasion and Aftermath*, pp. 24-25; Benjamin F. Schemmer, "JCS Reply to Congressional Reform Caucus' Critique of the Grenada Operation," *Armed Forces Journal*, July 1984, p. 13; Rick

Maze, "Report Faults Military Performance in Grenada," *Air Force Times*, April 23, 1984, p. 49; and Spector, *U.S. Marines in Grenada*, p. 21.

Don Bohning, an American newspaper correspondent, reported that the prison was initially "liberated" by three of his colleagues who simply walked quietly into the unguarded prison and freed ten political prisoners. Don Bohning, "The Invasion of Grenada: An Eyewitness Account," *Miami Herald*, October 30, 1983, p. 40.

88. Lieutenant Colonel Ray L. Smith interview, November 8, 1983 (Oral History Collection, MCHC, Washington, D.C.), pp. 44-46, cited by Spector, *U.S. Marines in Grenada*, p. 21.

89. Spector, *U.S. Marines in Grenada*, p. 21.

90. "President's Remarks, October 25, 1983," p. 67. Gabriel, *Military Incompetence*, p. 174. See also Charles Doe, "Grenada Rescuers Unaware of Students at 2nd Site," *Air Force Times*, March 12, 1984, p. 11.

91. Major General Schwarzkopf's recounting of the rescue at True Blue is remarkably candid. See his interview by Seymour Hersh on "Operation Urgent Fury," a PBS "Front Line" episode broadcast on February 2, 1988; and Schwarzkopf, *It Doesn't Take A Hero*, p. 252.

92. Cypher, "Urgent Fury," p. 103; and Fialka, "Commando Missions Didn't Go as Planned," p. 21.

93. Spector, *U.S. Marines in Grenada*, p. 17.

94. For more on the Grand Anse rescue, see Cypher, "Urgent Fury," p. 104; Gabriel, *Military Incompetence*, pp. 168-170; Spector, *U.S. Marines in Grenada*, pp. 17-18; and Uhlig, "Amphibious Aspects of the Grenada Episode," p. 94.

95. Schwarzkopf, *It Doesn't Take a Hero*, p. 254.

96. The scene was described this way by Joe Antario, one of the medical students awaiting rescue at Grand Anse. Mark Whitaker, "The Battle for Grenada," p. 4. See also Spector, *U.S. Marines in Grenada*, p. 18; and Schwarzkopf, *It Doesn't Take A Hero*, p. 255.

97. Spector, *U.S. Marines in Grenada*, p. 18.

98. "Address to the Nation, October 27, 1983," p. 1501.

99. On November 3, 1983, Vice Admiral Metcalf transferred his responsibilities to Major General Trobaugh, Commander of U.S. Forces Grenada, and Brigadier General Rudyard E. C. Lewis, Commander of the OECS established Caribbean Peace Force. By December 15, 1983, the U.S. presence on Grenada consisted of only about 300 military police, technicians, and support troops. Cypher, "Urgent Fury," p. 106.

100. Weinberger, "Grenada Invasion Was a Military, Political Success," p. 34. In his memoir, Weinberger would dub the Grenada invasion "the complete model for future such activities." Weinberger, *Fighting for Peace*, p. 126.

101. "Remarks to Citizens, February 20, 1986," *Weekly Compilation of Presidential Documents* 22 (February 24, 1986): 249.

102. Reagan, *An American Life*, p. 455.

103. Kenneth Adelman et al., "Where We Succeeded, Where We Failed: Lessons from Reagan Officials for the Next Conservative Presidency," *Policy Review*, no. 43 (Winter 1988), p. 52.

104. Figures cited by Lou Cannon, "President Welcomed in Grenada," *Washington Post*, February 21, 1986, p. A14. For a listing of Grenada casualties, see U.S. Army Public Affairs Office, Consolidated List, June 1984. More than two-thirds of the Americans were killed by friendly fire, mistaken bombing attacks, helicopter crashes, and other accidents. In addition, twenty percent were wounded in these accidents. See the *Providence Evening Bulletin*, November 7, 1984, p. C7. If U.S. "special operations" casualties are included, the American death toll jumps to twenty-nine. Gabriel, *Military Incompetence*, p. 182.

105. Figures cited in "Auditing an Invasion," *Time*, July 23, 1984, p. 49. Although $134.4 million seems a modest figure compared to the American annual defense budget, it should be noted that Grenada's current annual budget is fixed at $96 million, approximately seventy percent of the three-day cost of "Urgent Fury." See Schanche, "Grenada struggles to shake off recent past," p. 16.

106. Schwarzkopf, *It Doesn't Take A Hero*, p. 258. A Senate Armed Service Committee staff report in February of 1986 and a classified Department of Defense assessment in July of the same year detailed a number of significant problems of the Grenada mission, *inter alia*:

(1) poor communications;

(2) an almost total lack of accurate intelligence; and

(3) logistical problems.

Because of incompatible equipment and technology, there was virtually no contact between Rangers and Army airborne troops on the island and the naval task force offshore. Every time a ship would turn, communication was lost until the antennas could be manually adjusted. Accordingly, Army officers resorted to ham radios, sent couriers to vessels by helicopter, and in one case, used an AT&T credit card to place a call on a civilian telephone to Fort Bragg. Because a CIA operative got cold feet and refused to fly to Grenada, the lack of intelligence on the island was almost crippling. Moreover, U.S. forces lacked proper maps of the island. The map lockers on board the assault ships contained no maps of Grenada; the "maps" which did arrive were photos which had to be glued together on the ships, and which turned into a jellified mess when wet. Finally, the decision that the Rangers attack at daylight instead of at night was based on the mistaken belief that they were unable to do so.

For more on the problems of "Urgent Fury," see especially Adkin, *The*

Battle for Grenada; Cushman, "Pentagon Study Faults Planning," pp. A1-A4; Emerson, "What went wrong?" p. 42; Gabriel, *Military Incompetence*, pp. 173-184; Lehman, *Command of the Seas*, pp. 291-305; Schemmer, "Grenada Highlights," pp. 50-52; Hedrick Smith, *The Power Game: How Washington Works* (New York: Random House, 1988), p. 197; and Wilson and Weisskopf, "Shortcomings Exposed," p. A24.

107. Testimony of Sally Shelton, former Deputy Assistant Secretary for Inter-American Affairs, in *United States Policy toward Grenada*, p. 56.

108. *United States Policy Toward Grenada*, p. 56.

109. Frank V. Ortiz, "Letter to the Editor," *Harper's*, June 1984, p. 7.

110. Schoenhals and Melanson, *Revolution and Intervention*, pp. 112-116.

111. Lars Schoultz, *National Security and United States Policy Towards Latin America* (Princeton: Princeton University Press, 1987), p. 240. See, for example, Robert S. Leiken, "Eastern Winds in Latin America," *Foreign Policy*, no. 42 (Spring 1981), p. 101.

112. "The UN vote on Afghanistan was perceived in the eyes of Washington and many western capitals as the crossing of the Rubicon by the Grenadian revolutionary leaders." Manigat, "Revolutionary Shockwave, Crisis, and Intervention," in *The Caribbean in World Politics*, eds. Jeine and Manigat, p. 185.

113. Maurice Bishop, "In Nobody's Backyard, National Broadcast by Maurice Bishop on RFG on April 13, 1979," in *Selected Speeches*, p. 9.

114. See Payne et al., *Revolution and Invasion*, 50-53; Magnuson, "D-Day," p. 26; and Latin American Bureau, *Whose Freedom?*, p. 46.

115. See Magnuson, "D-Day in Grenada," p. 26; Payne et al., *Revolution and Invasion*, pp. 50-53; and Schoultz, *National Security and United States Policy*, pp. 240-242.

116. Schoenhals and Melanson, *Revolution and Intervention*, p. 116.

117. Payne et al., *Revolution and Invasion*, pp. 54, 61.

118. For a discussion of the Reagan administration's policy toward Grenada, see Davidson, *A Study in Politics*, pp. 29-39; Latin American Bureau, *Whose Freedom?* pp. 47-53; Robert Pastor, "Grenada and the American Foreign Policy Context," in *American Intervention in Grenada*, eds. Dunn and Watson, pp. 15-28; Payne et al., *Revolution and Invasion*, pp. 43-70; Schoenhals and Melanson, *Revolution and Invasion*, pp. 117-136; Lars Schoultz, *National Security and United States Policy Towards Latin America*, pp. 238-248; and *United States Policy toward Grenada*.

119. *United States Policy toward Grenada*, p. 1

120. Payne et al., *Revolution and Invasion*, p. 63; Schoultz, *National Security and U.S. Policy*, p. 242.

121. *United States Policy toward Grenada*, p. 13.

122. "National Security: Address to the Nation, March 23, 1983," *Weekly Compilation of Presidential Documents* 19 (March 28, 1983): 445.

123. When Bishop arrived in Washington, he was apparently rebuffed by the State Department until Senators Claiborne Pell and Lowell Weicker intervened on his behalf. Schoenhals and Melanson, *Revolution and Intervention*, p. 136.

124. Magnuson, "D-Day in Grenada," p. 27. Dam later testified: "What he was proposing is that we move toward better relations, and we said that we would be pleased to do so. We thought that the first step would be that he should stop what was quite a campaign of attacks on the United States, and that would indicate that he had a desire for better relations, and that is where the matter was left." U.S. Congress, Senate, Committee on Foreign Relations, *The Situation in Grenada*, 98th Congress, 1st session, 1983, p. 12.

125. "Bishop may have pulled the trigger on himself by pushing a modicum of detente with his Caribbean neighbors and with the United States." McNeil, *War and Peace in Central America*, p. 173.

126. Caleb Rossiter, "The Financial Hit List," *International Policy Report*, February 1984, p. 4.

127. See especially, Schoenhals and Melanson, *Revolution and Intervention*, pp. 130-131.

128. Schoultz, *National Security and U.S. Policy*, p. 242.

129. Schoultz, *National Security and U.S. Policy*, p. 242.

130. An administration spokesman dismissed Grenadian perceptions as unfounded: "Grenada has charged on numerous occasions and without a shred of evidence that the U.S. is preparing an invasion of Grenada and that various U.S. military and naval exercises in the region are part of those operations." *United States Policy Toward Grenada*, p. 39.

131. Gerald Hopple and Cynthia Gilley, "Policy Without Intelligence," in *American Intervention in Grenada*, eds. Dunn and Watson, p. 61; Payne et al., *Revolution and Invasion*, p. 65.

132. Cited in *Transafrica Forum*, November-December 1983, p. 7.

133. "U.S. Preparing to Invade Grenada," Statement by Maurice Bishop, reported in El Salvador Solidarity Campaign, *El Salvador News Bulletin*, no. 10 (September 1981).

134. "Address to the First Conference of Journalists from the Caribbean Area, April 17, 1982," People's Revolutionary Government, Grenada, mimeo, p. 12, cited by Payne et al., *Revolution and Invasion*, pp. 66-67.

135. Cited by Schoultz, *National Security*, p. 243.

136. See *Washington Post*, February 27, 1983, p. A11.

137. The most detailed indictment of the Bishop regime by the Reagan administration was made on June 15, 1982 by Stephen D. Bosworth, Principal Deputy Assistant Secretary of State for Inter-American Affairs. See his testimony in *United States Policy toward Grenada*.

138. United States Department of State, Bureau of Public Affairs, "Caribbean Basin Initiative, February 24, 1982," Current Policy No. 370. Reprinted in "Address Before the Permanent Council of the Organization of American States, February 24, 1982," *Weekly Compilation of Presidential Documents* 18 (March 1, 1982): 217-223.

139. "Remarks at Bridgetown, Barbados, April 8, 1982," *Weekly Compilation of Presidential Documents* 18 (April 19, 1982): 463.

140. "Central America and El Salvador, March 10, 1983," *Weekly Compilation of Presidential Documents* 19 (March 14, 1983): 377.

141. *Latin America Regional Report: Caribbean*, RC-83-03, March 31, 1983, cited by Payne et al., *Revolution and Invasion*, p. 67.

142. Because of its surprising conclusion, a proposal for strategic defense, Reagan's address on March 23 would subsequently be dubbed by journalists his "Star Wars" speech.

143. "National Security: Address to the Nation, March 23, 1983," p. 445.

144. The Cuban contribution to the international airport did not exceed $15 million, only a fraction of the $70 million total cost. Manigat, "Grenada: Revolutionary Shockwave, Crisis, and Intervention," p. 188.

145. See Payne et al., *Revolution and Invasion*, pp. 34, 67; Schoenhals and Melanson, *Revolution and Intervention*, p. 56; and Valenta and Valenta, "Leninism in Grenada," pp. 18-19.

146. Antigua, St. Lucia and Trinidad had runways of around 9,000 feet; Curacao, Barbados and Guadeloupe had ones all in excess of 11,000 feet. Figures cited in Embassy of Grenada, "Proceedings of Aid Donors Meeting Held in Brussels at ACP House, April 14-15, 1981," *International Airport Project --Grenada*, Appendix 1.

147. Quoted by Edward Cody, "Grenada's Leaders Veer Left, Engendering Wrath of U.S.," *Washington Post*, April 22, 1983, p. A18.

148. McNeil, *War and Peace in Central America*, p. 172. Emphasis mine. Assistant Secretary of State similarly described Grenada as having been "a minor irritant." Seymour Hersh's interview with Ambassador Motley, "Operation Urgent Fury," from the PBS series "Front-line," February 2, 1988.

149. McNeil, *War and Peace in Central America*, pp. 172-173.

150. Manigat, "Grenada: Revolutionary Shockwave, Crisis, and Intervention," p. 187.

3

The Public Rationale

The test of law lies not in the assertion of abstract principles but in the application of universal norms to specific situations. A court that cannot distinguish between lawful and criminal use of force — between force used to protect the innocent and force used to victimize the innocent — is not worthy to sit in judgment on anyone.[1]
— Jeane Kirkpatrick, November 2, 1983

One hundred nations in the United Nations have not agreed with us on just about everything that's come up before them where we're involved, and [their condemnatory resolution] didn't upset my breakfast at all.[2]
— Ronald Reagan, November 3, 1983

International law is to be determined "through reference to carefully constructed and enduring principles of universal applicability."[3]
— Davis Robinson, State Department
Legal Adviser, February 10, 1984

Given the widespread international criticism that was heaped upon the United States for the Grenada invasion, it is not surprising that the Reagan administration spent a great deal of time attempting to justify its commission of American military forces to the operation. Indeed, between October 1983 and February 1984, at least a dozen significant public statements were made before various American and international fora to articulate the government's rationale for its action.[4] For several reasons, it is worthwhile to scrutinize carefully the content and evolution of all these statements made by President Reagan and six different administration officials.[5]

First, a comprehensive examination of the public justification for "Urgent Fury" may help in a general way to suggest what motives informed Reagan administration decisionmaking. Although the contents of speeches, public statements, and published letters of governmental officials must necessarily be viewed with a certain measure of skepticism, one cannot peremptorily dismiss their accuracy. To be sure, governments may deliberately choose either to distort or not to reveal the facts when deception suits their purposes; indeed, history is rife with "big lies." Nevertheless, the national interest may often be served, or at least not frustrated, by a straightforward presentation of the facts. Particularly in the United States, where the major foreign policy decisions of the executive branch are regularly subject to close scrutiny by the legislative branch and the media, public misrepresentation can ultimately prove perilous. Accordingly, the Reagan administration's rationale for its action, in whole or perhaps only in part, may actually be revealed by its rhetoric.

Second, a thorough review of the administration's public rationale will help to establish its basic attitude toward international law *per se*. If, for example, little or no specific reference to "international law" is found in governmental statements, this may signify a general disregard for international law. At a minimum, it will suggest a disdain for the utility of public legal justification. Conversely, if consistent appeals by the Reagan administration to international law are encountered, this may indicate a genuine respect for legal norms. At the least, it will suggest a desire for the appearance of lawful behavior.

Finally, a careful examination of the Reagan administration's public rationale will allow a testing of its consistency over time, and indirectly, may suggest the degree to which law played a role in the decisionmaking process. A shifting or self-contradictory legal argument may indicate one or perhaps several things: that the administration's public statements were composed in an uncoordinated fashion over a four-month period; that the statements were written with different audiences in mind, and therefore, emphasized different motives for the military action; that the administration's argument changed as material circumstances changed;

that administration officials disagreed about the justification for U.S. action; or even that law played little or no role in the decision to act, and hence, that the administration's legal considerations were *post facto*. Conversely, an unwavering legal argument may support several conclusions: that the Reagan administration carefully orchestrated its public statements; that material circumstances never changed; or perhaps even that international law played an early role in the determination to employ force.

This chapter will trace the evolution of the Reagan administration's public rationale for "Urgent Fury" — from President Reagan's first disclosure of the operation on Tuesday morning, October 25, 1983, until the publication of State Department Legal Adviser Davis R. Robinson's letter to Professor Edward Gordon, dated February 10, 1984. It will begin with a discussion of the contemporary international law relating to the recourse to force, the *jus ad bellum*. Once this framework has been set out, it will turn to a chronological examination of the administration's justification for military action.

The *Jus ad Bellum*

The U.N. Charter and the lawful use of force

Although the law governing the recourse to armed force is, on its face, relatively straightforward, international legal scholars have spent no little ink since 1945 attempting to advance a universally accepted interpretation of the *jus ad bellum*. Such extensive scholarly activity would seem to reflect three factors: first, the manifest significance of the question; second, the inherent difficulties of treaty interpretation;[6] and third, the fundamental transformation of the international system since World War II.[7]

Any discussion of the contemporary *jus ad bellum* must begin with Article 2(4) of the United Nations Charter. Article 2(4) is generally construed as proscribing the use of military force in international relations. Moreover, it is considered by many legal scholars to be a rule of customary international law binding on all states,[8] and has been submitted as a candidate for classification as a norm of *jus cogens*, a peremptory norm of international law from which no derogation is permitted.[9] Article 2(4) provides that:

All Members [of the United Nations] shall refrain in their international relations from the threat or use of force against the territorial integrity or political independence of any State, or in any manner inconsistent with the purposes of the United Nations.

Despite its general prohibition of "the threat or use of force" by states, the U.N. Charter provides three circumstances[10] under which the use of force is permissible:

1. Article 51 - the right to individual or collective self-defense;
2. Chapter VII - a Security Council action to maintain or restore peace and security; and
3. Chapter VIII - collective action by regional arrangements or agencies to maintain peace and security.

As will be seen, each of these exceptions to Article 2(4) is, in its own way, problematic.

Article 51 of the Charter affords one legal basis for the state's use of force. It specifically provides that:

Nothing in the present Charter shall impair the inherent right of individual or collective self-defense if an armed attack occurs against a Member of the United Nations, until the Security Council has taken the measures necessary to maintain international peace and security. Measures taken by Members in the exercise of this right of self-defense shall be immediately reported to the Security Council and shall not in any way affect the authority and responsibility of the Security Council under the present Charter to take at any time such action as it deems necessary in order to maintain or restore international peace and security.

Given various practical problems associated with Chapters VII and VIII of the Charter, which shall be noted, the provisions of Article 51 have emerged as the primary basis for lawful resort to armed coercion under the United Nations system.[11]

As one might anticipate, the interpretation of Article 51 has been fraught with difficulties.[12]   Some scholars have argued that aggression can be "indirect" as well as direct, and that under circumstances of "indirect aggression," states retain the rights of individual and collective self-defense.[13]   Commentators[14] have also maintained that self-defense can be "anticipatory," and that a legitimate defender can lawfully launch a preemptive first strike provided there is sufficient evidence of an imminent threat of aggression.[15] A considerable body of opinion denies that such right exists, however.[16] Although a more detailed discussion of the interpretation of Article 51 could be undertaken, such discussion is superfluous here given that the Reagan administration did not publicly justify its use of force on the basis of Article 51.

Chapter VII of the Charter, Articles 39-51, deals with Action with Respect to Threats of the Peace, Breaches of the Peace, and Acts of Aggression. Under Article 39, the U.N. Security Council is authorized to "determine the existence of any threat to the peace, breach of the peace or act of aggression." If the Council so judges, it is empowered by Article 42 to direct U.N. member states to wield force against the refractory state.[17] Such an enforcement action, according to O'Brien, "would represent the operation of the collective security system that is supposed to be the heart of the U.N."[18]

Unfortunately, a constellation of factors has conspired to thwart nearly all efforts to make this system work as originally envisaged, *inter alia*: the widespread use of the veto power by the Security Council permanent members; the inability to establish formal mechanisms for collective action; and the general rejection by states of limited collective security.[19] Accordingly, "the model of a Security Council decision under Chapter VII of the Charter producing an 'international police action'" has remained largely "theoretical."[20] Indeed, before the Grenada invasion of 1983, the Security Council had authorized an "enforcement action" against an aggressor state only once — after North Korea's June 1950 attack on South Korea.[21]

Chapter VIII of the Charter, Articles 52 to 54, provides that regional arrangements may play a role in the management of international conflict. Article 52 permits regional arrangements to deal with "matters relating to the maintenance of international peace and security" provided "such arrangements or agencies and their activities are consistent with the Purposes and Principles of the United Nations." It likewise requires members of such arrangements to "make every effort" to settle local disputes before referring them to the Security Council. Article 53 empowers the Security Council to employ regional arrangements "where appropriate" to execute enforcement actions; however, it provides that "no enforcement action taken under regional arrangements or by regional agencies without the authorization of the Security Council."[22] According to Article 54, the Council must be fully informed of any actions

contemplated or undertaken by regional arrangements "for the maintenance of peace and security."

Chapter VIII's provisions on regional arrangements, like the Charter's
provisions of Article 51 and Chapter VII, are problematic. Clearly, the
framers of the Charter envisioned a role for regional arrangements in the
maintenance of international peace and security, albeit one limited by the
restriction that a regional organization action could not amount to an
"enforcement action" without the permission of the Security Council.
Yet, how an "enforcement action" is to be defined has been the subject
of significant scholarly controversy.[23]

Other claims for the lawful use of force

Although a strict interpretation of the *jus ad bellum* as articulated by
the U.N. Charter would appear to afford states little or no lawful
opportunity to intervene in the internal affairs of other states, examples
of "intervention" abound. Not surprisingly, legal scholars have advanced
at least four claims for lawful intervention besides the three expressed
exceptions to the Charter's general prohibition of the use of force: (1)
intervention by lawful invitation; (2) intervention to protect nationals; (3)
humanitarian intervention; and (4) intervention by treaty right.[24] Since
the first three claims are directly relevant to a legal evaluation of "Urgent
Fury," each will be considered in turn.

The right of a state to intervene *after lawful invitation* has been
claimed by a number of publicists.[25] If a duly constituted authority of
a state has requested assistance, they argue, such assistance would not
constitute a violation of Article 2(4). Consent "removes the taint of what
would otherwise be illegal."[26] While the right to intervention after
lawful invitation has certainly been asserted, the existence of such a right
is by no means universally accepted. Indeed, Gilmore submits that "the
right of a government to seek, and a foreign state to provide, military
assistance in a civil war" has been rejected by "perhaps a majority" of
modern writers.[27] To be sure, many commentators have been willing
to grant the permissibility of military assistance to the government of a
state experiencing civil turmoil, when such turmoil is at a "low level."
However, they have generally rejected the state's right to provide
assistance when such outside help might well prevent self-determination.

Scholars have recognized that the state's right to *intervene to protect
nationals* was part of the corpus of customary international law before
1945.[28] Nevertheless, many question whether such a right now

exists,[29] especially in light of the proliferation of international agreements that normatively sanction respect for nonintervention without exceptions or qualifications.[30] Those jurists who acknowledge the existence of such a right may be grouped into three categories[31]: first, those who argue that the purpose of Article 2(4) is not to protect the inviolability of the state, but only its "territorial integrity and its political independence," and therefore, that protection of nationals falls below the "2(4) threshold" of permissible use of force;[32] second, those who contend that Article 51 preserves the pre-Charter customary right of self-defense;[33] and third, those who maintain that protection of one's own nationals and those of other states is in keeping with the humanitarian principles of the U.N.[34]

Publicists have also claimed the existence of a state's right to undertake *humanitarian intervention* to protect a people from widespread human rights abuse, even genocidal treatment, by their government such as that which transpired in Cambodia under Pol Pot or in Uganda under Idi Amin.[35] That the right to undertake humanitarian intervention existed under customary international law was generally accepted by scholars writing in the nineteenth and early twentieth centuries.[36] Indeed, even as recently as 1955, Lauterpacht appeared to champion the concept of humanitarian intervention.[37] Recently, however, most scholars have condemned as illegal such forcible action.[38] This general rejection of humanitarian intervention seems well justified based on a traditional reading of the U.N. Charter and a close examination of the actual practice of states.[39]

A Succession of Public Justifications

The first public explanation for Operation "Urgent Fury" was tendered by the President himself at 9:07 A.M. on October 25 — fully a day before any of the American medical students on Grenada had been evacuated.[40] Reagan's brief statement, delivered as the chair of the OECS stood at his side and Shultz and Weinberger looked on, cited three reasons for his "decisive action":

First, and of overriding importance, to protect innocent lives, including up to a thousand Americans, whose personal safety is, of course, my paramount concern. Second, to forestall further chaos. And third, to assist in the restoration of conditions of law and order and of governmental institutions to the island of Grenada.

The invasion, he emphasized, was a "multinational effort," a "collective action." Among the other prominent themes of the presidential announcement were the "unprecedented" character of the events on Grenada, the "chaos" and "violence" there, and significantly, the goal of restoring "democratic institutions" to the island.[41] Reagan's announcement seemed deliberately to underscore what some legal scholars would subsequently maintain had been the "humanitarian underpinnings of the mission."[42]

The President's first public account was noteworthy as much for what it did *not* say as for what it did. First, Reagan made no mention of Soviet or Cuban influence on the island of Grenada or of the strategic airport which Cuba had been helping to build there. Second, he did not refer specifically either to "international law" or to the United Nations. He did, however, contend in the subsequent "question-and-answer session" that the action was "being taken under the umbrella of an existing treaty." Finally, the President said nothing of his fears that American hostages might have been taken or of Sir Paul Scoon's invitation of assistance.

As one might expect, the President's letters to the Speaker of the House and to the President Pro Tempore of the Senate, dated October 25, were similar though not identical in content to his first statement.[43] In the duplicate letters, Reagan listed two objectives of the U.S. action: "to join the OECS collective security forces in assisting the restoration of conditions of law and order and of governmental institutions to the island of Grenada, and to facilitate the protection and evacuation of United States citizens." This latter goal, the President once again noted, was "of overriding importance." As in his Tuesday morning announcement, Reagan stressed the "unprecedented threat" posed by "the vacuum of authority on Grenada." Again, he cited the "violent series of events" there, but did not explicitly discuss the role of Cuba and the Soviet Union, the international legality of the American action, his hostage fears, or the Scoon invitation. Interestingly, no reference was made in Reagan's letter to the restoration of "democratic institutions" to Grenada, only to that of "governmental" ones.

Also on Tuesday, October 25, Secretary Shultz explained the American rationale for invasion at a White House press conference.[44] Here, Shultz elaborated upon and amplified Reagan's earlier statement. According to the Secretary of State, the administration had "basically two" objectives in launching its military operation:

* To secure the safety of American citizens, and, for that matter, the citizens of other countries, and to assure that any who wish to leave may do so; and

* To help the OECS states establish law and order in the country and establish again governmental institutions responsive to the will of the people of Grenada.

In his discussion of the "two basic reasons that determined the President's decision," Shultz referred *four* separate times to the atmosphere of "violent uncertainty" on Grenada. He also reiterated the argument that there had been a "vacuum of governmental authority." The United States Government could see, he said, "no responsible government in the country." Here again the Secretary alluded to the humanitarian motives which had informed American objectives. Yet, like Reagan had already twice done, Shultz made *no* explicit reference to "international law." In a departure from Reagan's first statement, but in conformity with the President's letter, Shultz did not mention restoring "democratic" institutions to Grenada, only "governmental" ones. Finally, Secretary Shultz observed for the first time that the administration had been concerned about the possibility of Americans being taken "hostage."

October 26 at the OAS
The next day, William J. Middendorf, Jr. addressed the Permanent Council of the Organization of American States.[45] In his statement to the OAS special meeting, the United States Ambassador echoed many of the themes already introduced by Reagan and Shultz: the "unprecedented" nature of the Grenada situation; the "menacing uncertainty" on the island; and the administration view that there had been no "coherent group ... in charge" there. Characterizing the American action as part of a "regional collective security" effort, Middendorf cited several objectives of the "collective security force": "to restore law and order and help the people of Grenada restore functioning institutions of government and to facilitate the departure of those who wish to leave." Although the United States had shared the concerns of the OECS states, he observed, it had "also had a particularly humanitarian concern." According to Middendorf, the "lack of respect for human rights and the degenerating conditions" on the island had posed a threat not only to foreign nationals but also "to the people of Grenada." Consistent with

previous Reagan administration statements, the American Ambassador seemed here to be making a tentative legal case for "humanitarian intervention."

Certainly, Middendorf's address was the first significant administration statement explicitly to present an international legal justification for the Grenada invasion, if a rather unsophisticated one. The US/OECS action was, he said, "a reasonable and proportionate reaction [to events on Grenada,] ... consistent with the purposes and principles of the Charters of the United Nations and the Organization of American States." Ambassador Middendorf maintained that the "regional security measures" just taken were of the sort "expressly contemplated by Article 52 of the U.N. Charter." The US/OECS action was similarly permitted under Articles 22 and 28 of the OAS Charter, he asserted. Moreover, pursuant to Article 8 of the OECS Treaty, the Grenadian invasion was consistent with Article 19 of the OAS Charter.

Thursday, October 27: Kirkpatrick and Reagan

On Thursday evening, October 27, Jeane Kirkpatrick addressed the U.N. Security Council. Here, the American Ambassador delivered a sharp rebuke to a condemnatory resolution which had earlier been introduced by Guyana, Nicaragua and Zimbabwe.[46] Kirkpatrick's lengthy statement, the most overtly ideological thus far, underscored several themes which had already been introduced by the Reagan administration: that there had been a "vacuum of responsible government authority" on Grenada; that there had been "a unique combination of circumstances prevailing" there; and that the "collective action" had been aimed at restoring "democratic government." The U.S. Ambassador noted, as had Secretary Shultz two days earlier, that the U.S. Government had feared with good cause that Americans might be held "hostage."

Taking a bit of rhetorical license, Kirkpatrick introduced a new but ephemeral theme to the American rationale for its action: terrorism. Specifically referring to a form of the word "terror" *seven* separate times, Kirkpatrick argued that in Grenada "terrorists [had] murder[ed] the leading citizenry and leadership of their country." Under such circumstances, the United States and Caribbean states were not legally prevented from taking military action for "the charter does not require that peoples submit supinely to terror, nor that their neighbors be indifferent to their terrorization."

Kirkpatrick's legal defense of United States actions was in some respects more elaborate and innovative than her OAS colleague's had been the day before. Although she did not cite any specific articles from the U.N. Charter or the OECS Treaty, Kirkpatrick argued that the Grenada mission "was fully compatible with relevant international law and practice." Rejecting the common criticism that the Grenada action had been "a simple case of intervention in the internal affairs of others," she asserted that "the events of the past days" had posed no "legally simple questions." According to Kirkpatrick, "the prohibitions against the use of force in the UN Charter" were "contextual, not absolute." Hence, the Charter's contextual prescriptions "provide[d] ample justification for the use of force in pursuit of the other values also inscribed in the charter — freedom, democracy, peace."

Ambassador Kirkpatrick submitted three circumstances which, she maintained, had justified U.S. military measures: the "danger to U.S. nationals, the absence of a minimally responsible government in Grenada, and the danger posed to the OECS by the relatively awesome military might those responsible for the murder of Bishop now had at their disposal." Quoting extensively from Jamaican Prime Minister Edward Seaga, she now appeared to introduce a new theme into the legal argument: the self-defense of the OECS countries. The United States had joined the OECS to "eliminate the threat to the security of the entire region ... a combination of brutal men with awesome might." The OECS had been "spurred to action because, as the result of the murder of Mr. Bishop and almost his entire cabinet, the military power which Grenada had amassed with Cuban and Soviet backing had fallen into the hands of individuals who could reasonably be expected to wield that awesome power against its neighbors." Ambassador Kirkpatrick would be the only administration official to make an apparent appeal to OECS self-defense.

Kirkpatrick also observed — this, for the first time by a Reagan administration official — that "the Governor-General of Grenada, the sole remaining symbol of governmental authority on the island, [had] invited OECS action."[47] By October 27, it would later be asserted by the administration, the United States could safely reveal Sir Paul's request for assistance. Even the day before, Davis Robinson would explain, "his home was still surrounded by heavily armed forces."[48]

Besides its legal novelties, Kirkpatrick's address was notable for its characterization of Grenada under Maurice Bishop. Here, the Ambassador's rhetoric was strikingly similar to that of President Reagan in the three years before the invasion:

> Maurice Bishop was a man of strong ideological commitments. Those commitments identified him and allied him with Cuba, the Soviet Union, the member states of that empire which invokes Marxist principles to justify tyranny.
>   Bishop freely offered his island as a base for the projection of Soviet military power in this hemisphere. The familiar pattern of militarization and Cubanization was already far advanced in Grenada. More than three dozen Soviet officials have been detained in just the past 3 days. Truly enormous arsenals of Soviet weapons have been discovered in the past three days. The total number of Cuban military personnel in Grenada is still unknown, but it is clear that there were more than 1,000 — more than one Cuban for every 100 Grenadians.

Turning the intervention charge on its head finally, Kirkpatrick concluded: "Grenada's internal affairs had fallen under the permanent intervention of one neighboring and one remote tyranny. Its people were helpless in the grip of terror." The United States intended, she pledged, "to leave Grenada just as soon as law [was] restored and the instrumentalities of ... democratic government [had] been put in place."

At 8:00 P.M. that Thursday evening, President Reagan publicly broached for the third time the subject of Grenada — now, while simultaneously discussing the recent tragedy in Beirut.[49] In his thirty-minute televised "Address to the Nation," Reagan touched upon virtually every significant theme that had thus far been introduced by himself and by members of his administration. Seated behind his Oval Office desk, the President argued: that "Grenada [had been] without a government"; that his administration had feared U.S. citizens would "be harmed or held as hostages"; and that the OECS, "joined by Jamaica and Barbados, had sent an urgent request that we join them." The US/OECS action, having been proposed under the terms of "a treaty, mutual assistance pact," would "restore order and democracy" to the island.

In his televised speech, Reagan referred briefly to Sir Paul Scoon, the Grenadian Governor-General, whom the administration anticipated would "participate in setting up a provisional government." Curiously, however, he did *not* mention Scoon's request for American military assistance that Eugenia Charles had made public the day before. "The legitimacy of [the OECS] request, plus my own concern for our citizens, dictated my decision" to take action, the President explained. Also noticeably absent from Reagan's "Address to the Nation" was any explicit allusion to "international law."

Reagan's October 27 speech, delivered while 202 American medical students on Grenada still awaited rescue, reflected ideological and U.S. geostrategic considerations to a far greater extent than had his earlier public statements. The President charged that Maurice Bishop had been "a protege of Fidel Castro" and that the Point Salines airport had "looked suspiciously suitable for military aircraft, including Soviet-built long-range bombers." Alluding to the security fears of the OECS states, he contended that the Grenadian Army, "greater than all of theirs combined," had "obviously" been "not purely for defense." Reagan told his American audience that forces had "discovered a complete base with weapons and communications equipment, which [made] it clear a Cuban occupation of the island had been planned." Moreover, a "warehouse contain[ing] weapons and ammunition stacked almost to the ceiling" had been found. Here was "enough to supply thousands of terrorists." In the end, the President concluded, Grenada had been "a Soviet-Cuban colony, being readied as a major military bastion to export terror and undermine democracy." The United States had "got there just in time."

Wednesday, November 2: Kirkpatrick and Dam

On November 2, 1983, hostilities on Grenada officially ceased. That same day, after an anti-American resolution had been passed without debate by an overwhelming majority, Jeane Kirkpatrick addressed the General Assembly of the United Nations.[50] Here, she again defended the international legality of "the collective regional security action":

> We believe that the use of force by the task force was lawful under international law and the UN Charter, because it was undertaken to protect American nationals from a clear and present danger, because it was a legitimate exercise of regional collective security, because it was carried out with due concern for lawful procedures and carried out in the service of values of the charter, including the restoration of the rule of law, self-determination, sovereignty, democracy, respect for human rights of the people of Grenada.

Ambassador Kirkpatrick maintained that an examination of the facts was necessary before a final determination of legality. She reiterated now her contention of October 27: the "test of law lies not in the assertion of abstract principles but in the application of universal norms to specific situations." In the case of Grenada, a distinction had to be made "between force used to protect the innocent and force used to victimize the innocent." The "failure to preserve such distinction," Kirkpatrick averred, "does not preserve law as an instrument of justice and peace but erodes the moral and legal foundations of civilized existence."

Kirkpatrick presented a variety of evidence to support her argument that the United States had employed force to protect the innocent: first, Bishop and his supporters had been "murdered;" second, between 1980 and 1982 five secret military assistance agreements had been executed between Grenada and the Soviet Union, Cuba, and North Korea; and finally, these clandestine pacts had provided for "delivery, free of charge, of millions of dollars in military supplies." Kirkpatrick concluded her address by accepting, in only an ironic sense, the parallel drawn by some states "between the action in Grenada and the Soviet action in Afghanistan." According to the U.S. Ambassador:

> Just as Maurice Bishop was murdered in Grenada because he tried to free himself from the Soviet stranglehold, so too was Mohammed Daud murdered in Afghanistan. And after him, Hafizollah Amin was murdered in Afghanistan. They too discovered that the only thing more dangerous than embracing the Soviet bear is trying to break loose from its deathly grip. They too learned that the price of trying to "reverse" Soviet conquest is violent death. This, and this alone, is the parallel between Grenada and Afghanistan. The difference is that the people of Grenada have now been spared the cruel fate of the people of Afghanistan.

On November 2, 1983, the same day that Kirkpatrick's highly politicized defense of American actions was made at the United Nations, Deputy Secretary of State Kenneth Dam delivered the most carefully drafted legal justification thus far offered by the administration for its military undertaking.[51] According to legal scholar Scott Davidson, a severe critic of "Urgent Fury"'s legality, Dam's statement was "one of fairly closely argued legal principles."[52] Presented before the House Foreign Affairs Committee, it would be presented again by him two days later, after only minor revision, to the Associated Press Managing Editors' Conference in Louisville, Kentucky.[53]

The Deputy Secretary's twin public statements repeated virtually every significant theme that had thus far been offered in administration accounts of Grenada: the "extraordinary," "unprecedented" nature of events there; the "climate of uncertainty and fear" on the island; American fears that "a hostage situation" might develop; the "absence of a functioning government" on Grenada; the "overriding concern" for "the safety of U.S. citizens;" and even Grenada's potential to become "an armed fortress."

In a subtle but significant departure from prior justifications, Kenneth Dam's statements recast the "two fundamental objectives" that had "motivated the President's decision." According to Dam, the United States had acted:

— to protect the lives of U.S. citizens; and

— to help Grenada reestablish governmental institutions capable of restoring order, protecting human rights and maintaining peace and stability.

In his succinct description of American goals, Dam made no mention of restoring "democratic institutions" to Grenada. Indeed, the Deputy Secretary appeared explicitly to contradict four previous statements to that effect by the President and Ambassador Kirkpatrick. Observing that U.S. objectives had been "precise and limited," Dam contended that they did "not encompass the imposition on the Grenadians of *any particular form* of government."[54] Dam did, however, list some of the desired attributes of a reconstituted Grenadian regime: the capacities to restore "order," protect "human rights," and maintain "peace and stability." Presumably, any legitimate government, whatever its form, would possess such abilities.

In his two public statements, Deputy Secretary Dam also backed away somewhat from the administration's earlier, technically inaccurate characterization[55] of its action as one of "regional collective security" or simply of "collective security."[56] The American undertaking had been, in Dam's words, a "collective effort," a "rescue operation." This modification reflected perhaps the generally more sophisticated legal approach of the Deputy Secretary's justification. The "U.S. actions," he explained, had "been based on three legal grounds": (1) the invitation of the Grenadian Governor-General; (2) the request of the OECS states, under the OECS Treaty; and (3) the protection of American nationals. "We have not made," Dam emphasized, "and do not seek to make, any broad new precedent for international action; we think the justification for our actions is narrow, and well within accepted concepts of international law."

In his discussion of the Scoon invitation, Kenneth Dam revealed that the United States had been informed on October 24 "by Prime Minister Adams of Barbados that Governor-General Scoon had used a confidential channel to transmit an appeal for action by the OECS and other regional states to restore order" on Grenada. "Since the arrival of the joint security force," Scoon had "confirmed this invitation to take action." According to Dam, Sir Paul Scoon's invitation had been "an important element — legally as well as politically — in the decision of the U.S. and the other countries participating in the joint force." Because the "legal authorities of the Governor-General remained the sole source of governmental legitimacy," the United States and the OECS states had "accorded his appeal exceptional moral weight." Secretary Dam concluded: "[t]he invitation of lawful governmental authority constitutes a recognized basis under international law for foreign states to provide requested assistance."

The invitation of the OECS states, Dam contended, was also a lawful basis for American action. The OECS states had decided "to take action under the 1981 Treaty establishing that organization." The OECS Treaty functioned as "a regional security arrangement":

> It contains a number of provisions, in Articles 3, 4 and 8, which deal with local as well as external threats to peace and security. The appeal of the Governor-General for OECS assistance provided a legitimate basis for collective action under the framework of this regional treaty. Both the OAS Charter, in Articles 22 and 28, and the UN Charter, in Article 52, recognize the competence of regional security bodies in ensuring regional peace and stability. Article 22 of the OAS Charter in particular makes clear that action pursuant to a special security treaty in force does not constitute intervention or use of force otherwise prohibited by Articles 18 or 20 of that Charter.

Given the circumstances, Dam maintained that "the actions of the OECS were consistent with the purpose and principles of both the UN and OAS Charters." Since their collective action was lawful, the OECS states "were entitled to call upon friendly states for appropriate assistance, and it was lawful for the United States, Jamaica and Barbados to respond to this request."

Finally, Deputy Secretary Dam presented what was probably the least controversial legal basis for American action: protection of nationals. The rescue of American citizens on Grenada, Dam asserted, had been "undertaken in accordance with well-established principles of international law regarding the protection of one's nationals." International law did not require that the United States "await further deterioration of the situation that would have jeopardized a successful mission." Nor, he concluded, did it require the United States "to await actual violence against U.S. citizens."

Despite its more sophisticated legal nature, the argument made by Dam was similar in at least two respects to that made by his administration colleague on November 2. First, like Ambassador Kirkpatrick did, Dam carefully distinguished American actions in Grenada from Soviet actions in Afghanistan: the U.S. had participated in a "genuine collective effort"; the action had been "justified by an existing treaty and by the express invitation of the Governor-General"; the U.S. government's concern for the safety of American citizens had been "genuine"; the Grenadian people would freely choose their governmental institutions; and the United States would withdraw as soon as circumstances permitted, or immediately upon the request of Grenadian authorities. Dam concluded: "Those who do not see, or do not choose to see, these signal distinctions have failed to analyze the facts."

Second, like the U.S. Ambassador to the United Nations did, Dam made a geostrategic appeal to bolster his justification of U.S. actions. In both his statements, Dam acknowledged that the Reagan administration had feared that "Grenada could be used as a staging ground for subversion of nearby countries, for interdiction of nearby shipping lanes, and for transit of troops and supplies from Cuba to Africa and from Eastern Europe and Libya to Central America." Likewise, in both he cited a number of disturbing finds on Grenada: secret military treaties with the Soviets, Cubans and North Koreans; secret military fortifications; extensive arms caches; and communications facilities. These discoveries, he told the Foreign Affairs Committee, had dramatized "just how important it [was] that Grenada have governing institutions responsible to its own people." That, Dam concluded, was "precisely

what Grenada's neighbors, and the United States, had in mind in
launching our joint rescue mission."[57]

"Didn't upset my breakfast at all"

On Thursday, November 3, after announcing that Defense Secretary
Weinberger had informed him that "hostilities in Grenada [had] ended,"
Ronald Reagan participated in a brief "question-and-answer" session.[58]
Here, the President abandoned his earlier description of the recent
American action; now, he described it as a "rescue mission," not as a
"collective security" action. Reagan went to great lengths to emphasize
the uniqueness of the circumstances surrounding the U.S. invasion:

> I can't foresee any situation that has exactly the same thing that this one
> had. It had exactly what we announced in the beginning — the need to
> protect the lives and the safety and the freedom of about 1,000 Ameri-
> cans, most of them students down there in a medical school, and in
> answer to a request on the part of the other nations bound by treaty
> together in the east Caribbean that we lend our support to them in freeing
> this up because they lacked the strength and capability of doing it.

When asked if he would be willing to invade another state if he were
again requested to do so, Reagan replied, "If all the conditions were the
same, I don't see why our reason would be any different. But I don't
foresee any similar situation on the horizon."

In answer to another query, the President contrasted U.S. actions in
Grenada with Soviet ones in Afghanistan, just as Kirkpatrick and Dam
had already done. The Soviets had "installed their choice of head of
state," had "used every vicious form of warfare, including chemical
warfare," and were "still there after a long period of time." Referring
to the "massive hoard of Soviet weapons" found on the island, Reagan
mused: "Who knows what evil the liberation of Grenada achieved for
us [sic], or averted in years to come." Perhaps the most notable feature
of the President's remarks was his response to the challenge of one
journalist: "Why did one hundred nations in the United Nations not
agree with you that this was a worthwhile venture?" Rejoined Reagan
rather flippantly, "One hundred nations in the United Nations have not
agreed with us on just about everything that's come up before them
where we're involved, and it didn't upset my breakfast at all."

Also on November 3, the White House released a more politic
response to the recent U.N. General Assembly resolution "deploring" the

Grenada action: "We find it sad that the United Nations sees fit to 'deplore' actions taken for humanitarian reasons, to save innocent lives, in full accord with the UN Charter."[59] This statement of the White House, like several others made the week before, appeared to suggest "humanitarian intervention" grounds for the American action.

Assistant Secretary Motley's statement

On January 24, 1984, Langhorne A. Motley spoke before the House Armed Services Committee.[60] In his lengthy statement, the Assistant Secretary of State for Inter-American Affairs set out the "circumstances which [had] led to U.S. participation in the collective security and rescue operation on the island of Grenada."[61] Specifically, Motley sketched for the first time in some detail the decisionmaking process that had preceded the forcible American action, reviewed the administration's key decisions, and provided some particulars on the requests for assistance of the OECS and the Grenadian Governor-General. The fundamental premise of Motley's statement was that there had been "no alternative to the President's decision."

Motley listed three reasons for "U.S. participation in the collective security and rescue operation." For the first two, he simply cited President Reagan's identical letters of October 25 to Tip O'Neill and Strom Thurmond: American objectives had been "to join in the OECS collective security forces in assisting the restoration of conditions of law and order and of governmental institutions to the island of Grenada, and to facilitate the protection and evacuation of United States citizens." It is possible that Motley quoted here Reagan's Congressional letters instead of the President's first statement of October 25 since the former lacked any problematic reference to the restoration of "democratic institutions." The third reason for American action, Motley submitted as had Kenneth Dam three months before, "could not be publicized at the time." Nevertheless, Governor-General Sir Paul Scoon "had appealed to Grenada's Caribbean neighbors for assistance in restoring civil order to the island." Scoon's request, Motley explained, had been "made through confidential channels, to Prime Minister Adams of Barbados, who informed us." The United States "could not publicly reveal the Governor-General's request until his safety had been assured."

According to Motley, "Inter-agency assessment meetings had reviewed developments in Grenada several times during 1983." Nevertheless, the U.S. military operation had been "an unexpected emergency response to sudden drastic deterioration of conditions on the island." Inter-agency group (I/G) meetings had been held on October 13, 14, and 17 to consider the developing situation on Grenada. On Wednesday, October 19, serious planning for a "nonpermissive evacuation" began. The next day, October 20, U.S. ships were diverted toward Grenada as a "precautionary measure" and "contingency plans which included the use of military assets [were] triggered." On Saturday, October 22, President Reagan "signed orders to prepare for a broader mission" although the United States "retained the ability to halt final implementation until the last moment." On the evening of October 24, after it had become apparent that a peaceful evacuation of Grenada would be impossible, "the President ordered U.S. participation in the operation to proceed." Reagan did so only after receiving confirmation of the OECS request and after he had dispatched Ambassador Francis J. McNeil and Major General George B. Crist as emissaries to the eastern Caribbean.

Given the potential for violence on Grenada, Motley contended, an "evacuation, permissive or not, would have been fully justified." Nevertheless, the Reagan administration "did not limit [its] efforts to an evacuation of our citizens," although "their safety" had remained the administration's "paramount concern." Instead, the U.S. government decided to pursue a broader military mission. The impetus for this more ambitious operation, Motley suggested, had come from the requests of the OECS and the Grenadian Governor-General.

The OECS decision to request U.S. help was made on October 21, Motley reported, and was formally transmitted on October 23. The OECS states had "viewed the breakdown of civil order on Grenada and the island's movement toward still more violent and undisciplined behavior to [have been] an imminent threat to regional security." Because they could not have confronted the military strength of Grenada alone, he explained, they had requested assistance from the United States, Jamaica, and Barbados.

The administration's "resolve to protect the security of the eastern Caribbean democracies and restore stability to the region received additional impetus," the Assistant Secretary argued, when it "received the appeal from Governor-General Scoon to assist him in stabilizing the situation in Grenada." As Kenneth Dam had earlier reported,[62] Prime Minister Adams had informed the United States of Scoon's appeal on October 24. "On October 27, after the Governor-General had been rescued" by American forces, the United States "received a copy of a letter to Prime Minister Adams, dated October 24, confirming his request."[63]

Motley concluded his January 24 statement to the Armed Services Committee with a glowing review of the American military action:

> By any standard, the collective security and rescue operation in Grenada was a success. American citizens were protected. American interests were preserved. The island democracies of the region are safer today than they were three months ago. And the people of Grenada have spoken clearly of their happiness and relief at the restoration of legitimate, humane, democratic government.

The State Department Legal Adviser

On February 10, 1984, the State Department Legal Adviser sent a letter to Professor Edward Gordon, Chair of the "Grenada Committee" of the American Bar Association's Section on International Law and Practice.[64] In his lengthy missive, Davis R. Robinson "reiterate[d] the legal position of the United States" concerning the Grenada mission it had undertaken almost four months before. Robinson's was by far the lengthiest, most complicated, and most carefully crafted legal defense ever offered by the Reagan administration for its actions. Despite his suggestion that it merely constituted a "reiteration," Robinson's letter to Gordon differed in many critical respects from earlier administration justifications.

Robinson did repeat certain previously submitted arguments: the "unique and almost unprecedented circumstances presented" on Grenada; the "collapse of functioning institutions of government" there; the distinction between Soviet actions in Afghanistan and U.S. ones in Grenada; and the three legal bases for American action — Scoon's invitation, the OECS decision to take collective action, and protection of U.S. nationals. Robinson even dubbed the military undertaking a "collective security action," as many of his administration colleagues had previously done. Nevertheless, his memorandum made a number of vital additions and alterations.

To the Reagan administration's legal defense, Robinson added four notable elements, each apparently intended to bolster his fundamental contention that the actions taken by the United States had been well within the narrow confines of established international law. First, he maintained that "the way in which States articulate[d] and interpret[ed] *principles of international law* [was] perhaps even more important to the development and maintenance of an effective international legal order than [were] debates as to whether *the facts* in a particular case [had] warranted the invocation of such principles."[65]   Hence, the United States had "consciously eschewed arguments which might [have] impl[ied] a weakening of established international legal constraints concerning the use of force."   Here, Robinson departed from Kirkpatrick's earlier, rather facile dismissal of "abstract legal principles"[66] while reinforcing Dam's contention that the United States had not sought "to make any broad new precedent for international action."[67]   One could quibble about the facts, Robinson suggested, but not about the law *per se.*

Second, Robinson noted that the "United States, *both before and after* the collective action," had "regarded three well-established legal principles as providing a solid legal basis for the action."[68]   Deliberate regard for international legality, he intimated, had been part of the Grenada decisionmaking process.   Robinson specifically suggested that "our internal legal analysis" had been proceeding since at least "October 23."   If so, then presumably the Legal Adviser's Office at the State Department had become involved before the invasion was launched.[69]

Third, Robinson argued that the United States had "not taken a position as to whether any *one* [of the three grounds presented by the administration] standing alone would have provided adequate support for the action."   Perhaps, he hinted, no single ground would have been considered legally sufficient by the administration for all of its actions in Grenada.   Certainly, the United States had "not asserted that protection of nationals alone would [have] constitute[d] a sufficient basis for all of the actions taken."

Finally, he listed four specific international legal arguments upon which the United States did *not* rely:

(1)   We did not contend that the action in Grenada was an exercise of the inherent *right of self-defense* recognized in *Article 51* of the U.N. Charter for the same reason that the United States eschewed such arguments in support of the actions taken by the United States and other Rio Treaty members in response to the Cuban missile crisis.

(2)   We did not assert that *Article 2(4)* had somehow *fallen into disuse* or been *overtaken by the practice of states*; we regard it as an important and enduring principle of international law.

(3)   Nor did we put forward *new interpretations of the language of Article 2(4).*

(4)   We did not assert a *broad new doctrine of "humanitarian intervention."* We relied instead on the narrower, well-established ground of protection of U.S. nationals.[70]

Robinson's dismissal of the last two would seem tantamount to a repudiation of arguments made earlier by the White House and by Ambassadors Middendorf and Kirkpatrick.   Middendorf, it will be recalled, had submitted on October 26 that the United States had been motivated by "a particularly humanitarian concern,"[71] while a November 3 White House statement had claimed that the Grenada action had been "taken for humanitarian reasons."[72]   On their face at least, these and other early administration statements would seem to have been appeals to "humanitarian intervention."   Kirkpatrick had asserted on October 27 that "the prohibitions against the use of force in the UN Charter" were "contextual, not absolute,"[73] and on November 2 that qualitative distinctions had to be drawn "between force used to protect the innocent and force used to victimize the innocent."[74]   The Ambassador's arguments would seem clearly to have constituted "new interpretations of the language of 2(4)."

Besides his general elaboration of the American legal case, Robinson offered other significant modifications as well.   First, the Legal Adviser made no mention of the American goal of restoring "democratic institutions," only of restoring "internal order."   And second, Robinson subtly altered the three grounds for action by the United States:

(1)   *The request of the Governor-General* had been "regarded by the United States as entitled to great moral and legal weight," according to Robinson.   Indeed, the administration's "internal legal analysis" had "relied heavily upon this request from the time we were first apprised of it on October 23."   Here, Robinson rather curiously shifted the date of Scoon's invitation: from October 24, as reported by Dam and Motley,[75] to October 23.   Sir Paul's request, Robinson submitted, "was clearly an important factor in the decision reached by the President on October 24 to respond favorably to the request of the Organization of Eastern Caribbean States (OECS) for U.S. assistance."   The critical observer might conclude from Robinson's change that it had been done to make Scoon's invitation appear to have exerted a disproportionate impact upon the President's decision.

"The request of lawful authority is a well-established basis for provided military assistance," Robinson added, "whether the requesting state is seeking assistance in the exercise of its inherent right of self defense as recognized in Article 51 of the U.N. Charter, or for other lawful purposes, such as maintenance of internal order." In support of this contention, Robinson cited Lauterpacht's edition of Oppenheim's *International Law*.[76] Although Robinson conceded that a determination of who constituted the "lawful authority" was sometimes difficult in a situation of factional strife, such was not the case in Grenada. "Under both the Constitution of Grenada as well as the law and practice of the British Commonwealth, the Governor-General [had] possessed a necessary residuum of power to restore order" when "confronted by the breakdown of government in his nation." Scoon had been "a recognized head of state of longstanding tenure."[77]

(2) The October 21 *decision by the OECS to take collective action* had provided "further legal support for the U.S. action," according to Robinson. Here, the Legal Adviser broached three separate issues: Had the action been consistent with the terms of the OECS Treaty? Did regional organizations have the capacity to take such actions? And, had the OECS been a competent regional organization?

(a) To bolster his argument that the Grenada invasion was consistent with the terms of the OECS Treaty, Robinson submitted that Article 6, not 8, was the relevant one: Article 8 defined "the jurisdiction of the Defense and Security Committee of the OECS, a subordinate body under that treaty. The decision to take military action on Grenada was reached by the heads of government of the OECS nations, who — unlike the Defense and Security Committee — [had] plenary authority under Article 6." In making this point, Robinson seems to have contradicted earlier statements by Ambassador Middendorf and Deputy Secretary Dam that had cited Article 8 of the Treaty. All the OECS heads of state, Robinson maintained, had "voted in favor of collective action." In another legal innovation, he held that Scoon's request for collective action had "manifestly constituted ratification on the part of Grenada." To those who had questioned whether the OECS had acted in conformity with its constitutive treaty, Robinson responded that "the views of the members of a regional treaty on questions of treaty interpretation are entitled to a weight greater than those of third-state commentators."

(b) The OECS had been competent to act because the Grenadian Governor-General had first requested its assistance. Under these circumstances, the OECS member states had been "doing no more collectively than they could lawfully [have done] individually." Hence, Robinson concluded, "the limits of what action a regional organization [might] properly take" absent a request for outside assistance had not been tested by the Grenada case. This broader "issue require[d] careful analysis in circumstances where an organization [had acted] on its own initiative."

(c) The OECS was, finally, legally competent to take collective action under Article 52 of the U.N. Charter and also under the OAS Charter. Robinson argued that the OECS had been "in effect the regional security arrangement of the Eastern Caribbean states." The OECS Treaty was, he asserted, an analogue to the Rio Treaty. The United States "attached no weight whatsoever to the relatively small size of the OECS member states" since all were sovereign and equally "entitled to enjoy the benefits of regional security arrangements." Robinson concluded: "If it were the case that the OAS Charter stood as a bar to the OECS states taking collective security action, then it would seem that OAS membership would impose burdens uniquely on these states which have the greatest need for collective security."

(3) The *need to protect American citizens* was "the third basis for U.S. participation." According to Robinson, "protection of nationals" was "a well-established, narrowly drawn ground for the use of force which [had] not been considered to conflict with the U.N. Charter." Protection of American nationals, he concluded, had "clearly" justified "the landing of U.S. military forces," if not all the actions taken by the United States in Grenada.

Robinson's letter to Gordon was slavish in its appeal to "well established legal principles." The United States did not stand, Robinson proclaimed, "for the proposition that international legal restraints on the use of force [had] been eroding." It did not believe that international law should be "determined by the policies of the large powers or by transitory voting majorities in international fora." Rather, Robinson concluded, law was to be determined "through reference to carefully constructed and enduring principles of universal applicability." The Grenada mission had been simply a unique case: "We have emphasized the mutually reinforcing nature of the elements of the position we did take, and the unusual circumstances posed by the breakdown of lawful authority and the request of the head of state."

Conclusions

A comprehensive study of the content and evolution of the post-invasion justification for Operation "Urgent Fury" supports four tentative conclusions about the Reagan administration's decision to invade Grenada and about the role played by international law in that decision. These four conclusions presuppose *no knowledge* of the decisionmaking process that preceded Reagan's determination to authorize military action.

1. More than "two basic objectives" appear to have informed Reagan administration decisionmaking.

If public discourse is any indication, Washington decisionmaking was driven by two fundamental objectives: first, and foremost, to ensure the safety of the American students on Grenada who, it was feared, might be harmed or taken hostage by the RMC; and second, to replace the chaos and violence on the island with law and order and functioning governmental institutions. Without exception, every significant public statement offered by the Reagan administration from October 25, 1983 until February 10, 1984 included explicit reference to these ends. Four statements, the more ideological ones offered by Reagan and Kirkpatrick, were more specific about the sort of government sought by the administration: a "democratic" one. Other statements were less specific. Presumably, these were designed to dispel the adverse impression that the United States had sought to impose its own preferred regime type upon the Grenadian people. Caspar Weinberger, for example, observed after Shultz's October 25 news conference: "The form of government that we want to get into Grenada is a form of government that enables the people to choose the kind of government they wish."[78] And Kenneth Dam seemed explicitly to reject the objective of "democratic" government, maintaining that American goals did "not encompass the imposition on the Grenadians of any particular form of government."[79]

Although the Reagan administration never argued that its action had constituted a "humanitarian intervention" *per se*, and while Davis Robinson's letter to Edward Gordon expressly rejected such a legal position, the administration's post-invasion public rationale clearly expressed humanitarian motives, nevertheless. According to jurist Fernando Tesón, the "whole logic of [the Reagan administration action], evidenced not only by the conduct of the United States and her Caribbean allies, but also by statements by the highest United States officials, denote[d] the humanitarian underpinnings of the mission."[80]   As we have seen, the first spoken and written statements issued by Washington on October 25 emphasized the goals of restoring order and forestalling chaos, surely "humanitarian" objectives. On October 26, Ambassador Middendorf submitted that the United States had been prompted by "a particularly humanitarian concern."[81] And a week later, a White House statement claimed that the Grenada action had been "taken for humanitarian reasons."[82] Once again, if public justification at all suggests private intent, then Washington's actions may have reflected humanitarian aims, at least, in part.

While the Reagan administration may indeed have pursued the "two basic objectives" enumerated by George Shultz and his governmental colleagues, it would seem from its rhetoric almost certainly to have pursued a third less humanitarian objective as well: the elimination of Soviet and Cuban influence on Grenada. As we have seen, a number of prominent public statements by the administration, before both domestic and international fora, included explicitly geopolitical appeals. In his October 27 televised address to the American people, for example, Ronald Reagan charged that Prime Minister Bishop had been "a protege of Fidel Castro" and that the Point Salines airport had "looked suspiciously suitable for military aircraft, including Soviet-built long-range bombers." The island of Grenada, the President maintained, had been "a Soviet-Cuban colony, being readied as a major military bastion to export terror and undermine democracy." Hence, the United States military had "got there just in time."[83] Similarly, in her October 27 speech to the U.N. Security Council, Ambassador Kirkpatrick had noted how Maurice Bishop had "freely offered his island as a base for the projection of Soviet military power in this hemisphere." In Kirkpatrick's words, "the familiar pattern of militarization and Cubanization [had been] already far advanced in Grenada."[84]   And in both his November statements,[85] Kenneth Dam conceded that the Reagan administration had feared that "Grenada could be used as a staging ground for subversion of nearby countries, for interdiction of nearby shipping lanes, and for transit of troops and supplies from Cuba to Africa and from Eastern Europe and Libya to Central America." Likewise, in both he cited troubling discoveries on Grenada: secret military treaties with the Soviets, Cubans and North Koreans; secret military fortifications; extensive arms caches; and communications facilities. These finds, he told the House Foreign Affairs Committee, had dramatized "just how important it [was] that Grenada have governing institutions responsible to its own people."[86] Dam's reference to these discoveries in his legal defense of American actions would seem to dramatize just how important it was to the Reagan administration that Grenada be freed from Cuban and Soviet influence.

2. The Reagan administration was sufficiently concerned about international legality to pay it rhetorical attention. Nevertheless, a close inspection of the administration's public rationale reveals a rather indifferent attitude toward the law.

"International law" played a fairly prominent role in the Reagan administration's *post facto* rationale for the Grenada operation. In virtually every public explanation tendered by the administration, some reference was made to international legal agreements, norms, or institutions. Particularly in the days following D-day, October 25, appeals to "law" were ubiquitous. At first glance, such a consistent pattern of rhetoric would appear to suggest a certain degree of respect for international legality; the Reagan administration would seem at least to have wished a law-abiding reputation. A closer inspection of its public rationale, however, reveals the administration's rather nonchalant, cavalier attitude toward international law.

The most egregious example of the administration's indifference toward international law and institutions was provided by the President, himself, on November 3, 1983. Then, he rather glibly asserted that the U.N. General Assembly's 108-9 condemnation of the American action as a "flagrant violation of international law" had not "upset [his] breakfast at all."[87] Continuing the joke, the White House press office promptly produced Reagan's breakfast menu: one poached egg, fruit, toast, and coffee.[88] November 3 was not the first time that international law had been publicly rebuked in administration discussions of the Grenada operation, however, but only the most obvious time.

On the very day that "Urgent Fury" was launched, no statement offered by the Reagan administration, either by the President or his Secretary of State, ever explicitly mentioned "international law." Given the circumstances, one might well have expected a government genuinely concerned about international legality to have made some specific reference to "law," however fleeting. Yet, no allusion was made. In fact, President Reagan never referred expressly to "international law" in *any* of his official explanations for his invasion decision.

Nor did Reagan refer to Sir Paul Scoon's invitation of assistance in his nationally-televised "Address to the Nation."[89] By October 27, Scoon had been rescued and his invitation had already been revealed; hence, an appeal by the President to the Governor-General's invitation would not have put the Grenadian at risk. One must question, therefore, whether the administration had actually accorded Scoon's request the "great moral and legal weight" that would later be claimed by Robinson. If the invitation had in fact been deemed so significant, why would Reagan not have made any appeal to it whatsoever in his most prominent accounting of his invasion decision? International legal justification would seem then to have been among Reagan's lesser priorities.

3. The Reagan administration's legal justification for action was inconsistent, both in its expression of specific legal arguments and in its general articulation of the *jus ad bellum*.

Throughout its public justification for action, the Reagan administration emphasized without contradiction three themes of legal import: its concern for the safety of U.S. nationals on Grenada; the uniqueness of the circumstances surrounding its military action; and the essential distinction to be drawn between the American use of force in Grenada and the Soviet use of force in Afghanistan. While these arguments did not change with the passage of time, the legal rationale for "Urgent Fury" took many twists and turns, nevertheless.

There were, for example, at least six noteworthy discrepancies of fact or argument in the Reagan administration's legal "case": (1) the *date given for Sir Paul Scoon's invitation* of assistance — Robinson reported October 23 while Motley and Dam reported October 24; (2) Ambassador's Kirkpatrick's apparent legal appeal on October 27 to the *self-defense* of the OECS states,[90] which was not prominently made in any other administration statement; (3) the *article of the OECS Charter* cited as legally relevant to the joint military action — Article 6 was cited by Robinson, Article 8 by Middendorf and Dam; (4) the *second U.S. objective* of Operation "Urgent Fury" — the restoration of "democratic institutions," according to Reagan and Kirkpatrick, the restoration of "governmental" ones, according to Shultz, Dam, Middendorf, and Motley; (5) the *appeal to Sir Paul's invitation* — not until October 27, after four public explanations for U.S. action had already been offered, did the administration cite the Grenadian Governor-General's request; and finally, (6) the administration's apparent claim of *humanitarian intervention* — although a variety of public statements suggested such legal grounds for the American recourse to force, Robinson's letter explicitly rejected "humanitarian intervention."

In addition to these six discrepancies, the Reagan administration's articulation of how the *jus ad bellum* was to be understood and applied by states was inconsistent. Statements by Jeane Kirkpatrick underscored the significance of the specific *factual situation* and expressed the war decision law in a broad, manifestly untraditional fashion. In contradistinction, statements by Kenneth Dam and Davis Robinson emphasized the importance of international legal *principles* and interpreted the *jus ad bellum* in an essentially traditional, if decidedly permissive, way.[91]

On October 27, Kirkpatrick told the United Nations Security Council that the U.N. Charter's prohibitions against the use of force were "contextual, not absolute."[92] Hence, they provided "justification for the use of force against force, in pursuit of other values also inscribed in the Charter, such values as freedom, democracy, and peace." A state might take recourse to force, the U.S. Ambassador implied, if its cause were just and consistent with Charter values. Kirkpatrick's understanding of the modern *jus ad bellum* was apparently not shared by most of her Security Council colleagues, however, as eleven state representatives supported a resolution "deeply deploring" the U.S.-led invasion of Grenada and labeling it a "flagrant violation of international law." Six days later, on November 2, Ambassador Kirkpatrick argued before the U.N. General Assembly that the "test of law [lay] not in the assertion of abstract principles but in the application of universal norms to *specific situations*."[93] There was a qualitative and legally significant distinction, she suggested, "between force used to protect the innocent and force used to victimize the innocent." This argument, like that made by her earlier before the Security Council, would seem to reflect more the *jus ad bellum* criteria of "just war" analysis than those of the U.N. Charter framework.[94] If taken to its logical conclusion, Kirkpatrick's argument would appear to sanction the use of force by states under a variety of circumstances not traditionally seen as legally sufficient to justify such action.

In marked contrast to Kirkpatrick's rather expansive, nontraditional rendition of the contemporary *jus ad bellum*, Deputy Secretary Dam stated on November 2 that the United States had "not made, and [did] not seek to make, any broad new precedent for international law."[95] The American justification for its action, he stressed, was "narrow, and well within the accepted concepts of international law." Unlike Kirkpatrick, Dam expressed an apparently high regard for abstract legal principles, explicitly enumerating those considered valid and germane: the invitation of lawful government authority as a basis for state intervention; the capacity of a regional security arrangement to call upon other states for assistance; and the state's right to protect its nationals. Three months later, Davis Robinson's letter to Edward Gordon averred that "the way in which States articulate[d] and interpret[ed] *principles* of international law [was] perhaps even more important" than factual debates.[96] Accordingly, he wrote, the United States had chosen not to "put forward new interpretations of the language of 2(4)." Instead, law was to be ascertained "through reference to carefully constructed and enduring principles of universal applicability." Here, the State Department Legal Adviser would seem to have strayed far from Kirkpatrick's earlier expression of the contemporary *jus ad bellum*. Indeed, Robinson's letter to Professor Gordon, like Dam's twin addresses four months before,[97] may well have been a conscious effort to limit the damage wrought by Kirkpatrick's ideologically rich but legally tenuous addresses before the U.N. Security Council and General Assembly.

Without knowledge of the Grenada decisionmaking process, how might one explain the many conspicuous inconsistencies of the Reagan administration's public rationale? In part, the inconsistencies would seem to reflect a certain *lack of bureaucratic coordination*. Reagan's first address to the nation on October 25 and his identical letters to Thurmond and O'Neill dated October 25 must have been prepared during the same general time frame: sometime shortly before the morning of October 25. Nevertheless, the President's speech refers to restoring "democratic" institutions to Grenada and his letters to restoring "governmental" ones. Since the administration would presumably not contradict itself by conscious choice, such a rhetorical discrepancy may well suggest a lack of bureaucratic coordination. Certainly, one might expect a certain degree of confusion within the government with the State Department, Pentagon, JCS, and NSC all participating in the policy process.

The legal inconsistencies exhibited by the administration's public rationale for "Urgent Fury" probably also reflect the *different audiences* for which the various statements were intended. It is perhaps not coincidental, for example, that the most tightly reasoned legal argument was composed for the Chair of the "Grenada Committee" of the ABA's Section on International Law and Practice. What audience might have

greater concern for legality than the ABA? Nor is it likely accidental
that the public statement which arguably savored least of international
law was delivered by Reagan in a nationally-televised speech treating
simultaneously the Grenada mission and the recent Beirut massacre.
What audience might be least troubled by the absence of legal niceties
than the American public shortly after two hundred and forty-one of
"their boys" had been slaughtered by terrorists?   Public statements,
whether written or oral, are almost invariably composed with a specific
audience in mind. It would indeed be surprising if this were not true
here.

In one instance, *changed material circumstances* explain an obvious
inconsistency found in the administration's public rationale: not until
Thursday, October 27, two days after "Urgent Fury" was launched, did
the Reagan administration publicly acknowledge Sir Paul Scoon's
invitation of assistance.   This delayed acknowledgment has led scholars
to question "whether the argument had not at that time been formulated
or, alternatively, that Sir Paul Scoon had not yet signed the letter of
invitation."[98]   As we have seen in Chapter Two, Sir Paul had in fact not
been rescued from Government House until Wednesday, October 26, at
which time he transmitted his written request to American FSO Lawrence
Rossin.   Before then, it would have been inappropriate for the administration to make note of his invitation lest his life be unnecessarily
endangered.[99]

Another possible explanation for the variance in legal justifications is
that they reflected *divergent legal and policy perspectives* within the
Reagan administration. Governments are not monolithic entities; rather,
they are composed of many individuals with differing personalities,
backgrounds and predilections.   Hence, it would seem reasonable to
hypothesize that Reagan administration officials in Washington, New
York and elsewhere lacked a single, unified perception of Operation
"Urgent Fury," its policy underpinnings, and its lawfulness.   Such
differences in viewpoint, in turn, could manifest themselves in dissimilar
public rationales.

Finally, *time constraints* faced by the State Department Legal
Adviser's Office may explain in part why the Reagan administration's
public legal rationale lacked homogeneity, and also why that rationale
became increasingly sophisticated in the days following the Grenada
invasion.   If Assistant Secretary Motley's testimony before the House
Armed Services Committee[100] is accurate, legal study could only have

commenced on or after Thursday, October 13 — the first day that the Grenada situation was considered by the administration. More likely, such analysis would only have been undertaken after Wednesday, October 19, when, according to Motley, serious planning for a "non-permissive evacuation" began. Even then, "L" may not have been made privy to administration deliberations.

If Robinson's letter is reliable,[101] the international legal aspects of the Grenada operation were considered sometime on or before October 23 since State's "internal legal analysis" had been proceeding since at least then. If legal study commenced on Sunday, October 23, and not beforehand, then "L" would have had at most two days to prepare before the administration's first public justification need be tendered — an unhappy situation, indeed. Under such tight temporal constraints,[102] one would expect its legal argument to be rather thin at first and to become more nuanced and tightly-reasoned with the passage of weeks, then months. No matter when the legal aspects of "Urgent Fury" were first examined, however, Robinson's letter reveals one essential fact: international law was considered at least two days before the start of the Grenada operation.

4. Even the Reagan administration's most sophisticated legal justification relied upon a rather liberal rendition of the *jus ad bellum*.

Davis Robinson's letter to Edward Gordon arguably constituted the Reagan administration's most sophisticated legal rationale for "Urgent Fury." Prepared four months after the fact, the letter must surely have been written with far less haste and after far more consideration than had previous justifications. As the distinct product of the Legal Adviser's Office, it very likely represented the Reagan administration's "best effort" to provide a legal defense of the Grenada invasion. But how well did Robinson's rendition of the *jus ad bellum* square with prevailing interpretations of the law? Was it "well within accepted concepts of international law,"[103] as Kenneth Dam had earlier contended?

A careful review of the contemporary *jus ad bellum* and of Robinson's letter to Gordon suggests that the Reagan administration's "best" legal justification may indeed have fit within the confines of mainstream international legal thought, but only narrowly so. Robinson defended U.S. actions in Grenada on the basis of what he termed three "well-established legal principles": (1) "the request of lawful authority;" (2)

"collective action under Article 52 of the U.N. Charter;" and (3) "protection of nationals." The first and third "principles" cited, intervention after lawful request and intervention to protect nationals, are not unchallenged bases for the permissible use of force; the two are not explicitly provided for in the U.N. Charter and have been rejected by numerous publicists. Nevertheless, both "principles" have prominent scholarly advocates. Robinson's second principle, collective action under Article 52, is provided for in the U.N. Charter, although how that "collective action" is to be understood has also been vigorously disputed by publicists. Accordingly, Davis Robinson's citation of legal principles was not implausible, if perhaps ultimately unpersuasive. The Legal Adviser's Office was surely concerned that its rendition of the *jus ad bellum* not be considered illegitimate, for as Robinson contended, "the way in which States articulate[d] and interpret[ed] principles of international law [was] perhaps even more important" than factual debates. Presumably, it was at least in part for this reason that appeals to "humanitarian intervention" and to "new interpretations of Article 2(4)" were specifically rejected by Robinson.

An analysis of the lawfulness *per se* of American actions will be undertaken in the final chapter of this study. A preliminary assessment of Davis Robinson's letter to Edward Gordon suggests that, at the very least, the administration's "best case" relied upon the invocation of legal concepts that enjoy some measure of scholarly support.

The Need to Examine the Decisionmaking Process

In an effort to determine how and why the United States decided to invade Grenada and the role played by international law in that decision, this chapter and the previous one have examined in some detail four distinct factors: the pre-invasion conditions on Grenada; the conduct of Operation "Urgent Fury;" the relationship between the United States and the Bishop regime; and the Reagan administration's public justification for its military action. As we have seen, these four factors, while significant, yield a suggestive but incomplete picture of Reagan administration motives. They are, more importantly, only marginally indicative of the actual decisionmaking process that preceded "Urgent Fury."[104] Many critical questions about the decisionmaking process remain unaddressed, *inter alia*: Which specific decisionmakers were most intimately involved? What were the attitudes of the various departments of the national security bureaucracy? How did the decision to use force evolve? What particular role did the President play in that decision? Was the administration ignorant of the multiple locations of the medical students? If it had known of their locations, then why had the American invasion forces not known? What role did the leaders of the Caribbean states play?

Furthermore, the four factors we have thus far considered reveal precious little about the specific role of law in the foreign policy process. If the public accounts given by Motley and Robinson are accurate, then administration lawyers were brought in at some point between October 13 and 23. But when specifically was legal counsel sought? For what reason? Was it listened to, and if so, by whom? What was the origin of the OECS request and what role did the United States play in it? What of the mysterious Scoon invitation? Why was Ambassador McNeil sent to Barbados and what were his findings? The answers to these essential questions can only be found in a careful reconstruction of the thirteen-day decision process that preceded "Urgent Fury." It is to such a reconstruction that the next two chapters of this study will be devoted.

Notes

1. "Ambassador Kirkpatrick's Statement, UN General Assembly, November 2, 1983," *Department of State Bulletin* 83 (December 1983): 76-77.
2. "President's Remarks and Question-And-Answer Session (Excerpts), November 3, 1983," *Department of State Bulletin* 83 (December 1983): 78-79.
3. Letter from Davis R. Robinson, State Department Legal Adviser, to Professor Edward Gordon, Chairman of the "Grenada Committee" of the American Bar Association's Section on International Law and Practice, dated February 10, 1984. Reprinted in full in Moore, *Law and the Grenada Mission*, pp. 125-129 (hereafter cited as "Robinson letter").
4. The post-invasion justifications included: (1) President's Remarks, October 25, 1983, (2) President Reagan's Letter to Congress, October 25, 1983, (3) Secretary Shultz's News Conference, October 25, 1983, (4) Ambassador Middendorf's Statement, OAS, Permanent Council, October 26, 1983, (5) Ambassador Kirkpatrick's Statement, UN Security Council, October 27, 1983, (6) President Reagan's Address to the Nation, October 27, 1983, (7) Deputy Secretary Kenneth Dam's prepared statement before the House Committee on Foreign Affairs, November 2, 1983, and Deputy Secretary Dam's Remarks, Louisville, November 4, 1983, (8) Ambassador Kirkpatrick's Statement, UN

General Assembly, November 2, 1983, (9) President's Remarks and Question-and-answer Session, November 3, 1983, (10) White House Statement, November 3, 1983, (11) Assistant Secretary Langhorne Motley's statement before the House Armed Services Committee, January 24, 1984, and (12) State Department Legal Adviser Davis R. Robinson's letter to Professor Edward Gordon, February 10, 1984. Full citations will follow.

5.   For a study of the role of public rhetoric in the Grenada episode, see Denise M. Bostdorff, "The Presidency and Promoted Crisis: Reagan, Grenada, and Issue Management," *Presidential Studies Quarterly* 21 (Fall 1991): 737-750. See also David S. Birdsell, "Ronald Reagan on Lebanon and Grenada," *The Quarterly Journal of Speech* 73 (August 1987): 267-279; and William F. Lewis, "Telling America's Story: Narrative Form and the Reagan Presidency," *The Quarterly Journal of Speech* 73 (August 1987): 280-302.

6.   The "widespread doctrinal controversies which surround many central aspects of the Charter regime ... stem, in the main, from the ambiguities of wording found in the textual provision in question; ambiguities which states have, in practice, sought to exploit to their own advantage." Gilmore, *Analysis and Documentation*, p. 41.

7.   Among the significant changes in the system: the advent of nuclear weapons; the rise of the "Developing World;" the changed nature of international conflict, including the proliferation of wars of national liberation; the increased significance of terrorism; and the forty-five year "Cold War" relationship between the United States and the Soviet Union.

8.   Natalino Ronzitti, *Rescuing Nationals Abroad through Military Coercion and Intervention on Grounds of Humanity* (Dordrecht: Martinus Nijhoff, 1985), p. xiii. See also Hermann Mosler, "The International Society as a Legal Community," *Recueil des Cours* 140 (1974-IV): 283; and Andrzej Iacewicz, "The Concept of Force in the United Nations Charter," *Polish Yearbook of International Law* 9 (1977-1978): 138.

9.   Davidson, *A Study in Politics*, p. 89; Ronzitti, *Rescuing Nationals Abroad*, p. xiii. See also Arnold Duncan McNair, *The Law of Treaties* (Oxford: Clarendon Press, 1961), p. 216; Alfred Verdross, "*Jus Dispositivum* and *Jus Cogens* in International Law," *American Journal of International Law* 60 (1966): 60; and Gamal M. Badr, "The Exculpatory Effect of Self-Defence in State Responsibility," *Georgia Journal of International and Comparative Law* 10 (1980): 13.

10.   There are two explicit exceptions to Article 2(4) which have virtually no practical significance: force undertaken by the five major powers before the Security Council is functional — Article 106; and force undertaken against "enemy" states of the Second World War — Articles 107 and 53. Anthony Clark Arend, "International Law and the Recourse to Force: A Shift in Paradigms," *Stanford Journal of International Law* 27 (1990): 1-2.

11. William V. O'Brien, *U.S. Military Intervention: Law and Morality*, Washington Papers No. 68 (Beverly Hills, Calif.: Sage/Center for Strategic and International Studies, Georgetown University, 1979), p. 29.

12. See Davidson, *A Study in Politics*, pp. 102-107. See also Anthony Clark Arend and Robert J. Beck, *International Law and the Use of Force: Beyond the U.N. Charter Paradigm* (London: Routledge, 1993).

13. Such was the American contention at the outset of the Vietnam war. See William V. O'Brien, *The Conduct of Just and Limited War* (New York: Praeger, 1981), p. 260. See also John Norton Moore, "The Secret War in Central America and the Future of World Order," *American Journal of International Law* 80 (January 1986): 43-127.

14. Derek Bowett, *Self-Defense in International Law* (Manchester: Manchester University Press, 1958), pp. 31, 58, 256; Claude H. M. Waldcock, "The Regulation of Force by Individual States in International Law," *Recueil des Cours* 81 (1952-II): 463; and Myres S. McDougal and Florentino P. Feliciano, *Law and Minimum World Public Order* (New Haven, Conn.: Yale University Press, 1961), pp. 207-244.

15. For an excellent discussion of anticipatory self-defense, see Richard J. Erickson, *Legitimate Use of Military Force Against State-Sponsored International Terrorism* (Maxwell Air Force Base, AL: Air University Press, 1989), pp. 136-143. See also Arend and Beck, *International Law and the Use of Force*, pp. 71-79.

16. See Ian Brownlie, *International Law and the Use of Force by States* (Oxford: Clarendon Press, 1963), pp. 275-278; Michael Akehurst, *A Modern Introduction to International Law*, 5th ed. (London: Allen and Unwin, 1985); and Louis Henkin, "Force, Intervention and Neutrality in Contemporary International Law," *Proceedings of the American Society of International Law* (1963): 150.

17. Article 42 provides: "Should the Security Council consider that the [non-military] measures provided for in Article 41 would be inadequate or have proved to be inadequate, it may take such action by air, sea, or land forces as may be necessary to maintain or restore international peace and security. Such action may include demonstrations, blockade, and other operations by air, sea, or land forces of Members of the United Nations."

18. O'Brien, *U.S. Military Intervention*, p. 27.

19. Arend, "International Law and the Recourse to Force," pp. 6-10.

20. O'Brien, *U.S. Military Intervention*, p. 27.

21. Since the end of the Cold War, the Security Council has taken a more active role in matters of international peace and security. It has, for example, authorized forcible actions by U.N. member states in the Persian Gulf War, Somalia, and Bosnia. For a more elaborate discussion of collective uses of force under the U.N. Charter, see Arend and Beck, *International Law and the*

Use of Force, pp. 47-68, 188-194.

22. "[W]ith the exception of measures against any enemy state [of World War II]."

23. Leland Goodrich, Edvard Hambro, and Anne Patricia Simons, *Charter of the United Nations*, 3rd ed. (New York: Columbia University Press, 1969), pp. 364-368; John Norton Moore, "The Role of Regional Arrangements in the Maintenance of World Order," in *The Future of the International Legal Order*, Vol. III, eds. Cyril E. Black and Richard A. Falk (Princeton: Princeton University Press, 1971), pp. 122-164; John Norton Moore, "Toward an Applied Theory for the Regulation of Intervention," in *Law and Civil War in the Modern World*, ed. John Norton Moore (Baltimore: Johns Hopkins University Press, 1974), pp. 3-37; and Moore, *The Grenada Mission*, p. 23.

24. See O'Brien, *U.S. Military Intervention*, pp. 15-25.

25. Ann Van Wynen Thomas and A. J. Thomas, Jr., *Non-Intervention: The Law and Its Import in the Americas* (Dallas: Southern Methodist University Press, 1956), pp. 91-97; Brownlie, *Use of Force*, p. 317.

26. Davidson, *A Study in Politics*, pp. 92-93.

27. Scholars reject intervention as illegal "at least in those cases where there is no evidence to suggest that the insurgents are benefitting from the assistance of a foreign power." Gilmore, *Analysis and Documentation*, p. 72.

28. See Hugo Grotius, *De Jure Belli Ac Pacis*, vol. 2, *The Translation*, ed. James B. Scott, trans. Francis W. Kelsey et al. (Oxford: Clarendon Press, 1925), p. 627; L. Oppenheim, *International Law: A Treatise*, vol. 1, *Peace*, 5th ed., ed. Hersh Lauterpacht (London: Longman, 1955), (hereafter cited as "Oppenheim, *International Law*"), p. 309; Thomas and Thomas, *Non-Intervention*, pp. 305-306; Bowett, *Self-Defense*, p. 97; and Philip C. Jessup, *A Modern Law of Nations* (New York: Macmillan, 1958).

29. See Brownlie, *Use of Force*, pp. 298-301; J.L. Brierly, *The Law of Nations* (Oxford: Oxford University Press, 1963); Jessup, *A Modern Law of Nations*, pp. 169-170, Michael Akehurst, "The Use of Force to Protect National Abroad," *International Relations* 5 (May 1977): 3; and Ronzitti, *Rescuing Nationals Abroad*.

30. Joyner, "Reflections on the Lawfulness of Invasion," p. 134. Joyner cites the U.N. Charter, the OAS Charter, and the Rio Treaty as examples of international agreement specifically prohibiting intervention.

31. For a citation of authorities supporting "intervention to protect nationals," see J.B.L. Fonteyne, "Forcible Self-Help by States to Protect Human Rights: Recent Views from the United Nations," in *Humanitarian Intervention and the United Nations*, Richard B. Lillich, ed. (Charlottesville: University of Virginia Press, 1973), p. 197.

32. Ronzitti discusses but rejects this view in *Rescuing Nationals Abroad*, p. 1.

33. See Gilmore, *Analysis and Documentation*, p. 57; and Davidson, *A Study in Law*, p. 113.

34. See, for example, Fernando Tesón, *Humanitarian Intervention*; Michael Reisman and Myres S. McDougal, "Humanitarian Intervention to Protect the Ibos," in *Humanitarian Intervention and the United Nations*, ed. Richard B. Lillich (Charlottesville: University of Virginia Press, 1973), p. 167; and Moore, "Toward an Applied Theory for the Regulation of Intervention."

35. See Reisman and McDougal, "Humanitarian Intervention to Protect the Ibos"; Moore, "Toward an Applied Theory for the Regulation of Intervention"; and Tesón, *Humanitarian Intervention*.

36. Brownlie, *Use of Force*, p. 338.

37. Oppenheim, *International Law*, p. 312.

38. See Akehurst, "Use of Force," pp. 9-19; and Ian Brownlie, "Humanitarian Intervention," in *Law and Civil War in the Modern World*, John Norton Moore, ed. (Baltimore: Johns Hopkins Press, 1974), p. 217.

39. Davidson, *A Study in Politics*, pp. 119-124. For an excellent recent study, see Ronzitti, *Rescuing Nationals Abroad*.

40. Reagan's remarks are reprinted in *Department of State Bulletin* 83 (December 1983): 67. The President's "Remarks and Question-and-Answer Session with Reporters" are contained in the *Weekly Compilation of Presidential Documents* 19 (October 31, 1983): 1487-1489.

41. Only near the end of his statement, in a reiteration of American goals, did Reagan mention "the restoration of democratic institutions." He reported: "Let me repeat, the U.S. objectives are clear: to facilitate the evacuation of those who want to leave, and to help in the restoration of democratic institutions in Grenada."

42. Tesón, *Humanitarian Intervention*, pp. 188-200. See also Davidson, *A Study in Politics*, p. 167.

43. Identical letters were addressed to Thomas P. O'Neill, Jr., and Strom Thurmond. They are reprinted in the *Weekly Compilation of Presidential Documents* 19 (October 31, 1983): 1493-1494.

44. "Secretary Shultz's News Conference, October 25, 1983," *Department of State Bulletin* 83 (December 1983): 69-72. Hereafter cited as "Shultz's News Conference."

45. "Ambassador Middendorf's Statement, OAS, Permanent Council, October 26, 1983," *Department of State Bulletin* 83 (December 1983): 72-73.

46. "Ambassador Kirkpatrick's Statement, UN Security Council, October 27, 1983," *Department of State Bulletin* 83 (December 1983): 74-76.

47. Prime Minister Charles had first mentioned the Scoon invitation on Wednesday, October 26, in a speech delivered at the United Nations. Payne et al., *Revolution and Invasion*, p. 157.

48. Robinson letter, p. 126. See also Motley, "The Decision to Assist Grenada," p. 70.

49. "Address to the Nation," *Weekly Compilation of Presidential Documents* 19 (October 31, 1983): 1497-1502.

50. "Ambassador Kirkpatrick's Statement, UN General Assembly, November 2, 1983," pp. 76-77.

51. Dam had come to State from the University of Chicago Law School, on whose faculty he had served for many years.

52. Davidson, *A Study in Politics*, p. 167.

53. "Statement by the Honorable Kenneth W. Dam, Deputy Secretary of State, Before the Committee on Foreign Affairs, U.S. House of Representatives, November 2, 1983," reprinted in Moore, *Law and the Grenada Mission*, pp. 101-105. "Secretary Dam's Remarks, Louisville, November 4, 1983," *Department of State Bulletin* 83 (December 1983): 79-82.

54. Emphasis mine.

55. As originally conceived, "collective security" required the universal membership of all the states of the international system. Hence, to speak of "regional collective security" is to blur the distinction between "collective security" and "regional collective defense." See Inis L. Claude, Jr., *Power and International Relations* (New York, NY: Random House, 1962), pp. 115.

56. As has been noted, Middendorf's October 26 statement and Kirkpatrick's November 2 statement used the term "regional collective security" to describe the American action. In Reagan's letter to Congress and Shultz's press conference, "collective security" was used. Motley would also describe the US operation as part of a "collective security" action. See below.

57. "Statement by the Honorable Kenneth W. Dam, November 2, 1983," reprinted in Moore, *Law and the Grenada Mission*, p. 105.

58. "President's Remarks and Question-And-Answer Session (Excerpts), November 3, 1983," pp. 78-79.

59. "White House Statement, November 3, 1983," *Department of State Bulletin* 83 (December 1983): 78.

60. Motley, "The Decision to Assist Grenada," pp. 70-73.

61. Motley used the specific phrase "collective security and rescue operation" four separate times. In his statement, the Assistant Secretary was now employing both descriptions for the U.S. operation which had been tendered by the administration.

62. "Secretary Dam's Remarks, Louisville, November 4, 1983," p. 80.

63. The letter is reprinted in Moore, *Law and the Grenada Mission*, p. 87.

64. Robinson's letter, pp. 124-129.

65. Emphasis mine.

66. "Ambassador Kirkpatrick's Statement, UN General Assembly, November 2, 1983," p. 77.

67. "Secretary Dam's Remarks, Louisville, November 4, 1983," p. 81.

68. Emphasis mine.

69. The precise involvement of "L" will be discussed in Chapters 4, 5 and 6 below.

70. Enumeration and emphasis mine.

71. "Ambassador Middendorf's Statement, OAS, Permanent Council, October 26, 1983," p. 73.

72. "White House Statement, November 3, 1983," p. 78.

73. "Ambassador Kirkpatrick's Statement, UN Security Council, October 27, 1983," p. 74.

74. "Ambassador Kirkpatrick's Statement, UN General Assembly, November 2, 1983," p. 77.

75. "Secretary Dam's Remarks, Louisville, November 4, 1983," p. 80; and Motley, "The Decision to Assist Grenada," p. 73.

76. Oppenheim, *International Law*, p. 305.

77. Here Robinson was compelled to cite less venerable authorities than Lauterpacht: Stanley A. de Smith, *The New Commonwealth and its Constitutions* (London: Stevens, 1964), pp. 90-100; *The Guardian*, October 28, 1983, p. 6; and *The Economist*, November 9, 1983, p. 45.

78. Cited in *New York Times*, October 26, 1983, p. 1.

79. "Statement by the Honorable Kenneth W. Dam, House of Representatives, November 2, 1983," pp. 101-105; and "Secretary Dam's Remarks, Louisville, November 4, 1983," pp. 79-82.

80. Tesón, *Humanitarian Intervention*, p. 192.

81. "Ambassador Middendorf's Statement, OAS, Permanent Council, October 26, 1983," p. 73.

82. "White House Statement, November 3, 1983," p. 78.

83. "Address to the Nation, October 27, 1983," pp. 1497-1502.

84. "Ambassador Kirkpatrick's Statement, UN Security Council, October 27, 1983," pp. 74-76.

85. "Statement by Kenneth W. Dam, Before the Committee on Foreign Affairs, November 2, 1983," pp. 101-105; and "Secretary Dam's Remarks, Louisville," pp. 79-82.

86. "Statement by Kenneth W. Dam, Before the Committee on Foreign Affairs, November 2, 1983," pp. 101-105.

87. "President's Remarks and Question-And-Answer Session (Excerpts), November 3, 1983," p. 79.

88. Ed Magnuson, "Now to Make It Work," *Time*, November 14, 1983, p. 20.

89. Reagan likewise said absolutely nothing of the Scoon invitation in his memoir account of the Grenada invasion. Reagan, *An American Life*, pp. 449-458.

90. "Ambassador Kirkpatrick's Statement, UN Security Council, October 27, 1983," p. 75-76.

91. According to Davidson, "each of the grounds [cited by Dam and Robinson] justifying the intervention depended on a liberal interpretation of existing norms." Nevertheless, both officials were careful "to state precise legal grounds for the action, which, they argued, were acceptable interpretations of existing norms." A Study in Politics, pp. 167-168.

92. "Ambassador Kirkpatrick's Statement, UN Security Council, October 27, 1983," p. 74.

93. "Ambassador Kirkpatrick's Statement, UN General Assembly, November 2, 1983," pp. 76-77. Emphasis mine.

94. Kirkpatrick's appeal was more to "just cause" and "right intention" than it was to Articles 2(4) and 51 of the U.N. Charter. On the just war jus ad bellum, see O'Brien, The Conduct of Just and Limited War, pp. 13-36. For recent studies of the evolution of just war doctrine see James T. Johnson, Just War Tradition and the Restraint of War (Princeton, NJ: Princeton University Press, 1981); and O'Brien, The Conduct of Just and Limited War.

95. "Secretary Dam's Remarks, Louisville, November 4, 1983," p. 81.

96. Robinson's letter, p. 125.

97. According to Davidson, "Dam's statement of the legal basis for US intervention was designed not so much to legitimate, but rather to minimize the damage which may have been done, from a legal point of view, by [Kirkpatrick's] initial statement in justification." A Study in Politics, p. 167.

98. Davidson, A Study in Politics, p. 167.

99. So it was argued by Robinson and Motley. See Robinson's letter, p. 126; and Motley, "The Decision to Assist Grenada," p. 70.

100. Motley, "The Decision to Assist Grenada," pp. 70-73.

101. Robinson's letter, pp. 125-129.

102. This interpretation has been offered by Scott Davidson: "the arguments in justification have the appearance of being constructed 'at a gallop' with little forethought." A Study in Politics, p. 166.

103. "Secretary Dam's Remarks, Louisville, November 4, 1983," p. 81.

104. Only Motley's January 24 statement to the House Armed Services Committee is of much help here.

4

The Stage Is Set

I didn't want nine thousand years of [post-invasion] Security Council debate.[1]
— Assistant Secretary of State Motley

International law's impact on deliberations: *"Not much."*[2]
— Undersecretary of State Eagleburger

This chapter and the next will retrace a thirteen-day period in October 1983. During this brief span, the Reagan administration decided to launch the invasion of Grenada, code-named Operation "Urgent Fury." Drawing upon memoir accounts and upon interviews and correspondence with key participants, Chapters Four and Five will reconstruct as carefully as possible the complicated decisionmaking process that preceded the President's startling disclosure Tuesday morning, October 25, that he had decided to authorize a military action. The story of the "Urgent Fury" decision takes place in a variety of settings: Bridgetown, Barbados; Washington, D.C.; St. George's, Grenada; Augusta, Georgia; Port-of-Spain, Trinidad; and Beirut, Lebanon. At least in part, it is a story of little-known individuals and lesser-known states. It is, more importantly, a story in which international law plays a role.

This chapter will consider specifically the events of Thursday, October 13 through the early morning of Saturday, October 22. During this eight-day interval, the tiny island of Grenada assumed an increasingly prominent role in Reagan administration deliberations. Five events then were of particular import: U.S. Ambassador Milan Bish's offer on Saturday, October 15, of an airplane to facilitate the rescue of Maurice

Bishop; Maurice Bishop's murder on Wednesday, October 19; the first Cabinet-level meeting devoted to Grenada on Thursday, October 20; the OECS invitation of American military assistance on Friday, October 21; and the very early morning discussions on Saturday, October 22, that followed receipt of word of the OECS invitation. For the sake of clarity, Chapter Four will be divided into four chronologically-arranged sections: (1) Early Deliberations; (2) Concerns Intensify; (3) "Bloody Wednesday;" and (4) Cabinet-level Involvement.

Early Deliberations

In the years since Ronald Reagan's decision to launch "Urgent Fury," commentators have justifiably criticized his administration for the insufficiency of its pre-invasion intelligence. More and better information should certainly have been gathered. Nevertheless, the U.S. government apparently knew almost from the beginning that factional battles were plaguing the People's Revolutionary Government.[3] Indeed, by Wednesday, October 12, the day the coup against Bishop was launched, officials in Washington had already been receiving reports of discord within the Grenadian regime.[4]

Among the sources of this intelligence was the U.S. Embassy in Bridgetown, Barbados, which had long been following events on nearby Grenada. According to Kenneth Kurze, a Foreign Service Officer stationed at Bridgetown, "our information came *from the island*, mainly from people telephoning to Barbados, newspapers, radio station talk shows, and friends."[5] Unfortunately, however, virtually no American embassy intelligence was first-hand. As George Shultz has observed in his 1993 memoir:

> We ... charged our ambassador on Barbados, Milan Bish, to keep track of events [on Grenada] through occasional visits and other means. We found [during the Grenada deliberations] that Bish had recently prohibited embassy political and U.S. Information Agency officers from even visiting Grenada to do the normal contact and reporting work. His rationale, as we learned it, seemed to be: these are Communists; therefore, they are evil and not trustworthy; therefore, we shouldn't talk to them. This is hardly what we needed. The upshot was that we had neither current information nor good contacts with whom to talk.[6]

Nor was information available from any Central Intelligence Agency source on Grenada. As John F. Lehman, Jr., Secretary of the Navy in 1983, would later explain:

> Over the opposition of Frank Carlucci, then deputy director of the CIA, the Carter administration had ended its last intelligence efforts in Grenada as part of a shriveling of the CIA. The fact is, we did not really have any on-scene sources on the island but had to depend solely on overhead pictures and other technical intelligence.[7]

The paucity of reliable "human intelligence" on the evolving Grenada situation would prove significantly to influence Reagan administration decisionmaking. Computer-enhanced satellite images could reveal something of Grenada's physical topography, but nothing of its shifting political landscape.

The RIG

On Thursday, October 13, the political conflict on Grenada began formally to be discussed at Foggy Bottom. There, the Restricted Interagency Group (RIG) first considered the growing unrest on the island and the dangers it might pose to U.S. citizens.[8]

This State-chaired group was typically composed of the following five Reagan administration officials: Langhorne A. "Tony" Motley, Assistant Secretary of State for Inter-American Affairs and the RIG Chair; Nestor D. Sanchez, Deputy Assistant Secretary of Defense for Inter-American Affairs; Vice Admiral Arthur S. Moreau, Jr., Assistant to the Chairman of the JCS; Duane R. "Dewey" Clarridge, Latin American Division Chief of the CIA's Directorate of Operations; and Lieutenant Colonel Oliver L. North, the NSC's Deputy Director of Political-Military Affairs. In addition, depending on the circumstances, RIG meetings might also be attended by one or more of the following Deputy Assistant Secretaries of State for Inter-American Affairs: L. Craig Johnstone; Charles A. "Tony" Gillespie; and James H. Michel.[9] During Motley's tenure, the group normally met once or twice a week in the afternoon to consider Latin American affairs and made key decisions on covert operations and other central policy questions. At one RIG meeting in late 1983, for example, the suggestion to mine Nicaraguan harbors was introduced by Dewey Clarridge.[10]

The RIG itself was Tony Motley's creation.[11] When Motley succeeded Thomas O. Enders as Assistant Secretary in May of 1983, the former Ambassador to Brazil secretly reorganized his predecessor's "Core Group" in an effort to regain control of policy. George Shultz had wanted the Restricted Interagency Group to report directly to him. However, because of President Reagan's reticence to delegate decision-making responsibility to the Secretary of State, the RIG members reported separately to their respective bosses: Clarridge to William Casey, the Director of Central Intelligence; Moreau to the Joint Chiefs and to General Paul Gorman, Commander of U.S. Southern Command, Panama; North to William P. Clark, the President's National Security Adviser; and Sanchez to Caspar W. "Cap" Weinberger, the Secretary of Defense. Only Motley reported to Shultz. Of the five principal RIG members, Sanchez apparently occupied the weakest position. "Nestor would play along, but Moreau was the heavy," one RIG participant would later recall.[12]   Although the Vice Admiral was reserved in public appearances, he would later be described by an associate as "very bright" and "very powerful" because he had the ear of General John W. "Jack" Vessey, the JCS Chairman.[13]

On Thursday, October 13, Maurice Bishop had not yet been placed officially under house arrest; accordingly, the Restricted Interagency Group's discussions were essentially precautionary. Indeed, Grenada had not even been a planned agenda item.[14]   In the next two weeks, however, as the situation on Grenada seemed to grow increasingly volatile, Motley would convene RIG meetings on a daily basis.[15]

The National Security Council Staff

The National Security Council began its own consideration of developments on Grenada at a 7:30 A.M. senior staff meeting on Thursday, October 13.   The daily meetings were held in the White House Situation Room and were typically attended by National Security Adviser William Clark, Robert C. "Bud" McFarlane, Clark's deputy, Vice Admiral John M. Poindexter, and about ten other senior staff members.[16]   This Thursday morning, in the two or three minutes he was customarily allotted, National Security Assistant for Latin American Affairs Constantine Menges described the instability that now appeared to threaten the Grenadian regime.

Last Saturday, Menges explained, Maurice Bishop had returned from Cuba after having visited his friend, Fidel Castro.   Now that the Prime Minister was back on Grenada, his life might well be in danger.   The pro-Soviet hardliners in the Central Committee were apparently planning a coup to oust him. This plot reflected, it seemed, "a tactical quarrel between Havana and Moscow and their respective Grenadian allies." Menges then told his colleagues what responses the Soviet Union and Cuba had taken to the changing Grenada situation. Among other things, it is possible that Menges reported Bishop's visit on the morning of October 12 to the Cuban Ambassador to Grenada, Julian Torres Rizo.[17] A new NSC staff member,[18] Menges concluded by discussing the concerns which had already been raised by the democratic leadership in the Caribbean.[19]

Clark is replaced

On Thursday afternoon, October 13, Judge Clark convened an unusual afternoon meeting of the NSC staff in the Roosevelt Room. Now, Reagan's second National Security Adviser announced that he had decided to resign his position and that he would accept the President's nomination as Secretary of the Interior Department.[20] Though it was not known on Thursday afternoon, Clark would be succeeded the following Monday by his deputy, Robert McFarlane. At first, President Reagan had planned to appoint James Baker as his National Security Adviser, and Michael Deaver as his Chief of Staff.[21] Given very strong opposition from William Clark, Caspar Weinberger, William Casey, and Ed Meese, however, the President "reversed [himself] and scrap[ped] the change."[22] In his 1990 memoir, Reagan called his decision not to appoint Baker "a turning point for my administration, although I had no idea at the time how significant it would prove to be."[23]

Friday, October 14

On Friday, Assistant Secretary Motley convened another RIG meeting at the State Department. Now, for the first time, Grenada was part of the scheduled agenda.[24] After receiving unconfirmed reports of Bishop's arrest and other disruption on the island, State began to review its standard evacuation plan for the island. In addition, the Joint Chiefs of Staff office was asked through Vice Admiral Moreau to review its contingency plans for evacuation.[25] Accordingly, the JCS office made a "what if" telephone call Friday to Admiral Wesley McDonald's CINCLANT headquarters in Norfolk "requesting possible options for show of force/presence operations in the vicinity of Grenada and possible noncombatant evacuation operations."[26]   The Restricted Interagency Group's consideration on October 14 of a possible American evacuation of Grenada, it should be noted, was far from that of a full-scale invasion.[27]

That evening on Barbados, British Deputy High Commissioner David Montgomery telephoned the American Embassy in Bridgetown. Ludlow "Kim" Flower, the charge d'affaires and Deputy Chief of the U.S. Mission (DCM), took the call. Montgomery had very important news to report: Maurice Bishop had been placed under house arrest by the NJM's Central Committee.[28]   After this intelligence was conveyed, Montgomery and Flower spoke for some time about the general situation on Grenada. Such discussions about Caribbean politics were common between the British High Commissioner's office and the American Embassy. Once their conversation was finished, Flower thanked Montgomery for his call and immediately informed Ambassador Milan D. Bish, a Reagan political appointee whose embassy was responsible for Grenada. Fearing that Americans on the island might now be in danger, Ambassador Bish promptly sent a cable drafted by his deputy to Washington.[29]

Saturday, October 15

The next day, Ambassador Bish tentatively approached the Barbadian Permanent Secretary of Defence and Security.[30]   Bish told him that the United States would provide one transport aircraft to evacuate Prime Minister Bishop from Grenada. Bish's offer appeared "to cover both a [voluntary] release of Bishop" or "Bishop's forcible freeing by a raid being contemplated by several Caribbean states." When the Permanent Secretary asked whether the United States might provide helicopters for a raiding party, the former Nebraska banker responded that the offer was only for one airplane.[31]

Although the State Department would subsequently deny that Bish had done so, it is clear that the Ambassador did make such an offer, that he did so "with U.S. government authority,"[32] and that nothing ultimately came of it. What remain uncertain are the origin and the rationale for Bish's offer. As to its origin, it has been reported that Lieutenant Colonel North was responsible for planning the Bishop rescue mission.[33] Given what is known of North's fondness for covert activity, it is possible, perhaps even likely, that he proposed the mission. As to the rationale of Bish's offer, it has been speculated that Reagan administration officials feared Bishop's continued detention would lead him to request Cuban intervention to oust Hudson Austin. If Maurice Bishop could be transported safely to a third country, then pressure for a Cuban intervention might wane.[34] Alternatively, it has been suggested that if Prime Minister Bishop could be saved from his more radical PRG colleagues, the United States might realize political benefits upon Bishop's restoration to power.[35]

Also on Saturday, Kim Flower spoke by telephone with Barbadian Prime Minister Tom Adams.[36] The Deputy Chief of the U.S. Mission had been at the home of Rudyard "Rudy" Lewis, the commander of the Barbadian Defence Force, when Adams had phoned there. At first, Adams spoke privately with General Lewis. Then, when Lewis apprised the Prime Minister of Flower's presence, Adams asked to speak directly with the American diplomat. In the course of their ensuing twenty-minute discussion of the Grenada situation, Adams told Flower that he wished to speak with Ambassador Bish on Monday.

Concerns Intensify

Monday, October 17, proved to be a crucial day in the Grenada decisionmaking process. It was still two days before Maurice Bishop and his colleagues would be murdered; nevertheless, from now until October 24, American planning would take place in an interagency forum with representatives of all relevant agencies participating on a daily basis. Moreover, the Inter-American Bureau of the State Department would begin its advocacy of serious planning for a peaceful "noncombatant evacuation operation" or "NEO." Finally, the President and Vice President would now be kept personally informed of all developments.[37] Ronald Reagan, whose principal foreign policy focus remained on Lebanon, had just returned to Washington from a weekend at Camp David, Maryland.[38] George Bush, coincidentally, was on a tour of the Caribbean.[39]

In Bridgetown, Barbados, Tom Adams met "informally" on Monday with Ambassador Bish and Kim Flower. This would be the first sit-down, heart-to-heart conversation between Bish and Adams regarding the Grenada situation.[40] The Barbadian Prime Minister had spoken with Caribbean colleagues over the weekend about the possibility of taking military action against the leaders of the coup against Maurice Bishop.[41] Now, the conservative Prime Minister suggested that the current situation on Grenada might offer the United States the opportunity to reduce the influence of the Soviet Union and Cuba in the Caribbean. Issuing an implicit invitation to the American diplomats, he encouraged the United States to help launch a military operation. Ambassador Bish now reiterated to Adams the offer he had made on Saturday of an airplane to facilitate Bishop's evacuation. Adams appeared dissatisfied with the modest American proposal, however, hoping instead for more substantial action.[42] Although they were noncommittal, Bish and his DCM promised Adams that they would relay his request to the proper authorities. Immediately following the meeting, Ambassador Bish cabled a "memcon" to Washington drafted by Flower.[43]

Back at the State Department on Monday, Assistant Secretary Motley chaired a two-hour RIG meeting, the first devoted specifically to Grenada.[44] Among those who almost certainly attended the special meeting were Clarridge, Moreau, North, and Sanchez.[45] Although Maurice Bishop was still only under house arrest, Motley was concerned for the safety of the Americans on the island.[46] Accordingly, he now argued that "serious thought" should be given to a "noncombatant evacuation operation" (NEO).[47] Perhaps surprisingly, Vice Admiral Moreau, the JCS representative, was reluctant even to begin contingency planning. Memories of Vietnam still loomed large among the uniformed services. Moreover, the JCS office was not convinced that all nonmilitary options had been explored, and was displeased with the quality of intelligence thus far received.[48] As a consequence, it "preferred to await specific high-level authorization before considering a military operation."[49] In the event that military action were taken, the RIG members assumed that there would be an Entebbe-style operation with highly trained troops which would be dispatched on a specific rescue mission and then rapidly recalled.[50]

After the interagency meeting, and presumably after meeting with Lieutenant Colonel North, Robert McFarlane briefed Reagan.[51] McFarlane's appointment as National Security Adviser had been announced by the President that same day at 3:30 P.M.[52] Now, McFarlane apparently convinced Reagan of the gravity of the situation on Grenada since the President promptly ordered that planning for an "NEO" proceed.[53]

Tuesday, October 18

On Tuesday morning, Robert McFarlane presided over his first senior staff meeting as National Security Adviser; it was only one day before the murder of Bishop and his colleagues. When his turn came to speak, Constantine Menges claims he told McFarlane that the situation in Grenada "required the protection of U.S. citizens and offered the opportunity to restore democracy." Menges supposedly then related how he had written the outline of a political-military plan to accomplish this and had discussed it informally with a Defense Department colleague, probably Undersecretary for Policy Fred C. Ikle. Menges added that he planned today to discuss his scheme with William J. Middendorf, Jr., the U.S. Ambassador to the OAS, and also with the State Department.

McFarlane looked at Menges "with a quizzical expression." The new NSC chief then told his subordinate, "Well, that's okay," and called on the next staff person.[54] Menges apparently had not been apprised of Monday's RIG meeting or of McFarlane's subsequent briefing of the President.[55] The cold warrior, it now seems clear, had been perceived as a "loose cannon" and had therefore been deliberately cut out of the decisionmaking loop.[56]

At Foggy Bottom on October 18, Secretary of State Shultz took two critical steps. First, after a meeting that day with Assistant Secretary Motley, he decided to authorize the establishment of a special "Grenada Task Force" within the State Department. "This put into place a round-the-clock watch," Shultz would later write. "With Tony as our leader, [it] got us all mentally and administratively ready as the problem became more grave."[57] Second, Secretary Shultz made certain Tuesday to contact the Prime Minister of Dominica, Eugenia Charles. On Monday, Deputy Assistant Secretary of State Charles Gillespie had received a request from Mrs. Charles of U.S. military assistance to address the Grenada situation. Now, Shultz sought a "formal evaluation" by the Organization of Eastern Caribbean States. George Shultz's October 18 communication to Prime Minister Charles would serve several functions, he subsequently argued: it "attended to her request," demonstrated "that we were responsive and alert," and "set the stage for the United States to act in a manner consistent with our interests and with international law."[58] A formal OECS request for United States support, Shultz implied here, constituted a lawful basis for U.S. intervention.

Meanwhile on Tuesday, the aircraft carrier *Independence* left Hampton Roads, Virginia, and the 22nd Marine Amphibious Unit

(MAU) shipped out of Morehead City, North Carolina. Both were bound for the eastern Mediterranean, where the 22nd was scheduled to participate in an amphibious exercise in Spain before relieving the 24th MAU in Lebanon.[59] The Marines of the 22nd recognized that they would soon be assuming a hazardous assignment in an area torn by factional strife. What they could not then know was that within a week they would be facing Grenadian and Cuban gun barrels.

Coincidentally, the role of the Marines in Lebanon had been discussed in a top-level National Security Planning Group (NSPG) meeting that same Tuesday.[60] Among those in attendance then were President Reagan, Secretary of State Shultz, Secretary of Defense Weinberger, and the President's new National Security Adviser, Robert McFarlane. Here, Weinberger attempted unsuccessfully to convince the President to order a Marine redeployment to ships off Lebanon's coast. The Syrians and the various anti-Gemayel militias now viewed the American forces as combatants, Weinberger told Reagan. Hence, the Marines were "sitting on a bull's-eye"[61] and all the Joint Chiefs of Staff favored their removal from Beirut. Secretary Shultz, a former Marine, countered that it would be a mistake to extract forces at the very time that U.S. policy success seemed imminent. Reagan then solicited the advice of Robert McFarlane, who had recently served as special envoy in the Middle East. Like Shultz a former Marine, McFarlane supported the Secretary of State's case for a continued American presence. When Weinberger recognized how little support existed for his withdrawal proposal, the Defense Secretary did not call for a formal vote.[62] He would later bitterly regret not having been "more persuasive with the President."[63]

"Bloody Wednesday"

As we have already seen, October 19 marked the end of Maurice Bishop's life and of the People's Revolutionary Government of Grenada. It likewise marked the beginning of "serious planning" by the U.S. government for the possibility that a "nonpermissive evacuation" would prove necessary.[64] Such an action, Reagan administration officials recognized, "would require the use of military assets and the securing of military targets."[65] Put more simply, a "nonpermissive evacuation" meant an American "invasion" of Grenada.

On Barbados

Wednesday, October 19, proved to be an extremely busy day on Barbados. That morning, only hours before Bishop's murder, the Barbadian cabinet met in an emergency session "to consider what steps should be taken to deal with the obviously deteriorating situation" on Grenada. Here, the cabinet authorized Adams to arrange a collaborative mission.[66] Shortly thereafter, Adams spoke with Giles Bullard, the British High Commissioner on Barbados, about the possibility of British participation in a military action. Bullard gave no indication that Britain would assist in such an undertaking, however.

Around 1:00 P.M., Ambassador Bish and Kim Flower met with Tom Adams.[67] In the two days since he had spoken in person with the Americans, the hawkish Prime Minister had grown increasingly concerned about the Grenadian situation. "Would the United States consider invading Grenada?" he now asked hypothetically. "If not," Adams contended, "we will do so without you." Adams explained that he had already spoken with the entire eastern Caribbean leadership who had appeared ready to act alone if necessary, and with Giles Bullard, who had expressed his great skepticism. Later today, Adams told Bish and Flower, he would speak with Canadian High Commissioner Noble Power, from whom he expected a similarly unenthusiastic response. The Barbadian leader stressed that his request of U.S. military assistance must be kept confidential. Should it become public and should no action be taken, he and his state would be in an extremely vulnerable situation.[68] Bish and Flower remained noncommittal, but assured Adams that his message would be transmitted. After their meeting, therefore, Bish and Flower promptly sent a cable to Washington summarizing this very important development.[69] Bish would later recall also sending a message then through a "back channel" to the CIA in Washington.[70] Unknown to Ambassador Bish at the time of his cable was that while he had been speaking with Prime Minister Adams early on Wednesday afternoon, Bishop and seven others were being murdered in Fort Rupert.

Late Wednesday afternoon, October 19, Deputy Assistant Secretary of State Charles A. "Tony" Gillespie arrived in Bridgetown. Quite by chance, Gillespie had been on a familiarization tour of the Caribbean with Vice President Bush.[71] Motley had suggested some time earlier that Gillespie be dispatched to Bridgetown to assist the Ambassador and his DCM.[72] Shortly before Gillespie's arrival there, on October 17, the Deputy Assistant Secretary had spoken with Eugenia Charles. Like Tom

Adams, the Dominican Prime Minister had expressed then her interest in a collaborative military operation.[73] Gillespie had also spoken before Wednesday with John Compton, Prime Minister of St. Lucia. Compton had also urged that action be taken to protect St. Lucia and Dominica, and had invited Gillespie to attend an OECS meeting to be convened Friday on Barbados.[74]

Several hours after Tony Gillespie's arrival on Barbados, Ambassador Bish hosted a formal dinner party.[75] Among those attending was Barbadian Deputy Prime Minister Bernard "Bree" St. John. Toward the end of the meal, around 8:00 P.M., American Defense Attache Lawrence Reiman called. "Maurice Bishop has been murdered," the Lieutenant Colonel reported. Immediately, Bish called Prime Minister Adams, who confirmed the news.[76] Shortly thereafter, Bish and Flower drafted their second cable of the day and sent it to Washington.[77] The "red-coded" message warned:

> There appears to be imminent danger to U.S. citizens resident on Grenada due to the current deteriorating situation, which includes reports of rioting, personnel casualties (possibly deaths), automatic weapons being discharged, Soviet-built armored personnel carriers in the Grenadian streets and some loss of water and electricity on the island ... AmEmbassy Bridgetown recommends that the United States should now be prepared to conduct an emergency evacuation of U.S. citizens residing in Grenada.[78]

By the time of this second cable, American diplomats on Barbados were aware of two additional causes for American concern. First, the U.S. Embassy had received that day a response from Grenada to its inquiry the previous day about the status of American citizens on the island. "The interests of U.S. citizens" were, it had said, "in no way threatened by the present situation in Grenada which the Ministry [of External Affairs] hastens to point out is a purely internal matter."[79] Assistant Secretary Motley would later call Grenada's October 19 response "a bland assertion and a blunt slamming of the door ... containing no assurances, no concrete measures to safeguard foreign residents."[80] Second, the American Embassy had attempted midmorning Wednesday to send Foreign Service Officers Kenneth Kurze and Linda Flohr to Grenada "to make an on-the-ground assessment." Their regularly-scheduled Leeward Islands Air Transport (LIAT) plane had been refused permission to land at Pearls airport, however, in what Kurze would later term an "escalation of the first order."[81]

Perhaps reflective of his personal concern for the safety of the Americans on Grenada, at some point on Wednesday Milan Bish had also contacted Dr. Charles Modica in New York by telephone. In this brief conversation, the American Ambassador had sought to convince the Chancellor of St. George's Medical School to fly to Barbados and publicly to request U.S. intervention. Ambassador Bish's effort proved unsuccessful, however.[82]

In Washington

On Wednesday afternoon in Washington, the RIG was once again convened by Tony Motley.[83] Although Constantine Menges would later complain that "the Latin American bureau had 'forgotten' to tell [him] or anyone from the NSC" about the meeting,[84] Oliver North was presumably in attendance. The meeting may have been called after the CIA's receipt of Bish's "back channel" message reporting Adams' request for military assistance, or perhaps after word of Bishop's assassination had been received.[85] Hence, it is uncertain whether the Restricted Interagency Group knew during the course of its October 19 meeting what brutality had just transpired on Grenada.

For at least three reasons, accurate intelligence would remain sparse: the curfew imposed by the RMC on Grenada; the absence of a U.S. diplomatic presence there; and Britain's loss of contact with its diplomatic mission.[86] Given such uncertain circumstances, Motley and his RIG colleagues had cause for genuine concern about the welfare of the Americans. They must also have recognized that the unstable conditions on Grenada presented attractive opportunities: to remove a Marxist regime disliked both by Grenada's neighbors and Washington; and to expel Cuban and Soviet influence. Although earlier Admiral Moreau had not wanted even to consider contingency planning, he agreed at least to discuss contingency plans for a limited military action.[87] In addition, he provided a preliminary list of military resources that would be available if a rescue operation were to be undertaken.[88]

Late that evening, Motley briefed Secretary Shultz for about an hour.[89] Whether Motley had as yet received word of Bish's second cable is not clear. Nevertheless, the Assistant Secretary informed his boss that most members of the afternoon's interagency group had favored extending contingency planning to cover a military action. Although the generally hawkish Shultz "had to be convinced," he eventually agreed with Motley that such planning was necessary. Since the Pentagon had thus far been reluctant to undertake possibly unnecessary work, the Secretary would convince President Reagan to head off their qualms.[90] It may also have been decided now, but certainly sometime during the latter part of this week, that the European Bureau of the State Department would be excluded from Grenada deliberations.[91] Fears that the military option might be opposed or its security compromised appear to have driven this decision.

Cabinet-level Involvement

Thursday, October 20, was the first day that the possibility of an American invasion of Grenada was considered at a cabinet-level meeting. October 20 was also officially the "last day of unilateral planning," although as we have seen, American discussions with Caribbean leaders had been taking place "informally" since the previous weekend.[92] Now, Washington was seriously considering some American action — at least, an evacuation of U.S. citizens, but perhaps even a more ambitious undertaking. As Motley would tell the House Armed Services Committee in 1984, from October 20 on, the administration's "primary task regarding the safety of the U.S. citizens was to determine whether the situation on the ground was likely to improve by itself. Without clear indications of a return to civil stability, an evacuation would be prudent."[93] He would be more succinct in a 1988 interview: by October 20, "this thing was getting big."[94]

At 9:00 A.M. Thursday,[95] Vice Admiral John Poindexter convened the "Crisis Preplanning Group" (CPPG),[96] a working group designed to handle developing crises.[97] In attendance with the Deputy National Security Adviser were North and Menges of the NSC; Motley and Johnstone of the State Department; Sanchez and Ikle of Defense; Clarridge of the CIA; and OAS Ambassador Middendorf.[98] This select group of second echelon officials gathered in Room 208 of the Old Executive Office Building (EOB), the new "crisis management center," which included the most advanced computer, audiovisual and secure communications systems.[99]

The meeting opened with a briefing on the latest developments on Grenada, including news that the *Heroic Vietnam*, a Cuban weapon transport ship, was moored in St. George's harbor.[100] Next, the CPPG considered the military and logistical requirements for landing troops to rescue and to evacuate American citizens.[101] By this point, both State and Defense representatives were in agreement that planning a military operation was necessary.[102] As accurately as the CPPG could determine, the total armed strength available to Austin's Revolutionary Military Council was approximately four thousand Grenadians, and around six hundred armed Cubans. In addition, if he chose to do so, Fidel Castro could within days airlift to Grenada perhaps ten thousand Cuban troops.[103]

Secrecy, it was agreed, would be essential for any U.S. military operation lest Austin divine Washington's intentions and preemptively seize American students. For obvious reasons, no one wanted a Caribbean version of the Iran hostage crisis. The group spent some time considering the feasibility of a simple "quick in and out rescue." The CPPG appears also to have considered now the merits of a more ambitious military operation.[104] At length, Admiral Poindexter closed the meeting, announcing that there would be another that evening to discuss this issue further.[105]

Shortly thereafter, around 10:00 A.M., a secret conference was held in Undersecretary Ikle's office at the Pentagon. Here, the logistical requirements for a military operation were discussed in greater detail.[106]

Cabinet-level deliberations

At around 4:45 P.M. Thursday, October 20,[107] the first of several cabinet-level meetings to consider Grenada was convened by Vice President Bush, who had just returned from his brief tour of the Caribbean. Participants in the early evening meeting of the "Special Situations Group" (SSG)[108] included: McFarlane, North, and Menges of the NSC; Weinberger, Vessey, and Ikle of the Defense Department; Acting CIA Director John N. McMahon; Undersecretary for Political Affairs Lawrence S. Eagleburger of State; Middendorf; and White House Counselor Edwin Meese. Shultz and Motley would also attend, arriving halfway through deliberations.[109] The one-hour meeting was held in the Situation Room, located in the sub-basement of the west wing of the

White House beneath the Oval Office.[110] In the dark-paneled, window-less room, Bush took his place in the President's chair, with McFarlane seated at the opposite end of the conference table. Around the table sat the other cabinet members.[111]

The meeting of the SSG, the Reagan administration's highest-level crisis management unit, began with a factual update. Intelligence information suggested that those now in charge on Grenada were ruthless and might possibly try to hold American hostages.[112] Apparently, one important source of intelligence then was Sir Paul Scoon, the Governor-General of Grenada. A Senate source would relate after the invasion: "The Governor-General was feeding information to us through the U.K. [United Kingdom] on the nature of the guys who were taking over. Basically, his assessments were driving some of our considerations."[113] Given the pessimistic intelligence appraisal of General Austin and his RMC colleagues, Lawrence Eagleburger specifically raised the specter of the Teheran hostages. The Undersecretary of State argued that if the United States did nothing to rescue its citizens, the administration would lose face — this at the very time when toughness against the left-wing challenge in Nicaragua and El Salvador was essential.[114]

In time, the discussion turned to the availability of American forces for action and the time required to ready them. "The objective, right from the beginning," Menges would later recall, "was to plan a rescue that would guarantee quick success, but with a minimum of casualties on either side."[115] Accordingly, some meeting participants were stunned to discover that the military had as yet no contingency plan for invading Grenada and that the most recent aerial photos of the island had been taken five months ago.[116] General Vessey reportedly observed now that a surgical strike simply to remove the Americans would be extremely difficult without securing the entire island of Grenada.[117] With Secretary Weinberger's support, Vessey likewise sought improved intelligence and more time in which to plan a full-scale invasion.[118]

About 5:15 P.M., Secretary Shultz and Assistant Secretary Motley arrived.[119] The two had been on Capitol Hill most of the afternoon briefing a closed-door session of the Senate Foreign Relations Committee; ironically, the topic of their briefing had been the secret contents of the Kennedy-Khrushchev accords on Cuba.[120] State had already made clear to Reagan administration decisionmakers that the Caribbean leaders were deeply frightened by the bloodshed on Grenada and wanted action taken.[121]   Now, the requests by Prime Ministers Charles, Compton, and Adams for American military help must surely have been discussed.[122]   Some of the Caribbean's democratic leadership, it was also noted, would hold a summit meeting tomorrow on Barbados[123] to decide whether to issue a formal request for collective action under the terms of the OECS treaty.[124]

After a few more minutes of discussion, around 5:45 P.M., Vice President Bush called the meeting to a close.   In its course, at least six important decisions had been made.   First, the group determined that steps must be taken to improve intelligence, especially that of the military.   Up-to-date aerial reconnaissance of Grenada was necessary. Perhaps even more importantly, the CIA needed better human intelligence (HUMINT): it had to place an agent on the island.[125]   Second, the JCS office was formally directed to prepare a detailed operational plan for evacuation.[126]   Shultz had argued that it was necessary for Reagan to have the military option in his hand.[127]   Third, the group recommended that the President order navy vessels *en route* to Lebanon, and other naval units, to steam toward Grenada.[128]   With a sizeable American force off the Grenadian coast, Reagan would have at least the possibility of authorizing the use of force.   Despite the disagreement of McFarlane, the JCS had refused to redirect the flotilla without a formal presidential order.[129]   Fourth, it was decided that measures would be taken to insure the absolute secrecy of the operation.   Among other precautions, all government leaders would attempt to maintain their announced schedules.   It was probably also decided now that "measures of deception to mislead Grenadian leaders and Cubans about the military operation" should be authorized.[130]   Fifth, a draft "National Security Decision Directive" was ordered to be prepared.   Reagan's signature of an (NSDD) would be necessary before American forces could be committed to combat.[131]   Finally, although some advisers had suggested that immediate and direct military action should be taken, the group decided to limit American action temporarily to await the outcome of conversations with other Caribbean states.[132]   At this point, the administration lacked plausible legal grounds for a full-scale invasion.   The fear for American lives and the absence of a legitimate government were simply not enough: the group seems to have been reluctant "to say that the administration had just decided to violate international law."[133] Hence, a decision on a military operation would be delayed until at least Saturday.[134]

After Thursday evening's SSG meeting, McFarlane, Poindexter, North and Menges conferred briefly. Here, they outlined an NSDD that "would constitute the president's written prepare-for-action order." Shortly thereafter, Menges returned to his office and composed it, showing his draft to North for comments.[135] Then, Menges wrote a memorandum from McFarlane to the President, summarizing the facts, the discussion, and the consensus of opinion at the Thursday evening meeting.[136]

Sometime later that Thursday evening, Robert McFarlane carried the NSDD to Reagan. The President himself had spent the day engaged in various rather mundane activities: he had met with the Cabinet Council on Commerce and Trade, had presented Richard Helms with the National Security Medal, and had attended a reception for the U.S. Olympic Ski team.[137] Now, turning to weightier matters, he authorized the diversion of the flotilla and also ordered operational planning to proceed.[138] He later remembered:

> I asked McFarlane how long the Pentagon thought it would need to prepare a rescue mission on Grenada. He said the Joint Chiefs of Staff believed it could be done in forty-eight hours. I said, "Do it."[139]

The President did not yet sign an NSDD authorizing invasion *per se*, however.[140]

Toward midnight on Thursday, October 20, as his Marine amphibious task force was passing north of Bermuda, Navy Captain Carl R. Erie received orders to turn south and to take station approximately 500 miles northeast of Grenada. Although the message had given no reason at the time, a modified track pattern was adopted to keep the task force within easy sailing of Grenada until October 25. In the event that no further word arrived by midnight of October 23, the force would resume its transit to the Mediterranean.[141]

October 20 in the Caribbean

While important decisions were being made on Thursday in Washington, others were being made in the Caribbean. Sometime that day, John Compton, the Prime Minister of St. Lucia, telephoned Prime Minister Adams.[142] Compton, with whom Adams almost certainly had spoken the previous weekend, had decided that the Caribbean states could not allow the current situation on Grenada to continue: it was simply too dangerous for them.[143] The RMC on Grenada, he feared, would attempt to push the entire Caribbean community into the communist camp. Compton therefore believed that the Caribbean nations must take the "initiative to intervene in Grenada ... to restore law and order and to lead the country to an early election."[144] To this end, he called upon Barbados to help establish a multinational force. Tom Adams, pleased but not surprised by Compton's sentiments, immediately expressed his agreement.

Within a few hours, the Barbados government authorized the Prime Minister to commit Barbados to intervention. That night, the Barbadian Premier appeared on the ABC News "Nightline" program. Here, Adams told Ted Koppel that most West Indians hoped that the United States would intervene militarily in Grenada. Adams' words on American network television seem to have been designed deliberately "to signal the seriousness of the [Grenada] situation" and "to help smooth the way for U.S. action."[145]

Friday, October 21

At Friday morning's NSC staff meeting, Bud McFarlane was given a full report on the latest information regarding Grenada. Here, Menges noted that the State Department had been preparing a detailed plan related to the political aspects of an American military action. In a few hours, he explained, the plan for a rescue of Americans and the establishment of an interim government on Grenada would be reviewed at a Restricted Interagency Group meeting. "Fine," said McFarlane to his staffer, "but we also need to have a CPPG meeting in room 208 late this afternoon to prepare for Saturday morning's NSC meeting."[146]

From noon until 2:00 P.M. Friday, Assistant Secretary Motley led yet another RIG meeting at the State Department.[147] Among the matters apparently now discussed was the question of how to deal with those governments friendly to the United States.[148] Specifically, it had to be decided who would be informed about an American operation should there be one, and when those informed would be so. In addition, the post-invasion role played by Governor-General Scoon was considered here.[149] As the Grenadian Head of State, and arguably the sole authority on the island,[150] Sir Paul could play an important part in the establishment of an interim government.

Of greater significance for our purposes, the question of the domestic and international legal aspects of a forceful evacuation was probably also taken up at this RIG meeting. It is clear that at some point on Friday,

Deputy Assistant Secretary James Michel suggested that Reagan administration lawyers be brought into the Grenada decisionmaking process.[151] Tony Motley agreed with Michel, who had formerly been the State Department's Deputy Legal Adviser. Over the past several days, Motley had become convinced by Vessey and Moreau that a "surgical strike" operation would be insufficient. The American students on Grenada were dispersed in three different locations; Sir Paul Scoon, whose rescue might likewise be necessary, was located in a fourth. Thus, the seizure of the entire island would probably be necessary.[152] If the American military were to seize Grenada, the Assistant Secretary recognized that a plausible legal rationale would simplify matters later for the United States. He would later recall with deliberate hyperbole, "I didn't want nine thousand years of [post-invasion] Security Council debate."[153]   Accordingly, Motley directed his principal deputy to convene a group of government legal experts to consider the various legal implications of an American invasion of Grenada.[154] They would consider not only questions related to international law, but also those related to the War Powers Resolution.[155]

Motley also met Friday with Secretary Shultz.[156] The two discussed now the evolving situation on Grenada and the mood of the eastern Caribbean leadership. Adams, Charles and their colleagues were "out in front," Motley noted, "and we want to keep it that way." Meanwhile, the largest state proximate to Grenada, Venezuela, seemed unlikely to participate in any military action. Hence, "it would be a Caribbean effort if anything went forward," and that prospect appeared progressively more likely. Recalled Shultz: "Tony and I were both increasingly convinced we had run out of ways to accomplish a peaceful evacuation of the American students and that the situation on the ground was deteriorating into total anarchy." Both men feared conditions were "ripe for hostage-taking." Motley told Shultz, "I want to make sure you are on board." Replied the Secretary of State, "If we can bring this student rescue off, it would be a damn good thing."[157]

At 5:00 P.M. on Friday, Admiral Poindexter chaired another meeting of the Crisis Pre-planning Group in the EOB's "crisis management center."[158]   By now, State had revised its preliminary action plan, based upon those suggestions offered at the noon RIG meeting, and copies had been distributed. Although the United States had not yet been formally invited to do so by any plausibly competent authority, it now seemed fairly certain that the Reagan administration would take some sort of action. The individual requests of Charles, Compton, and Adams for American military assistance rested upon dubious legal footing at best. If the United States were to undertake any action beyond a simple evacuation of its citizens — a full-scale invasion of Grenada, for example — it would need an invitation of greater legal plausibility.

Of Friday's CPPG meeting Menges would later note, "the tone of our discussions had shifted from whether we would act to how this could be accomplished with minimum casualties while insuring speed to avoid Cuban or Soviet counteraction."[159] It reportedly remained an open question, however, whether the military should conduct an "NEO" or completely seize the island. Accordingly, the Joint Chiefs of Staff office was instructed to plan for both.[160]

For four and a half hours that Friday evening, North and Menges wrote background and decision memoranda for Saturday morning's planned meeting of the National Security Council. Early that evening, Deputy National Security Adviser Poindexter reviewed their first draft, making a few minor revisions. Then, the Grenada memoranda were transmitted to Augusta, Georgia.[161]

Late on Friday evening, Reagan, Shultz, McFarlane, Donald Regan, former New Jersey Senator Nicholas F. Brady and their wives had flown to the Augusta National Golf Club. The President was to be one of the guests there in the annual four-man "George Shultz Invitational Golf Tournament."[162] Before his departure, he had recorded that afternoon a radio address on "Arms Control and Reduction" for Saturday afternoon broadcast.[163] Reagan had also briefly considered whether to remain in Washington for the weekend. Ultimately, recalls Shultz, "he and the rest of us felt that the sudden cancellation of a long-planned trip would bring on intense and undesirable speculation."[164]

October 21 on Barbados

Although the meetings held in Washington on Friday played an important role in the American decision to invade Grenada, meetings convened on Barbados that same day were even more significant. Here, the leaders of the Organization of Eastern Caribbean States decided formally to request the help of the United States.[165]

Shortly after lunch, amid the strictest security measures ever seen in Barbados, representatives from six of the seven OECS states convened at Dover Convention Centre, a few miles south of Bridgetown.[166] Joining them in the meeting chaired by Prime Minister Eugenia Charles was Edward Seaga, the Prime Minister of Jamaica. Also present at the facility were the Americans Tony Gillespie and Milan Bish.[167] Halfway through the discussion, at nightfall, Prime Minister Adams arrived at the Conference Centre by the back door and joined the meeting.[168]

At first, the Defence and Security Committee of the OECS met to discuss the Grenada situation. Then, the Authority, the supreme organ of the OECS, was convened. During the course of the day's conversations, it became clear that the OECS states "were greatly shocked by what had happened in Grenada over the previous few days. They felt that such brutal behavior was as unprecedented in the Commonwealth Caribbean as it was unacceptable."[169] At length, the members "unanimously" agreed to invoke Article 8 of the OECS Treaty and to seek the assistance of friendly states to "stabilise the situation and establish a peacekeeping force."[170] The decision, Vaughan Lewis would later suggest, "was very, very difficult." The Caribbean leaders did not want to appear as "American lackeys," the OECS director general emphasized. "It was a decision in the last resort that was the only alternative."[171]

After the OECS vote was cast, Adams was requested to attend the organization's meeting. There, the Premier was issued an official invitation for Barbadian participation.[172] Late that evening, the meeting was finally adjourned. Then, a package of political and economic sanctions against Grenada was promptly made public, possibly to cloak the military intentions of the OECS.[173] These sanctions included the cutting off of further supplies of banknotes from the Eastern Caribbean Currency Authority and the suspension of all sea and air contacts between Grenada and the OECS countries.[174]

There is some doubt about the precise degree to which the prominent Americans present at the Dover Convention Centre influenced the OECS deliberations.[175] Although Gillespie and Bish may or may not have actively participated in the official OECS meetings *per se*, it seems clear they communicated the American predisposition to assist the OECS.[176] Indeed, Ambassador Bish may even have directly affected the outcome of the OECS vote. Lester Bird, Deputy Prime Minister and Foreign Minister of Antigua and Barbuda, had apparently questioned the prudence of military action and had abstained in the OECS vote. When Bish discovered this, he contacted by telephone Vere Bird, Antiguan Prime Minister and Lester's father, who withdrew Antigua's abstention.[177]

Constantine Menges recalls the sentiments in Washington that Friday afternoon:

> Since no final decision had yet been made by President Reagan, it was not possible to give them a guarantee that if they asked for American help, the United States would say yes. The answer could well be no, and then where would they be?
>
> However, ... Milan Bish could tell the Caribbean leaders that the probability of U.S. military action would be much higher if they requested military action collectively. Still, for them such a step would be risky. I really did not know what they would do. Two thousand miles away, in Washington, we wondered, "Will they or won't they?"[178]

Some time during or after the OECS meeting, the United States learned that "they would." According to one account, Eugenia Charles informed Gillespie of the OECS decision immediately afterward in an anteroom.[179] Whether or not this report is accurate, American diplomats were certainly briefed in full at a late night meeting at Adams' residence. There, in the Prime Minister's living room, Adams, Charles, and Seaga met with Gillespie, Bish and Flower.[180] Among those also in attendance were Adams' wife Genevieve, Jamaican Foreign Secretary Neville Gallimore, and Adams' Permanent Secretary. During the disjointed, generalized discussions, a number of questions were raised. In tomorrow's CARICOM meeting, how might Forbes Burnham, President of Guyana, and the Trinidadians react to the Grenada situation? What sanctions might CARICOM impose? What specific steps might the Caribbean Development Bank (CDB) and the Leeward Islands Air Transport take?[181]

After this late night Friday meeting, probably between midnight and 1:00 A.M. Saturday, Kim Flower drafted a cable which reported the OECS invitation. The cable was signed by Ambassador Bish and cleared by Tony Gillespie.[182] After the cable's receipt in Washington, Gillespie was reportedly instructed to inform the Caribbean leaders that the United States needed a request for intervention in writing.[183]

Back in the United States

After midnight on Saturday, October 22, the Bridgetown cable was received in Washington by Assistant Secretary Motley, who contacted John Poindexter around 1:00 A.M.[184] Poindexter in turn telephoned

Robert McFarlane in Georgia, briefing the National Security Adviser on the critical new Caribbean developments.[185]   Shortly thereafter, Vice President Bush and Secretary of Defense Weinberger were called from their beds to the White House.[186]   General Vessey, James Baker, Ed Meese, and John McMahon were likewise summoned.[187]   An exceptionally lengthy and demanding day for the Reagan administration had thus begun.

From a guest house at Augusta National Golf Club, Bud McFarlane called George Shultz at 2:45 A.M.[188]   He then strode to the adjacent six-bedroom Eisenhower cottage where Secretary Shultz and the Reagans were staying.[189]   When McFarlane arrived, he and Shultz reviewed the Bridgetown cable's contents and briefly considered its policy implications.   "The OECS states, and particularly Barbados, were prepared to call publicly for U.S. intervention in Grenada," the cable related.[190] It reportedly also expressed concern that leaks about the OECS request would tip off Grenadian and Cuban authorities, possibly leading to seizure of American hostages or other preemptive action. Hence, speed was essential and Sunday would be the best day for an operation, if practicable.[191]

Such concern over leaks was well-founded. By Friday, October 21, "news of U.S. planning had achieved wide currency in Caribbean capitals, giving Grenada's military leaders and a Cuban garrison crucial advance time to resupply their troops and fortify defenses." Opponents of intervention had been "leaking details of the proposed invasion from private council chambers to the news media and to supporters of Grenada's leftist government."[192]   Moreover, on Friday evening Eugenia Charles had acknowledged to reporters, perhaps imprudently, "that the question of a military solution" had been considered at Friday's OECS meeting.[193]

At 3:30 A.M., Vice President Bush met with Secretary Weinberger and other key national security advisers in the White House Situation Room.[194]   Joining them from Augusta through a secure conference call were Shultz and McFarlane.[195]   Secretary Shultz confirmed that the OECS states had brought Barbados and Jamaica into their counsels to request aid.[196]   Moreover, consistent with his generally hawkish inclinations and the advice transmitted from Barbados, Shultz apparently urged that an American invasion be launched on Sunday.   Secretary Weinberger, by contrast, was reluctant to act prematurely and therefore opposed a rushed operation in Grenada.[197]   The earliest reasonable time for such an action, he argued, would be Wednesday or perhaps Tuesday.[198]   Vice President Bush, meanwhile, feared the negative impression that an all-English-speaking operation might convey, and suggested that the United States solicit Venezuelan participation.[199] Despite some disagreement, the group determined ultimately that the United States should assist the OECS and that plans for a military action should be completed as quickly as possible. Then, mindful of past criticism that Reagan had sometimes been allowed to sleep while important discussions were being conducted, they decided to awaken the President and to inform him of their proceedings.[200]

Around 5:00 A.M., therefore, Robert McFarlane telephoned Ronald Reagan.[201] "He said it was urgent that I meet with him and George Shultz immediately in the living room of the Eisenhower Cottage," Reagan later recalled.[202] Still clad in his robe and pajamas, the President was told by Shultz and McFarlane that last evening the OECS had formally invited the United States to invade Grenada. Next, he was briefed on the various opinions that had been expressed by his advisers at their just-completed teleconference: while Weinberger had emphasized his reluctance to take military action, especially quick action, the others had favored the use of American force.

Just before 6:00 A.M., the secure phone line to the White House was reopened.[203] Weinberger now reiterated his position to the President but failed to alter Reagan's initial reaction that prompt military intervention in Grenada was politically desirable.[204] The President "was very unequivocal," McFarlane would later remember. "He couldn't wait."[205] Accordingly, before returning to his bed, Reagan ordered invasion plans to proceed, deciding that in the morning he would play golf as scheduled to avoid arousing suspicion.[206] "Under [the] circumstances, there was only one answer I could give to McFarlane and Shultz and those six countries who [had] asked for our help," Reagan would note in his memoir.[207] By early Saturday morning, October 22, the stage was set for "Urgent Fury."

Notes

1.   Author's interview with Langhorne Motley, September 20, 1988.
2.   Author's interview with Lawrence Eagleburger, March 15, 1993.

3.   According to Kenneth Kurze, Foreign Service Officer at the U.S. Embassy in Bridgetown, "rumors that the radicals led by Coard were discontent and planning something (at the very least, pressure on Bishop to conform) had been circulating for weeks." Kenneth A. Kurze's letter to the author, September 29, 1991.

4.   Among those officials was Constantine C. Menges, the National Security Assistant for Latin American Affairs.   Upon his receipt of this important news, Menges promptly asked all the U.S. foreign policy agencies for their latest facts on Grenada.   In addition, he sought information on related Soviet and Cuban activities.   Author's interview with Constantine Menges, September 21, 1988.

5.   Kenneth A. Kurze's letter to the author, September 29, 1991. According to John Lehman, the Reagan administration "right up to the invasion itself ... had to depend on intelligence, such as it was, shared from other nations; newspaper accounts; and most valuable of all, reports from returning tourists." John F. Lehman, Jr., *Command of the Seas* (New York: Charles Scribner's Sons, 1988), p. 300.

6.   George P. Shultz, *Turmoil and Triumph: My Years as Secretary of State* (New York, NY: Charles Scribner's Sons, 1993), p. 327.

7.   Lehman, *Command of the Seas*, p. 294. Prime Minister John Compton of St. Lucia told U.S. Ambassador Milan Bish that the CIA had a source within the Central Committee of the People's Revolutionary Government of Grenada. Author's interviews with Milan Bish, September 26, 1988; October 26, 1988. Selwyn Strachan, the PRG's Minister of Mobilisation, was accused of being a CIA agent.   Tim Hector, *The Outlet*, October 28, 1983. Cited by Payne et al., *Revolution and Invasion*, p. 129.

8.   Motley, "The Decision to Assist Grenada," p. 70.

9.   Michel was the Principal Deputy Assistant Secretary.   Gillespie became involved in intelligence-related matters.   Author's interview with Langhorne Motley, November 4, 1988.

10.   See Roy Gutman, *Banana Diplomacy: The Making of American Foreign Policy in Nicaragua, 1981-1987* (New York, NY: Simon and Schuster, 1988), pp. 194-198; Bob Woodward, *Veil: The Secret Wars of the CIA* (New York: Simon & Schuster, 1987); and Ben Bradlee, Jr., *Guts and Glory: The Rise and Fall of Oliver North* (New York, NY: Donald I. Fine, Inc., 1988), p. 169.

11.   For a discussion of the RIG, see Gutman, *Banana Diplomacy*, p. 138; and Keith Schneider, "North's Record: A Wide Role in a Host of Sensitive Projects," *New York Times*, January 3, 1987, pp. A1, A4.

12.   Cited by Gutman, *Banana Diplomacy*, p. 138.

13.   Cited by Gutman, *Banana Diplomacy*, p. 138.

14.   Author's interview with Langhorne Motley, November 4, 1988.

15. Author's interview with Langhorne Motley, November 4, 1988.

16. Menges, *Inside the NSC*, p. 55. The NSC senior staff included the Senior Directors of: Regional Affairs -- Europe and the Soviet Union, Asia, Africa, Latin America, and the Near East and South Asia; International Economic Affairs; Political-Military Affairs; Legislative and Legal Affairs; and Public Affairs.

17. The visit is noted in Schoenhals and Melanson, *Revolution and Intervention*, p. 72; and Davidson, *A Study in Politics*, p. 69.

18. Menges, who for the last two years had been National Intelligence Officer for Latin America at the CIA, had only joined the NSC this week. Menges, *Inside the NSC*, pp. 60-61.

19. According to his own account, Menges returned to the Old Executive Office Building immediately following the October 13 NSC staff meeting. There, the zealous anti-communist drafted a one-page plan "for the protection of our U.S. citizens and the restoration of democracy on Grenada." Supposedly, Menges' plan suggested action by "an international, legal, collective security force that would include democratic Caribbean countries." Menges, *Inside the NSC*, p. 61.

Such a proposal would have been extremely ambitious given the current circumstances: on the afternoon of October 13, Bishop was still alive; as yet, no state or individual had formally sought American intervention. Nevertheless, if his memoir is an accurate one, Menges intended to present the scheme to William Clark at next morning's staff meeting.

20. Menges, *Inside the NSC*, p. 61.

21. On the attempted "palace coup" that would have installed Baker as National Security Adviser and Deaver as White House Chief of Staff, see Hedrick Smith, *The Power Game: How Washington Works* (New York: Random House, 1988), pp. 320-324; Lou Cannon, *President Reagan: The Role of a Lifetime* (New York: Simon & Schuster, 1992), pp. 429-436; and Gerson, *The Kirkpatrick Mission*, pp. 218-220.

22. Reagan, *An American Life*, p. 448. See also Gerson, *The Kirkpatrick Mission*, p. 219.

23. Reagan, *An American Life*, p. 448.

24. Author's interview with Langhorne Motley, November 4, 1988.

25. Motley, "The Decision to Assist Grenada," p. 70.

26. Admiral Wesley L. McDonald, *Operation Urgent Fury: Lessons Learned* (Norfolk: Commander-in-Chief, The Atlantic Command, February 6, 1984), p. 1.

27. Also on Friday, Menges gave his preliminary plan for a Grenada invasion to Oliver North and Kenneth E. deGraffenried, the NSC's Senior Intelligence Director. Menges requested that both men kept his plan to themselves since it was still "only a personal idea." He asked North to think

about the military requirements of such an action, and deGraffenried to survey all available intelligence. Both NSC staff members reportedly expressed their strong skepticism that Reagan would take the dramatic action that Menges had in mind. Menges, *Inside the NSC*, p. 62. Indeed, there was as yet scarce political justification for such a bold American undertaking.

28. Author's interview with Milan Bish, October 20, 1988; author's interview with Kim Flower, July 6, 1989.

29. Author's interview with Kim Flower, July 6, 1989. On October 14, Barbadian Prime Minister Adams was informed of Bishop's arrest by a non-American but friendly diplomatic source, probably the British. Adams considered that the house arrest of a Prime Minister "was an act so extreme as to imply some measure of imminent violence and disorder." See "Address to the Barbadian People by Prime Minister Adams, October 26, 1983," reprinted in Gilmore, *The Grenada Intervention*, pp. 102-105.

30. Author's interviews with Milan Bish, October 20, 1988 and October 26, 1988; author's interview with Kim Flower, July 6, 1989. In a speech on October 26, Adams acknowledged: "an official of the Ministry of Defence and Security reported to me that he had been tentatively approached by a U.S. official about the prospect of rescuing Mr. Bishop from his captors and had been made an offer of transport." See "Address to the Barbadian People by Prime Minister Adams, October 26, 1983," reprinted in Gilmore, *The Grenada Intervention*, pp. 102-105.

See also John Burgess, "U.S. Reportedly Offered to Rescue Bishop Before His Execution," *Washington Post*, October 28, 1983, p. A10; and O'Shaughnessy, *Revolution, Invasion and Aftermath*, p. 153.

31. Burgess, "Rescue Bishop," p. A10.

32. The State Department denial is reported in Payne et al., *Revolution and Invasion*, p. 148. Ambassador Bish's actions on Saturday, October 15, 1983, were confirmed in an interview with him on October 26, 1988 and with Kim Flower on July 6, 1989.

Kenneth Kurze recalled that the U.S. Embassy had "had a visitor from Washington ... from State/INR [Bureau of Intelligence and Research] or CIA who in one of many 'what might U.S. do' sessions tossed [the rescue of Bishop] out as an idea." Kenneth A. Kurze's letter to the author, September 29, 1991.

33. Timothy Ashby, "The Reagan Years," in *The Caribbean After Grenada: Revolution, Conflict, and Democracy*, eds. Scott B. MacDonald, Harald M. Sandstrom, and Paul B. Goodwin, Jr. (New York, NY: Praeger, 1988), p. 278.

34. Burgess, "Rescue Bishop," p. A10.

35. Author's interview with Kim Flower, July 6, 1989.

36. Author's interview with Kim Flower, July 6, 1989.

37. Motley, "The Decision to Assist Grenada," p. 70.

38. Late on Friday afternoon, October 14, the President left the White House for a week-end stay at Camp David. On October 16, he returned to Washington. *Weekly Compilation of Presidential Documents* 19 (October 31, 1983): 1439, 1475.

39. *Department of State Bulletin* 83 (December 1983): 87.

40. Author's interview with Kim Flower, July 6, 1989.

41. Author's interview with Milan Bish, October 22, 1988. It is likely that Adams spoke with Prime Minister Seaga of Jamaica and Prime Minister John Compton of St. Lucia. See "Britain's Grenada Shut-out," *The Economist*, March 10, 1984, p. 31. He reportedly also spoke with Milton Cato, the Prime Minister of St. Vincent. According to Adams, Cato raised strong objections about the propriety of rescuing Bishop while ignoring "many other political prisoners in Grenada, put there by Bishop's government." Patrick E. Tyler, "The Making of an Invasion," *Washington Post*, October 30, 1983, p. A14.

Adams himself noted that on Saturday, October 15, "some of us discussed the [Grenada] situation. I concluded that, whatever our differences in the past, Mr. Bishop deserved the support of Caribbean governments in the circumstances and sought opinion on whether he could be got out of the hands of his enemies and the situation given an opportunity to stabilise." "Address to the Barbadian People," reprinted in Gilmore, *Analysis and Documentation*, p. 102.

42. Author's interview with Kim Flower, July 6, 1989.

43. Author's interviews with Milan Bish, September 26, 1988; October 20, 1988; October 26, 1988; author's interview with Kim Flower, July 6, 1989.

44. Author's interview with Langhorne Motley, November 4, 1988. See also Motley, "The Decision to Assist Grenada," p. 70; and Don Oberdorfer, "Reagan Sought to End Cuban 'Intervention,'" *Washington Post*, November 6, 1983, p. A21.

45. Bennett reports that middle-level representatives of the State Department, Central Intelligence Agency, the Joint Chiefs, the National Security Council, and the Secretary of Defense were in attendance. "Anatomy of a 'Go' Decision," p. 72. Menges was apparently not invited. See *Inside the NSC*, pp. 63-64.

46. Author's interview with Langhorne Motley, March 7, 1989.

47. Bennett, "Anatomy of a 'Go' Decision," p. 72; Leslie H. Gelb, "Shultz, With Tough Line, Is Now a Key Voice in Crisis," *The New York Times*, November 7, 1983, p. 15; Oberdorfer, "Reagan Sought," p. 21.

48. David K. Hall, "The Grenada Intervention," in *Selected Readings in Defense Economics and Decision Making* (Newport, Rhode Island: U.S. Naval War College, 1985), p. 18.

49. Oberdorfer, "Reagan Sought," p. A21. See also Gelb, "Shultz, Key Voice," p. A15.

50. Author's interview with Langhorne Motley, March 7, 1989. On October 17, the Director of the Joint Staff directed J-3 (Operations) to determine potential means of evacuating American citizens from Grenada under various conditions, from peaceful to hostile. The following day, Operations supplied an options paper on the subject. Admiral Robert P. Hilton, "Background Events on Grenada," unpublished briefing paper, p. 4.

51. Bennett, "Anatomy of a 'Go' Decision," p. 72. Motley's statement that from October 17 on, the President was kept personally informed of all developments would seem to corroborate this report. Motley, "The Decision to Assist Grenada," p. 70.

52. *Weekly Compilation of Presidential Documents* 19 (October 31, 1983): 1451. Earlier on Monday, Reagan asked his U.N. Ambassador, Jeane Kirkpatrick, to meet him in the Oval Office. In a one-hour conversation, the President attempted to persuade Kirkpatrick to remain at her post. While extolling her effectiveness, he explained that he had already determined to appoint Robert McFarlane as his third National Security Adviser. Reagan declared that he wished Kirkpatrick to continue as U.N. Ambassador, but that he was willing to establish a new White House position for her: Adviser to the President for National Security Affairs. Ambassador Kirkpatrick responded that she preferred to return to her U.N. position. Gerson, *The Kirkpatrick Mission*, p. 219.

53. Meanwhile, in a private meeting with a senior Defense Department official, probably Undersecretary for Policy Fred Ikle, Menges discussed his own more ambitious proposal. Here, Menges was told rather unceremoniously that his efforts were a "waste of time." His plan simply had "no chance whatsoever in this administration." Such pessimistic advice notwithstanding, he resolved to tell McFarlane about his scheme the next day. Menges, *Inside the NSC*, pp. 63-64.

54. Menges, *Inside the NSC*, p. 64. Later in the day, Menges met with Ambassador Middendorf. Middendorf, a proponent of activist foreign policy, thought Menges' idea was "great," but warned Menges not to get his "hopes up." Menges, *Inside the NSC*, pp. 64-65.

55. Later on Tuesday, Menges called the State Department and was told by an FSO that "not much [had] been done" at the Latin American bureau. Ambassador Bish had sent urgent cables describing the concern of all Caribbean democratic leaders. U.S. Ambassador to Jamaica, William Hewitt, had informed Washington that Prime Minister Seaga was planning to meet with six Caribbean prime ministers. Menges, *Inside the NSC*, p. 65.

56. According to one high-ranking official, Menges was permitted "virtually no role in the Grenada decision-making process." Background interview with author.

According to Gutman, Menges had "passionate convictions, a habit of lecturing his peers, and an 'I told you so' attitude that caused his tenure at most jobs to be short. In two years at the CIA he held the post of national intelligence officer for Latin America until Agency professionals could bear him no longer and was then assigned to a post concerned with paramilitary affairs, which was not filled after he departed. His move to the NSC was a cross between a firing and a promotion." *Banana Diplomacy*, p. 174.

57. Shultz, *Turmoil and Triumph*, p. 326.

58. Shultz, *Turmoil and Triumph*, p. 326.

59. Spector, *U.S. Marines in Grenada*, pp. 1-2.

60. Cannon, *President Reagan*, pp. 438-439. See also Weinberger, *Fighting for Peace*, pp. 157-161.

61. Weinberger, *Fighting for Peace*, p. 157; Cannon, President Reagan, p. 439.

62. Cannon, *President Reagan*, p. 439.

63. Lou Cannon's interviews with Colin Powell, April 17, 1990, and Caspar Weinberger, March 17, 1989, cited in Cannon, *President Reagan*, p. 444.

64. In his Congressional testimony on January 24, 1984, Motley defined a "non-permissive evacuation" as "one in which the host government impedes the departure of foreign citizens." Motley, "The Decision to Assist Grenada," p. 70.

65. Motley, "The Decision to Assist Grenada," p. 71.

66. "Address to the Barbadian People by Prime Minister Adams, October 26, 1983," reprinted in Gilmore, *Analysis and Documentation*, p. 102. See also Sandford and Vigilante, *The Untold Story*, p. 2.

67. Author's interviews with Milan Bish, September 26, 1988, October 20, 1988; author's interview with Kim Flower, July 6, 1989.

68. Menges would later observe: "I knew from our information that these leaders had a practical problem: what if they asked formally for military help from the United States and they were refused? Would the RMC take retaliatory actions? Might Castro? Their problem was very real." *Inside the NSC*, p. 72.

69. Author's interview with Milan Bish, October 22, 1988.

70. Author's interviews with Milan Bish, August 24, 1988 and October 26, 1988.

71. From October 16 to 19, Bush was in Jamaica at the invitation of Prime Minister Seaga. Afterward, the Vice President traveled to Puerto Rico to attend meetings with mayors of Latin American cities. *Department of State Bulletin* 83 (December 1983): 87.

72. Author's interviews with Langhorne Motley, September 20, 1988; and Francis McNeil, September 20, 1988.

73. Author's interview with Langhorne Motley, November 4, 1988.

74. Thomas Hammond's interview with Charles Gillespie, November 8, 1988. Notes of this interview were provided by Professor Hammond to the author.

75. Gillespie, whose arrival had not been anticipated, was not invited to the dinner and remained at his room at the Sands Hotel. Author's interview with Milan Bish, October 20, 1988.

76. Adams told Bish that he had been informed of Bishop's murder around 6:00 PM. Author's interview with Milan Bish, October 20, 1988.

77. Author's interviews with Milan Bish, September 26, 1988; October 20, 1988.

78. Motley, "The Decision to Assist Grenada," p. 71.

79. On October 18, the U.S. Embassy on Barbados had sent Grenada "a formal request for assurances of [American citizens'] well-being." Motley, "The Decision to Assist Grenada," p. 71.

80. Motley, "The Decision to Assist Grenada," p. 71. Larry Speakes reacted similarly: "What they told us, we simply did not trust. There was no way we could be at all assured that their promises would have been kept." *New York Times*, October 27, 1983, p. A20.

81. U.S. State Department Cable No. 06476. Kenneth Kurze's letters to the author, September 29, 1991; October 8, 1992.

82. *Covert Action Information Bulletin* 20 (Winter 1984): 8-10. This report was corroborated by the author's interview with Francis McNeil, November 11, 1988. See also Peter Bourne, "Was the U.S. Invasion Necessary?" *Los Angeles Times*, November 6, 1983, sect. 4, p. 1; and Robert Pastor, "The Invasion of Grenada: A Pre- and Post-Mortem," in *The Caribbean after Grenada: Revolution, Conflict and Democracy* eds. Scott B. MacDonald, Harald M. Sandstrom, and paul B. Goodwin, Jr. (New York: Praeger, 1988), p. 107.

83. Oberdorfer, "Reagan Sought," p. A21; Bennett, "Anatomy of a 'Go' Decision," p. 73. According to O'Shaughnessy, the meeting was in the afternoon. *Revolution, Invasion and Aftermath*, p. 154.

84. Menges, *Inside the NSC*, p. 66.

85. According to Bish, Motley arrived at the meeting unaware of Bish's message. Clarridge apparently received the message. Author's interviews with Milan Bish, August 24, 1988, October 26, 1988.

86. Tyler, "The Making of an Invasion," p. 14; Oberdorfer, "Reagan Sought," p. A21.

87. Gelb, "Shultz, Key Voice," p. A15.

88. Bennett, "Anatomy of a 'Go' Decision," p. 73; Oberdorfer, "Reagan Sought," p. A21. Moreau is not cited by name in these sources.

89. Motley usually had daily morning meetings or "cats and dogs sessions" with Secretary Shultz. Author's interview with Langhorne Motley, November 4, 1988.

90. Oberdorfer, "Reagan Sought," p. A21; O'Shaughnessy, *Revolution, Invasion and Aftermath,* p. 154; and Gelb, "Shultz, Key Voice," p. 15. The meeting between Shultz and Motley was confirmed in a background interview with a State Department official.

91. Author's interview with Fred C. Ikle, July 20, 1989; author's background interview with State Department official.

92. Motley, "The Decision to Assist Grenada," p. 71. In a State Department briefing on October 27, spokesman Alan Romberg disclosed that the United States "had been informally approached on an urgent basis by the Caribbean states as early as the weekend of October 15th and 16th, after the takeover ... on the 13th." The informal approaches, Romberg observed, "took the form of Caribbean leaders relaying to us through normal diplomatic channels their increasing concerns and apprehensions about the breakdown of order and growing violence and their belief that direct action might be necessary to prevent more deaths by a tyrannical, illegal government." When it was noted that by October 15 there had yet been no deaths, Romberg amended his statement to say that regional leaders were concerned about the "breakdown of order and, after October 19, growing violence" and the possibility of more deaths. See Patrick E. Tyler, "State Dept. Denies Reports That U.S. Sought Pretext for Invasion," *Washington Post,* October 28, 1983, p. A10.

93. Motley, "The Decision to Assist Grenada," p. 71.

94. Author's interview with Langhorne Motley, November 4, 1988.

95. According to Bennett, the meeting began at 8:00 AM. "Anatomy of a 'Go' Decision," p. 73. Menges gives the later time. *Inside the NSC,* p. 68.

96. Word of the murder of Bishop and Austin's curfew had reached Menges on late Wednesday afternoon. Given the significance of these new developments, he worked through the evening gathering all available Grenada information. He then prepared three one-page overviews: a factual summary of events; a summary of Caribbean attitudes; and a description of the pro-democratic leadership and institutions that could provide the basis for the restoration of democracy. Next, according to Menges' account, he met with Robert McFarlane and John Poindexter and urged them to convene the "Crisis Preplanning Group" (CPPG). After some discussion, Menges contends, the two chief NSC advisers agreed to do so the following day. Menges, *Inside the NSC,* p. 68. The degree to which he actually influenced McFarlane and Poindexter, however, was probably very slight.

97. One of Reagan's first acts in office was the creation of the Crisis Preplanning Group as an early warning mechanism to handle developing crises. Chaired by the Deputy National Security Adviser, the CPPG supported the "Special Situations Group." See Frederick H. Hartmann and Robert L. Wendzel, *Defending American Security* (Washington, D.C.: Pergammon-Brassey, 1988), p. 117; and Bennett, "Anatomy of a 'Go' Decision," p. 73.

According to Motley, the specific designation "Special Situations Group" was never used. Author's interview with Langhorne Motley, March 7, 1989.

98. Menges, *Inside the NSC*, p. 68; and Woodward, *Veil*, pp. 288-289.

99. The facility was infrequently used since every department had its own crisis facility. Author's interview with Langhorne Motley, November 4, 1988. North had supervised the creation of the center. Martin and Walcott, *Best Laid Plans*, p. 61.

100. Menges, *Inside the NSC*, p. 70; Woodward, *Veil*, p. 289. The unsuccessful effort of the U.S. Embassy on Barbados to send diplomats to Grenada was apparently not mentioned at the meeting and may not yet have been known in Washington. Menges, *Inside the NSC*, p. 70.

101. Menges, *Inside the NSC*, p. 69.

102. Oberdorfer, "Reagan Sought," p. A21

103. Menges, *Inside the NSC*, p. 69; Woodward, *Veil*, p. 70.

104. Six options for "NEO"s were reportedly reviewed on Thursday morning. From that time on, however, "the entire character of planning changed from NEO to active U.S. military involvement .... Planning now commenced for 'R and R, Rescue and Restoration of Democracy.'" Hilton, "Background Events on Grenada," pp. 5-6.

105. Menges, *Inside the NSC*, pp. 69-70; Bennett, "Anatomy of a 'Go' Decision," p. 73.

106. Author's interview with Fred Ikle, July 20, 1989. See also Bennett, "Anatomy of a 'Go' Decision," p. 73; and Oberdorfer, "Reagan Sought," p. A21.

107. Weinberger, *Fighting for Peace*, p. 110; Bennett, "Anatomy of a 'Go' Decision," p. 43; Oberdorfer, "Reagan Sought," p. A21.

108. On the "SSG," see Hartmann and Wendzel, *Defending America's Security*, p. 117; and Gutman, *Banana Diplomacy*, pp. 134-135.

109. Menges, *Inside the NSC*, p. 71.

110. According to Henry Kissinger, the "tiny, uncomfortable, low-ceilinged, windowless room ... owes its chief utility to its location next door to a bank of teletypes and other communications equipment linking the White House to embassies around the world. Its name derived from the illusion of an earlier President that the international situation could be represented currently by maps on the wall." *White House Years* (Boston: Little Brown, 1979), p. 315.

Inside the room is a conference table surrounded by twelve chairs. Around the wall are another fourteen chairs permitting each NSC participant to bring one staff person. Menges, *Inside the NSC*, p. 72.

111. Menges, *Inside the NSC*, p. 72.

112. Bernard Gwertzman, "Steps to the Invasion: No More 'Paper Tiger,'" *New York Times*, Oct. 30, 1983, p. 20; Schoenhals and Melanson, *Revolution and Intervention*, p. 140; "Britain's Grenada Shut-out," *The Economist*, p. 31.

113. Tyler, "The Making of an Invasion," p. A14.

114. O'Shaughnessy, *Revolution, Invasion and Aftermath*, p. 154. In a 1993 interview, Eagleburger conceded that "resolve" against the communist threat was the proper "button" to push. Author's interview with Lawrence Eagleburger, March 15, 1993.

115. Menges, *Inside the NSC*, p. 72.

116. See Oberdorfer, "Reagan Sought," p. A21; and Bennett, "Anatomy of a 'Go' Decision," p. 73.

117. Bradlee, *Guts and Glory*, p. 174.

118. Hall, "The Grenada Intervention," p. 18.

119. According to Shultz, his arrival was about "half-way through the meeting." "Shultz's News Conference, Oct. 25, 1983," p. 69. If the meeting lasted an hour and began at 4:45 PM, then Shultz and Motley arrived around 5:15 PM.

120. See "Shultz's News Conference," p. 69; Oberdorfer, "Reagan Sought," p. A21; Menges, *Inside the NSC*, p. 72; and Tyler, "The Making of an Invasion," p. A14.

121. Sandford and Vigilante, *The Untold Story*, pp. 2-3.

122. According to some accounts, the meeting's basic purpose was to consider Adams' request for U.S. invasion. See Schoenhals and Melanson, *Revolution and Intervention*, p. 140; "Britain's Grenada Shut-out," *The Economist*, p. 31; and Gwertzman, "Steps to the Invasion," p. 20.

John Compton, Prime Minister of St. Lucia, Eugenia Charles, Prime Minister of Dominica, and Tom Adams formed a "triad" of sorts, with Adams as intellectual leader, Charles as OECS chair, and Compton as the "engine that made it [the Grenada invasion] happen." Author's interview with Milan Bish, October 26, 1988.

123. Menges, *Inside the NSC*, p. 72. According to *The Economist*, Eugenia Charles was in Washington that Thursday, and returned to the Caribbean the following day. "Britain's Grenada Shut-out," p. 32. Schoenhals and Melanson speculate that the Prime Minister of Dominica was in Washington at the administration's request. *Revolution and Intervention*, p. 141.

According to a Senate source, "Charles had been consulting closely with U.S. officials before the invasion." Tyler, "The Making of an Invasion," p. A14. This is likely a reference to discussions between Charles and Gillespie. Author's interview with Langhorne Motley, November 4, 1988.

124. Throughout the meeting, Menges claims, the discussion had been framed in terms both of a "rescue mission" and of "democratic restoration." When the question was raised whether there existed any democratic leader or group on Grenada to replace the RMC, Menges briefed the group while copies of his one-page overview were distributed. The NSC staffer argued that there were genuine democrats who could establish an interim government leading to

fair and free elections. Menges, *Inside the NSC*, p. 72.

125. Bennett, "Anatomy of a 'Go' Decision," p. 73. In the hours before the invasion, the Army's office of Special Operations sought desperately to infiltrate an agent onto Grenada. Colonel James Longhofer flew to Barbados carrying a briefcase filled with $100,000 in cash to pay the agent. A civilian transport plane brought in a small Hughes 500D helicopter to airlift the agent to Grenada. At the last minute, however, the agent reneged. Martin and Walcott, *Best Laid Plans*, pp. 134-135.

126. Motley, "The Decision to Assist Grenada," p. 71.

127. Oberdorfer, "Reagan Sought," p. A21.

128. "Shultz's News Conference," p. 69. The diversion was recommended by General Vessey and approved by Secretary Weinberger. Weinberger, *Fighting for Peace*, p. 109.

129. Author's interview with Langhorne Motley, November 4, 1988. See also Shultz, *Turmoil and Triumph*, p. 327; and Woodward, *Veil*, p. 289.

130. Bennett, "Anatomy of a 'Go' Decision," p. 74; Menges, *Inside the NSC*, p. 73; Oberdorfer, "Reagan Sought," p. A1.

131. Oberdorfer, "Reagan Sought," p. A21; Schoenhals and Melanson, *Revolution and Intervention*, p. 140; and "Britain's Grenada Shut-out," *The Economist*, p. 31.

132. Author's interview with Lawrence Eagleburger, March 15, 1993. See also Davidson, *A Study in Politics*, p. 80; Bradlee, *Guts and Glory*, pp. 174-175.

133. Woodward, *Veil*, p. 290. *The Economist* tersely summarizes the situation on Thursday, October 20: "Three pressures now converged on the White House: its concern for the Americans on Grenada; the NSC's concern over Cuban penetration; and the desire of certain Caribbean states to end lawlessness on the island. Only the first of these, however, might justify the violation of foreign territory. Ideally, America needed an invitation from some plausible regional body." See "Britain's Grenada Shut-out," p. 32.

134. By Saturday, the results of the OECS meeting would be known. O'Shaughnessy has noted, the "assistance of the small islands of the eastern Caribbean was vital if legal justification for an invasion was to be found. An invitation from Grenada's neighbors would be of inestimable value in the diplomatic fallout that the State Department saw as inevitable after the US action." *Revolution, Invasion and Aftermath*, p. 155.

135. Menges, *Inside the NSC*, p. 73.

136. Menges, *Inside the NSC*, pp. 73-74.

137. *Weekly Compilation of Presidential Documents* 19 (October 31, 1983): 1476.

138. Motley, "The Decision to Assist Grenada," p. 71; Reagan, *An American Life*, p. 450; Shultz, *Turmoil and Triumph*, p. 327.

139. Reagan, *An American Life*, p. 450.

140. Oberdorfer, "Reagan Sought," p. A21.

141. Spector, *U.S. Marines in Grenada*, p. 2.

142. See "Address to the Barbadian People by Prime Minister Adams, October 26, 1983," reprinted in Gilmore, *The Grenada Intervention*, pp. 102-105. See also Sandford and Vigilante, *The Untold Story*, pp. 2-3.

143. Author's interview with Milan Bish, October 22, 1988. See also Adams' indirect acknowledgement in "Address to the Barbadian People," reprinted in Gilmore, *Analysis and Documentation*, p. 102.

144. "Adams Address," reprinted in Gilmore, *Analysis and Documentation*, p. 103.

145. Sandford and Vigilante, *The Untold Story*, p. 3.

146. Menges, *Inside the NSC*, p. 74.

147. Menges, *Inside the NSC*, p. 74; Oberdorfer, "Reagan Sought," p. A21.

148. Author's interview with Constantine Menges, September 21, 1988.

149. Author's interview with Langhorne Motley, November 4, 1988.

150. Author's interview with Langhorne Motley, September 20, 1988.

151. Author's interview with Michael Kozak, November 3, 1988.

152. Author's interviews with Langhorne Motley, September 20, 1988; November 4, 1988.

153. Author's interview with Langhorne Motley, September 20, 1988.

154. Author's interview with Langhorne Motley, November 4, 1988. Author's interview with Michael Kozak, November 3, 1988.

155. According to one Reagan administration official, Eagleburger did not want lawyers involved in the decisionmaking process for fear that the Grenada operation's security would be compromised. He discovered their involvement after the fact. Author's background interview with State Department official.

156. The following account is based on Shultz's in *Turmoil and Triumph*, p. 328.

157. Shultz, *Turmoil and Triumph*, p. 328.

158. Bennett, "Anatomy of a 'Go" Decision," p. 74. Menges says the meeting was in the "late afternoon." *Inside the NSC*, p. 76. Oberdorfer also reports the Friday CPPG meeting. "Reagan Sought," p. A21.

159. Menges, *Inside the NSC*, p. 76.

160. Bennett, "Anatomy of a 'Go' Decision," p. 74. *The Economist* confirms that meetings were held on Friday. Here, "orders were given to proceed with preparations for a 'non-permissive evacuation' of American citizens from Grenada." See "Britain's Grenada Shut-out," p. 32.

161. Menges, *Inside the NSC*, p. 76.

162. Magnuson, "D-Day in Grenada," p. 27; O'Shaughnessy, *Revolution, Invasion and Aftermath*, p. 158. See also Speakes, *Speaking Out*, p. 151; and Reagan, *An American Life*, p. 449.

163. "Radio Address to the Nation, October 22, 1983," *Weekly Compilation of Presidential Documents* 19 (October 31, 1983): 1479-1480. Also on Friday, Reagan conversed by telephone with Mrs. Martin Luther King, Jr., discussed the fiscal year 1985 Federal Budget with administration officials and White House staff, considered natural gas decontrol legislation with business leaders, and spoke with members of the National Bipartisan Commission on Central America.

164. Shultz, *Turmoil and Triumph*, p. 323.

165. Motley, "The Decision to Assist Grenada," p. 72.

166. O'Shaughnessy, *Revolution, Invasion and Aftermath*, p. 156. The six states represented were: Antigua-Barbuda; Dominica; Montserrat; St. Kitts-Nevis; St. Lucia; and St. Vincent and the Grenadines. For obvious reasons, no representative of Grenada participated in the October 21 meeting.

167. The presence at the Convention Centre of Bish and Gillespie was confirmed in author's interviews with Milan Bish, October 20 and 26, 1988 and with Francis McNeil, September 20, 1988. Bish reported that the Americans had been given a conference room at the facility.

168. O'Shaughnessy, *Revolution, Invasion and Aftermath*, p. 157. According to his own October 26 speech, Adams had spent the day on Friday in conversations with the High Commissioner for Trinidad and Tobago, with Giles Bullard, with Milan Bish, and with Noble Power. "Adams' Address," reprinted in Gilmore, *Analysis and Documentation*, p. 103.

169. Payne et al., *Revolution and Invasion*, p. 149.

170. "Adams' Address," reprinted in Gilmore, *Analysis and Documentation*, p. 104.

171. Cited by Juan Williams, "Jamaicans Indicate U.S. Signaled Will to Invade," *Washington Post*, October 27, 1983, p. A20.

172. "Adams' Address," reprinted in Gilmore, *Analysis and Documentation*, p. 104.

173. Payne et al., *Revolution and Invasion*, p. 151.

174. O'Shaughnessy, *Revolution, Invasion and Aftermath*, p. 157. The "OECS Press Release" of October 21, 1983 is reprinted in full in appendix no. 5 of Gilmore, *Analysis and Documentation*, p. 92.

175. Payne et al., *Revolution and Invasion*, p. 149; Davidson, *A Study in Politics*, p. 80.

176. The British Foreign Affairs Committee concluded that "although [they were] not present during the formal OECS meeting, representatives of the Governments of Barbados and Jamaica, and subsequently the United States Ambassador to Barbados, were invited to join the OECS representatives that evening." See "Second Report," p. xiii.

According to Prime Minister Seaga, American officials attending the meetings had voiced their "concern over the turn of events in Grenada and the expanding Cuban and Soviet influence on the island." Tyler, "The Making of an Invasion," p. A14.

177. O'Shaughnessy, *Revolution, Invasion and Aftermath*, pp. 157-158. While not confirming this story, Bish did not deny it. He emphasized Vere Bird's support for the Grenada mission, however. Author's interview with Milan Bish, October 26, 1988.

178. Menges, *Inside the NSC*, p. 76.

179. Oberdorfer, "Reagan Sought," p. A21; Bennett, Anatomy of a 'Go' Decision," p. 74.

180. Author's interview with Milan Bish, October 20, 1988; author's interview with Kim Flower, July 6, 1989.

181. Author's interview with Kim Flower, July 6, 1989.

182. Author's interview with Kim Flower, July 6, 1989.

183. Oberdorfer, "Reagan Sought," p. A21; Woodward, *Veil*, p. 290.

184. Gwertzman reports that Poindexter received word around 1:00 AM. "Steps to the Invasion," p. 20. Motley stated that once he received the cable from Bridgetown, he contacted Poindexter. Author's interview with Langhorne Motley, November 4, 1988.

185. Gwertzman, "Steps to the Invasion," p. 20.

186. "Britain's Grenada Shut-out," *The Economist*, p. 32.

187. Shultz, *Turmoil and Triumph*, p. 329.

188. Shultz, *Turmoil and Triumph*, p. 323; Edwin Meese III, *With Reagan: The Inside Story* (Washington, D.C.: Regnery Gateway, 1992), p. 216.

189. Cannon, *President Reagan*, p. 442.

190. Shultz, *Turmoil and Triumph*, p. 329.

191. Oberdorfer, "Reagan Sought," p. A21; O'Shaughnessy, *Revolution, Invasion and Aftermath*, p. 158.

192. Tyler, "The Making of an Invasion," p. A1.

193. Bridgetown CANA report by Albert Brandford, 8:30 PM Grenada time. Manuscript printed in *Unclassified FBIS - Latin America*, October 24, 1983, p. S2.

194. "Shultz's News Conference," p. 69; Tyler, "The Making of an Invasion," p. 14; "Britain's Grenada Shut-out," *The Economist*, p. 32; Reagan, *An American Life*, p. 449; Shultz, *Turmoil and Triumph*, p. 329.

195. "Shultz's News Conference," p. 69; Cannon, *President Reagan*, p. 441; Meese, *With Reagan*, p. 216.

196. Schoenhals and Melanson, *Revolution and Intervention*, p. 141.

197. Shultz, *Turmoil and Triumph*, p. 329.

198. O'Shaughnessy, *Revolution, Invasion and Aftermath*, p. 158. In his memoir, Weinberger acknowledged two significant facts: first, that on early Saturday morning he had raised the issue of the "shortness of time to gather intelligence;" and second, that on Friday General Vessey had advised him that

U.S. forces "could go in shortly after first light on Tuesday, October 25." Weinberger, *Fighting for Peace*, pp. 112, 114.

199. Shultz, *Turmoil and Triumph*, p. 329.

200. "Britain's Grenada Shut-out," *The Economist*, p. 32.

201. Bennett, Cannon, Tyler, Meese, Oberdorfer and Speakes all cite a 5:15 AM time. See "Anatomy of a 'Go' Decision," p. 74; *President Reagan*, p. 441; "The Making of an Invasion," p. 14; *With Reagan*, p. 216; "Reagan Sought," p. A21; and *Speaking Out*, p. 151.

According to his autobiographical account, Reagan and his wife were awakened "shortly after four o'clock." *An American Life*, p. 449. George Shultz reported in his October 25, 1983 news conference that President Reagan had been awakened "shortly" after the conference call discussions. "Shultz's News Conference," p. 70. Curiously, Shultz suggests in his memoir that Reagan had been awakened at 2:45 A.M. and had thereafter participated in administration deliberations. *Turmoil and Triumph*, p. 329.

202. Reagan, *An American Life*, p. 449.

203. Tyler, "The Making of an Invasion," p. 14.

204. "Shultz's News Conference," p. 70; Davidson, *A Study in Politics*, p. 81. According to Weinberger, "I sensed [the President] had just about decided we should go in." Weinberger, *Fighting for Peace*, p. 111. In his memoir account, Weinberger speaks only of making a secure call to the President with General Vessey around 2:00 AM. Weinberger, *Fighting for Peace*, pp. 111-112.

205. Lou Cannon's interview with Robert McFarlane, April 16, 1990, cited in Cannon, *President Reagan*, p. 441.

206. Gwertzman, "Steps to the Invasion," p. 20; Bennett, "Anatomy of a 'Go' Decision," p. 74. According to one account: "Reagan suggested that the presidential party return immediately to Washington. McFarlane pointed out that the Special Situations Group was already proceeding with invasion plans, and Shultz said that a change in Reagan's schedule might draw attention to the possibility of U.S. intervention. [Hence,] Reagan decided to remain in Augusta." Cannon, *President Reagan*, pp. 441-442. See also Shultz, *Turmoil and Triumph*, p. 330.

207. Reagan, *An American Life*, p. 449.

5

The Invasion Decision Is Made

Jokingly referring to U.S. invasion forces: *"[T]ell the State Department to inform Grenada that we will send some people to talk, and that they will arrive early next week."[1]*
— John Poindexter to Constantine Menges, October 22, 1983

[T]he costs of not doing Grenada were obviously greater than the cost of doing it. We didn't want students held 440 days as hostages.[2]
— Caspar Weinberger

On the secrecy of the Grenada operation: *"We didn't ask anybody, we just did it."[3]*
— Ronald Reagan

By Saturday morning, October 22, a number of related events had set the Reagan administration on a course toward the President's ultimate decision to launch "Urgent Fury." Only three days before, Prime Minister Bishop, seven of his colleagues, and scores of Grenadian citizens had perished at the hands of the People's Revolutionary Army. Since "Bloody Wednesday," Grenada had remained under a shoot-on-sight curfew imposed by General Austin.

Elsewhere in the Caribbean, government leaders had been growing increasingly restive about the conditions on Grenada. Even before Bishop's murder, Prime Ministers Adams of Barbados, Compton of St. Lucia, and Charles of Dominica had privately indicated to U.S. officials their interest in a collaborative military operation. And only last evening, the Organization of Eastern Caribbean States had formally requested the assistance of the United States.

Back in Washington, the administration had been considering for some time now how it should respond. Since Thursday, October 13, Motley's Restricted Interagency Group had been closely monitoring the Grenada situation. Just two days ago, on Thursday, October 20, the Special Situations Group had urged that steps be taken to enable a military operation. On that group's recommendation, President Reagan had Thursday evening ordered the diversion of U.S. naval forces toward Grenada and the commencement of operational planning. And yesterday, at his deputy's suggestion, Assistant Secretary Motley had directed administration lawyers to begin considering the legal ramifications of the contemplated American military action.

Despite all that had transpired in Washington and the Caribbean since October 13, however, it was not certain by Saturday morning that the United States would undertake a military operation. To be sure, a number of administration officials strongly favored immediate American action and critical steps had already been taken to facilitate such action. Moreover, around 6:00 A.M. Saturday, Ronald Reagan had made an "initial decision" to proceed.[4] Nevertheless, the President had as yet made no irrevocable decision. The next forty-eight hours would prove crucial.

This chapter will recount the many and diverse activities that took place between Saturday morning, October 22, and Tuesday morning, October 25. During this brief span, Grenada was finally reached by American envoys, a written invitation from the OECS issued, and a request of assistance from the Grenadian Governor-General relayed through diplomatic channels to the United States. While these events were quietly unfolding in the Caribbean, the President's tentative decision to invade Grenada was privately articulated, reconsidered in light of the Beirut massacre, finally confirmed, then carried out by American armed forces. In order best to illustrate the role played by international law in the Reagan administration's decisionmaking process, Chapter Five will be divided into four sections: (1) Saturday, October 22 and Sunday, October 23; (2) The Beirut Massacre and Its Repercussions; (3) The McNeil Mission; and (4) Final Preparations.

Saturday and Sunday

A critical meeting

At 9:00 A.M. Saturday, October 22, the Special Situations Group was reconvened by Vice President Bush.[5] To conceal any appearance of unusual activity, the second meeting on Grenada to be chaired by Bush was held in Room 208 of the Executive Office Building.[6] Present were Poindexter, Menges and North from the NSC; McMahon and Clarridge from the CIA; Eagleburger and Motley from State; and Weinberger, Vessey and Ikle from Defense.[7] On the golf course in Georgia, Reagan and Shultz would confer with Washington via a secure mobile telephone.[8] While the President and the Secretary of State played golf with Donald Regan and Nicholas Brady, McFarlane stood nearby to monitor the situation.[9]

As was customary, the meeting began with an overview and update.[10] Then, the State Department opened the two and a half hour discussion by addressing the political aspects of the prospective American action. The Organization of Eastern Caribbean States, Eagleburger and Motley reported, had last night officially requested U.S. military assistance. As yet, however, the organization had not issued a formal written invitation. State noted that Barbados and Jamaica had agreed to provide forces for a joint military operation,[11] although this information could not have been surprising in light of the cable traffic from Bridgetown over the past week. It is likely that State also discussed the CARICOM conference that would be held Saturday evening on Trinidad.[12] Here, an international organization larger, older, and better recognized than the OECS, though not a regional security organization, might decide to request American assistance.[13]

Next, the SSG turned its attention to the military aspects of a Grenada operation.[14] Despite intelligence limitations, there was a general consensus on the numbers and abilities of Grenadian and Cuban forces.[15] Weinberger and Vessey nevertheless wanted to learn more about the weapons the Grenadian military possessed, their willingness to fight, and the willingness of the Cubans.[16] In addition, Weinberger recommended now the use of Navy SEALs for pre-landing reconnaissance of the island.[17] The group also determined that as the first American troops landed on Grenada, U.S. Ambassadors would inform the governments of the Soviet Union, Cuba, and other "hostile" states that their "captured noncombat personnel would be treated correctly and repatriated as quickly as possible."[18]

A detailed hour-by-hour "action plan" was then distributed to the meeting participants. This "time-line" chart, which had been drafted by the State Department, was an elaborate checklist of actions to be taken by the United States in the days leading up to and including "D-Day."[19] While the meeting participants discussed the plan's various provisions in the "crisis management center," the President joined them by secure phone from Augusta. Reportedly, he would participate for about five minutes.[20] If the United States were to go beyond a simple "rescue mission" to a full-fledged invasion of Grenada, there would surely be risks involved.[21] One White House staff member warned that there would be "a lot of harsh political reaction" to an American strike at a small island nation. Reagan reportedly replied, "I know that. I accept that."[22] Carefully weighing the risks of a military action, the group determined that Tuesday morning would be the earliest practical date for a full-scale landing. An earlier invasion date simply could not ensure a rapid, low-casualty operation. If it became necessary to save Americans, however, the military could mount a commando airdrop more quickly.[23]

As the group deliberated over the scope of the contemplated American action, Vice President Bush asked Reagan about the mission's "threefold objective." According to the draft NSDD, the American operation would seek: to ensure the safety of American citizens; to restore democratic government to Grenada; and to eliminate current and future Cuban intervention on the island.[24] Certainly, a relatively strong case could be made for a short mission to rescue American citizens. But should the United States take the bold step of launching a full-scale invasion, thereby restoring democratic government and driving out the Cubans? Reagan reportedly replied, "Well, if we've got to go there, we might as well do all that needs to be done."[25] Throughout the SSG's morning discussions, Bush had given no indication of his own views, preferring only to report the opinions expressed by his colleagues.[26]

As the meeting continued, the War Powers Resolution was briefly discussed. The legislation did not appear to pose any serious difficulties, however. With any luck, the Grenada mission would be completed long before Congress could question the action's conformity with the resolution. After more deliberation, the meeting ended at 11:30 A.M. By now, there was a consensus.[27]

In the course of Saturday morning's meeting, at least four significant decisions were made. Most importantly, the President made clear his intention to accept the invitation of the OECS and to intervene in Grenada.[28] The hawkish view of the State Department and the White House had prevailed.[29] Reagan's decision, which he had reached very early that morning, constituted at least a "seventy-five percent" commitment to invade.[30] It implied several others.

First, military planning must be completed quickly and with absolute secrecy. Thus, the Joint Chiefs were instructed to proceed with invasion planning on the basis of a "go order."[31]

Second, steps must be taken to assess the position on Grenada and to clarify OECS cooperation. Accordingly, American diplomats would be dispatched from the Bridgetown Embassy to Grenada. Moreover, at Motley's suggestion, Ambassador Francis J. "Frank" McNeil and Marine Major General George B. Crist would be sent to Barbados to probe the OECS invitation and to liaise over support troops for an invasion. McNeil, a career foreign service officer and former Ambassador to Costa Rica, would make certain that the Caribbean leaders had in fact a common position and would secure from them a formal written invitation. It would not do for the United States to invade and subsequently to discover that the Caribbean leaders had changed their minds. General Crist, "a man with stars on his shoulders," would help signal to the Caribbean leadership Washington's serious intent and, in the event that the military option were taken, "make sure that the [Caribbean] flags" were brought into Grenada early.[32]

Third, especially in light of press reports that a Grenada invasion was imminent, steps must be taken to maintain the contemplated operation's secrecy. Thus, Shultz and Reagan would remain at Augusta and continue their golf weekend.[33] Moreover, an elaborate plan was hatched to postpone Shultz's departure for El Salvador and Brazil that had been scheduled for Monday morning.[34] Meanwhile, inquiries from the British embassy would be assured that American deployments were confined to providing for the security of American citizens, that America was proceeding "with extreme caution," and that London would be notified of any change in the plan.[35] Finally, Reagan administration spokespersons would not be informed of the President's decision, thus allowing them to deny that any invasion was planned.[36] Nor even were the senior civilian authorities for the three U.S. military departments to be made privy to Grenada planning. John Lehman, Secretary of the

Navy in 1983, remembered: "During the decisionmaking leading up to Grenada, and during the conduct of operations itself, the service secretaries depended on corridor gossip and the press" for information.[37]

A very busy Saturday afternoon

According to his account, Constantine Menges returned to his office after Saturday morning's meeting to participate in the drafting of two essential documents: first, the National Security Adviser's memorandum to the President; and second, the National Security Decision Directive (NSDD) that Reagan would use to order actions by the Departments of State, Defense and the CIA. Ollie North examined Menges' new draft NSDD before it was given to Deputy National Security Adviser Poindexter. Poindexter next made several changes. Then, Menges read the revised draft over a secure phone to several senior officials while Poindexter called others. Admiral Poindexter wanted to be certain that the NSC's draft accurately reflected Ronald Reagan's decisions and that its meaning was unambiguous.[38]

By 2:10 P.M. Saturday, McFarlane's decision memorandum and the NSDD were finished. According to Menges, acting National Security Adviser John Poindexter then "obtained authorization from the President" and transmitted signed copies to State, Defense, and the CIA. Assistant Secretary Motley would later confirm that on October 22, "the President signed orders to prepare for a broader mission to restore order in Grenada in cooperation with Caribbean forces."[39]

That Saturday afternoon at Augusta, Reagan administration efforts to maintain a normal atmosphere took a surreal turn.[40] Around 2:15 P.M., Charles Harris, an unemployed paper mill worker, crashed his pickup truck through an unguarded gate at the clubhouse, pulled a .38-caliber pistol and held seven men as hostages in the pro shop. Among them were David Fischer, Reagan's personal aid, and Lanny Wiles, a White House advance man. Uncertain of the extent of the incident and concerned that the gunman might have confederates, Secret Service agents pulled Reagan off Augusta's sixteenth hole and into his armored limousine. They next issued an order for emergency helicopter evacuation: "Launch Nighthawk Two." Within ten minutes, a helicopter was flying overhead and *Air Force One* readied on the tarmac.[41]

When Harris, who was reportedly drunk, demanded to speak with the President, Reagan broke his longstanding rule against negotiating with terrorists — the lives of two of his assistants appeared at stake. He later recalled:

> Normally, I wouldn't have made any response to demands by a terrorist. That only encourages more terrorism. But I was told that the gunman was very unbalanced and the lives of the hostages were in imminent danger.[42]

Reagan spent fifteen minutes attempting without success to converse with Harris by car phone:

> I said, "Hello, this is Ronald Reagan ..." There was a silence, then the man hung up without saying a word and the phone went dead. We dialed the pro shop again — in fact, four more times — but every time, he hung up on me. He was insisting on speaking to me face to face, which the Secret Service agents wouldn't permit.[43]

At length, the President was whisked by heavily-armed agents back to the Eisenhower cabin where he would later dine with Secretary Shultz. Ultimately, Harris was overpowered without anyone being hurt.[44] Three days later, the President would open his Tuesday cabinet session on Grenada with the crack, "You fellas ought to try golfing in Augusta sometime."[45]

Meanwhile at the State Department, William Montgomery, Lawrence Eagleburger's Executive Assistant, spent part of his afternoon attempting to contact Frank McNeil in Boston. The Tufts University Ambassador-in-Residence was finally reached around 1:30 or 2:00 P.M. on a nonsecure telephone line. McNeil was told then only that he was immediately needed and that he should bring tropical clothing.[46] Since his automobile had already been packed for a planned trip to Washington, McNeil declined an offer to be flown to the capital; instead, he drove through the night, arriving with his family in Washington around 2:30 or 3:00 A.M. Sunday. He then checked into the Howard Johnson's Hotel near the Watergate and called the State Department to report his arrival.[47]

Early Saturday evening, Deputy Assistant Secretary James Michel called Larry Rossin and asked the Foreign Service Officer to fly to Barbados the next day. "My instruction at the time of my departure," Rossin would later recall, "was to assist in any way necessary Ambassador McNeil in his special mission. I expected that I would stay in

Barbados a couple of weeks assisting with reporting from the Embassy there, though everything was very fluid and I quickly realized that nothing was firm."[48] On Saturday evening, though, the FSO almost certainly could not have guessed what role he would play in the attempted "special ops" rescue of Sir Paul Scoon.

Also on Saturday, the legal aspects of the contemplated American invasion of Grenada began seriously to be considered at Foggy Bottom.[49] There, at the bidding of Jim Michel, the senior career State Department lawyer, Deputy Legal Adviser Michael Kozak directed a small team of legal experts from the State, Justice, and Defense Departments. Among them were two State Department attorneys: K. Scott Gudgeon, Assistant Legal Adviser for Inter-American Affairs; and Mary E. McLeod, Assistant Legal Adviser for Politico-Military Affairs. Davis R. Robinson, the State Department Legal Adviser, was not directly involved but would be briefed by his deputy.

The State Department lawyers would spend much of the next three days and nights in the department's "operations center," exploring various questions of domestic and international law. Several tasks would be undertaken. First, they had to examine the OECS charter, and later, when it became an issue, the role of the Governor-General of Grenada. Second, in anticipation of Ambassador McNeil's mission to Bridgetown, the lawyers had to prepare an outline or list of essential points to be included in any formal OECS written request for assistance. This the President's Special Emissary could give to the Caribbean leaders on Sunday. Finally, the Legal Adviser's office would contribute to the administration's "time-line" chart a number of actions that would have to be undertaken by the administration — in the Congress, in the U.N., and in the O.A.S. — in the event that American military action were taken. During this time, as events in the Caribbean unfolded, Kozak periodically briefed George Shultz.[50]

Legal study was not the only investigation undertaken by the administration on Saturday afternoon. Then and thereafter, SR-71 and U-2 spy planes made repeated passes over Grenada while Grenadian radio transmissions were monitored. Meanwhile, the National Security Agency (NSA) took "snapshots" of the Caribbean island from repositioned reconnaissance satellites. One analyst would subsequently observe with hyperbole: the photographic scrutiny was so precise that "we [could] see where the roofs leak[ed] and the doorknobs [were] loose."[51] Marine leaders would later find, however, that aerial photos had given a false impression of the Grenadian terrain.[52] Moreover, according to John Lehman, "human agent intelligence — the most valuable kind" remained "totally absent."[53]

Oliver North spent Saturday afternoon continuing his work on the military aspects of the contemplated military action.[54] In the next several days he would work nearly around the clock.[55] The recently-promoted[56] Lieutenant Colonel "had as large a role [in the Grenada operation] as anyone in the White House did," Robert McFarlane would later recall.[57] "Ollie was kind of an in-house plans officer the Pentagon could call before they went into their own deliberations to get a very clear sense of what the President's sentiments were." North ensured that Ambassador Bish on Barbados worked with the military, and he facilitated relations between the intelligence community and the military:

> When the military came up with a problem they were too embarrassed to admit they didn't know the answer to — like specifics on the beach in Grenada, what is the beach gradient, where are some beaches we can get a track vehicle over — Ollie would get the answer from the CIA and put two guys together in the same room, whereas it wouldn't have happened if he didn't do it.[58]

At 10:00 P.M. Saturday evening, Captain Carl Erie, commodore of the Marine amphibious task force, received several significant messages. The first directed the amphibious ready group, which since late Thursday evening had been following a modified track pattern to keep it within easy sailing range of Grenada, to turn toward the island. The second message, received about the same time as the first, provided general information on the strength and disposition of forces on Grenada;[59] it also advised that an intelligence package was on its way from Roosevelt Roads, Puerto Rico, to the *Guam*. Meanwhile, a third message from Vice Admiral Metcalf advised Captain Erie that the U.S. Army was planning an airborne assault of Grenada.[60]

Saturday and Sunday in Trinidad

At 9:00 P.M. Saturday, a special meeting of the Heads of Government of the Caribbean Community was convened at the Trinidad Hilton in Port-of-Spain.[61] Present for the late evening meeting chaired by Prime Minister George Chambers were the representatives of all the CARICOM states except Grenada. The OECS representatives, Lester Bird, Eugenia Charles, John Osbourne, Dr. Kennedy Simmonds, John

Compton, and Milton Cato had arrived *en bloc* from Barbados; Seaga had shared the flight with them. Meanwhile, Prime Minister Adams had remained on Barbados and would be represented by Louis Tull, his Foreign Minister. Some time before an 8:15 P.M. picture call, George Price, Prime Minister of Belize, and Sir Lynden Pindling, Prime Minister of the Bahamas, had also arrived at the Hilton. Forbes Burnham, the President of Guyana, did not arrive until 9:00 P.M. sharp, however.[62]

Discussions that night at the so-called "upside-down hotel" focused upon a pacific settlement of the Grenada problem. Neither the OECS Heads of Government nor Prime Minister Seaga mentioned now that the OECS had decided the day before to undertake military intervention.[63] The Jamaican leader would later concede that nothing had been said "because we did not want anything to leak out."[64] Although Seaga maintained that CARICOM should not rule out the use of force, and the representatives of the OECS states and Barbados supported him, Chambers, Burnham, Pindling, and Price rejected the Jamaican Prime Minister's position. The four government leaders were convinced that force should not be used, at least in the first instance.[65]

At 3:06 A.M. Sunday, the CARICOM meeting adjourned. By this point, the meeting's chair believed that the organization had reached a consensus on a number of points. Chambers reported subsequently that the Caribbean Community had then agreed that there should be no external involvement in the solution of the Grenada crisis, that the crisis should be solved within CARICOM confines, that CARICOM should act in accord with international law and the U.N. Charter, and that all efforts should be directed toward restoring normality on Grenada. CARICOM had further agreed, Chambers later contended, that conversations would be carried on through Governor-General Scoon, lest the RMC construe negotiations with it as constituting its implied recognition. Specifically, the Caribbean organization had agreed upon the following objectives:

(a)   the immediate establishment of a broad-based civilian government of national reconciliation whose composition was acceptable to the Governor-General. The primary function of that Government would be the putting into place of arrangements for the holding of elections at the earliest possible date;

(b)   acceptance of a fact-finding mission comprising eminent nationals of CARICOM states;

(c)   the putting into place of arrangements to ensure the safety of nationals of other countries in Grenada and/or their evacuation where desired;

(d)   the acceptance of the deployment in Grenada of a peace-keeping force, comprising contingents contributed by CARICOM countries.[66]

After the conclusion of the formal deliberations, Charles, Seaga, Bird and Tull convened in secret caucus. Clearly, the CARICOM meeting had not gone as favorably as had been hoped: their colleagues seemed loath to use force. Until 4:00 A.M., therefore, the four considered how best they could bring plans for a military solution back to the forefront of CARICOM deliberations later that Sunday morning. From Bridgetown, Prime Minister Adams telephoned them to offer his own advice. Presumably, the Caribbean "hawks" now agreed that plans for intervention should proceed irrespective of any CARICOM decision.[67]

After breakfast on Sunday, the Caribbean Community reconvened an hour later than had been scheduled. Apparently, discussions with the U.S. Ambassador to Trinidad and Tobago had delayed the arrival of the representatives of Jamaica, Barbados and the OECS states.[68] Once the meeting began, certain heads of government "for the first time stated that there was no consensus on proposals." Instead, Eugenia Charles immediately placed the OECS agreed sanctions before the meeting for discussion, while Seaga resurrected a proposal he had made at the earlier Ocho Rios summit for a restructuring of CARICOM. After some discussion, a tougher line was ultimately "adopted."[69] Representatives from all Caribbean Community states but Guyana approved a package of sanctions similar to those that earlier had been accepted by the OECS. The measures were designed to isolate Grenada politically and to exert economic pressure upon the RMC. Of later significance, CARICOM had specifically supported the OECS cessation of all sea and air communication links with Grenada. Hence, all Leeward Islands Air Transport flights to Grenada would be suspended.[70]

Saturday and Sunday on Grenada

On the weekend of October 22 and 23, while critical meetings were being held in Washington, Port-of-Spain, and Bridgetown, the Revolutionary Military Council on Grenada was becoming increasingly anxious about the prospect of an invasion by the United States, and with some justification. General Hudson Austin, Lieutenant Colonel Ewart Layne, Major Leon "Bogo" Cornwall, and their colleagues knew that a U.S. naval task force had been diverted toward Grenada, that discussions about the Grenada situation were being held on Trinidad, and that the presence of American citizens could provide the United States with a ready justification for intervention.[71]   Perhaps even more unsettling, they learned Saturday afternoon that Fidel Castro, a close ally of Grenada since the revolution in 1979, had rejected as "impossible and unthinkable" the sending of Cuban reinforcements to Grenada.[72]   At the same time, Cuban Ambassador Julian Torres Rizo had also expressed Castro's advice to Austin and Layne: punish those responsible for Bishop's death and offer every facility for the evacuation of American, British, and foreign nationals.[73]   To follow Castro's first bit of advice would, of course, be impossible.

Given the precarious position in which they found themselves that weekend, the Revolutionary Military Council pursued a number of steps apparently designed to assuage the fears of foreign governments, especially those of the United States.[74]   Early Saturday, for example, arrangements were made for the reception of three diplomats: Kenneth Kurze and Linda Flohr from the American Embassy in Bridgetown; and David Montgomery, the British Deputy High Commissioner.[75]   At 6:40 P.M. that Saturday, Major Chris Stroude read the Council's "Statement of Intention" on Radio Free Grenada.   "A new cabinet will be appointed within ten to fourteen days," Stroude announced.   Moreover, the RMC pledged, "efforts made recently to improve relations with the United States Government will continue."[76]   Finally, the Council ordered Saturday that the American students be treated with the utmost consideration by the PRA.   Vehicles and escorts were provided to shuttle them between their two campuses.[77]   Indeed, "throughout the curfew period, Austin and other high-ranking officers repeatedly inquired about the welfare of the students, promising their safety and saying they could leave if they wanted."[78]   These efforts at improving the RMC's public image ultimately proved unconvincing to Reagan administration officials, however.   Austin and his colleagues were deemed untrustworthy.[79]

Late Saturday morning, October 22, Kurze, Flohr and Montgomery shared an Aeroservices flight from Barbados to Grenada.[80]   The trip would be the first official visit to Grenada by Americans since Bishop's death, although other earlier unofficial ones may also have been attempted.[81]   The diplomats' chartered plane arrived at Pearl's Airport around 12:45 P.M. Saturday, after a flight of perhaps forty minutes.[82] With Kurze and Flohr in one car and Montgomery in a second, the three representatives were driven to St. George's by soldiers loyal to the RMC. As the two vehicles proceeded along the bumpy road into town, Kurze noticed that the soldier sitting next to his driver was brandishing a machine gun.   On a perhaps less disquieting note, he observed that Grenadians were standing outside their homes, though in compliance with General Austin's curfew none had ventured into the streets.[83]

Upon their afternoon arrival at St. George's Medical School, Kurze and Flohr conferred with Vice Chancellor Geoffrey Bourne and his staff. Then, at around 6:00 P.M., they spoke to the American students on the island.   Kurze would later recall:

> [The students] were in a state of *panic*. We explained that grave events had occurred, that the area was in crisis, and that no one was sure where things would lead. We emphasized to them ... that no evacuation had been ordered, nor could one be arranged without the cooperation of the RMC. So we told them (and some visiting parents and friends) to stay calm and stay in touch with Bourne's office.[84]

After the conclusion of this meeting, Kurze and Flohr went to the Ross Point Inn, where each dined and thereafter retired for the evening.

Meanwhile on Saturday, David Montgomery toured the island by automobile with John Kelly, the British representative on Grenada. During his brief visit, the Deputy High Commissioner would find that between thirty and forty British residents wished to leave.   Upon his Sunday evening return to Barbados, he would assess the Grenada situation as "calm, tense and pretty volatile."[85].

Around 10:30 A.M. Sunday, Kurze and Flohr met at the Ross Point Inn with Leon Cornwall,[86] former Grenadian Ambassador to Cuba and probably second-in-command to General Austin.[87]   During their forty-five minute meeting, which was also attended by Dr. Geoffrey Bourne, Vice Chancellor of St. George's Medical School, and by British officials David Montgomery and John Kelly, Cornwall repeatedly offered assurances of the American students' safety.[88]   When Bourne suggested a two-week school holiday that would permit all the students to return home and to "come back when things settled down," Cornwall reportedly said that the proposal "wasn't a bad idea."[89]

The principal difficulty encountered during Sunday morning's discussions, and those that evening, stemmed from one question: How might the safe departure of *all* the American students be ensured? From the beginning, Cornwall had maintained that anyone wishing to leave could do so on "regularly scheduled" flights. Charter flights would not be permitted, however. The U.S. envoys pointed out that LIAT was not currently flying and that the largest craft capable of landing at Pearls airport could transport only forty-six persons. Moreover, the road to Pearls was long and difficult. Hence, an evacuation by airplane would be too time-consuming to assure security. Instead, the diplomats suggested an evacuation by U.S. naval ship, to be loaded by marine landing craft from Grenada's main harbor. Cornwall rejected the American recommendation as tantamount to allowing a military occupation of his state.[90]

On Sunday afternoon, two more American envoys were dispatched to Grenada from the U.S. Embassy at Bridgetown: Consul General James Budeit and Gary Chafin. They came with General Austin's approval to replace Ken Kurze, whose mother had just died.[91] As their airplane approached the island, however, the American diplomats were denied permission to land. General Austin's secretary, it was eventually learned, had misdialed the airport to alert it of the Americans' imminent arrival. At length, the problem was resolved with Dr. Bourne's assistance, and Budeit and Chafin were permitted to land.[92] While the newly-arrived American embassy officials rode into St. George's, Ken Kurze and David Montgomery flew back to Barbados. Upon their arrival at Grantley Adams Airport, the two diplomats were immediately swarmed by reporters frustrated at not being permitted into Grenada by the RMC and eager for any news on the developing Grenada situation.[93]

That Sunday evening on Grenada, American diplomats met again with Cornwall to discuss the question of evacuation. Cornwall now seemed disturbingly evasive. The United States, he repeated, would not be permitted to bring in charter airplane flights. Moreover, a nearby Cunard liner would not be allowed to dock in St. George's.[94] At some point that day he had reportedly agreed, at least in principle, to a suggestion to bring the cruise ship into port and to load it there.[95] If the United States decided to evacuate its citizens, the RMC would not waive customs inspection or any other technical details that customarily were relaxed during rapid evacuation procedures. "If it took hours or even days to process all 1,000 Americans, very well, they would have to wait."[96]

In retrospect, Cornwall's intransigence seems likely to have been a deliberate, if ultimately unsuccessful attempt, to stall. By Sunday evening, the RMC apparently feared that a peaceful evacuation would serve only as a prelude to American intervention.[97] The Cunard cruise ship had requested destroyer escort. Might that military vessel be used for invasion of Grenada once all the Americans were safe?

Indicative of the Council's perception of the situation, Radio Free Grenada repeated at 6:10 P.M. Sunday a communique reporting that the OECS had decided to "send military forces to invade Grenada," that some countries had "already sent armed forces to Barbados as a jumping off point for this invasion," and that an invasion was "expected tonight."[98] That same Sunday evening, the RMC sent a diplomatic note to the U.S. Embassy in Barbados restating its commitment to guaranteeing the safety of the U.S. nationals and reaffirming its intention not to use force against any other state. The note added that the RMC "would view any invasion of our country whether based on the decision of the CARICOM Governments or by any other government as a rude violation of Grenada's sovereignty and of international law."[99] The Revolutionary Military Council also attempted to transmit a telex to the British Foreign Office in London. Including a copy of the message it had dispatched to the American Embassy, the RMC asked the British Government to attempt to forestall the expected American invasion. Unfortunately for the Council, it had sent its missive to a telex number that had been reallocated to Scanplast, a London plastics company.[100]

That same Sunday, while the RMC fretted about its future, David Montgomery visited Sir Paul Scoon at Government House in St. George's.[101] There, in the Governor-General's Garden, the two men spoke privately for about an hour that afternoon.[102] According to the British Foreign Affairs Committee, which would subsequently interview both Scoon and Montgomery, "the details of the conversation between Mr. Montgomery and Sir Paul [were] not made available to us." Nevertheless, Sir Paul had been "evidently worried about the situation of his country." Despite his obvious concerns, the Committee would conclude, the Grenadian Governor-General "did not make any request to the Deputy High Commissioner for help."[103] Since such a request almost certainly would have been ignored anyway, Scoon probably did not ask Montgomery that Sunday afternoon for the assistance of Britain *per se*. As we shall see, however, he apparently did ask then for outside help.

The Beirut Massacre and Its Repercussions

Sunday, October 23, was a hectic day in the Caribbean and a tragic one in the Middle East. It was also arguably the most challenging day of the Reagan Presidency.[104] At 2:27 A.M., Robert McFarlane awakened the President with a phone call, just as he had done the day before. "We've had a terrible attack on the Marines with a substantial loss of life," McFarlane reported. "I believe we should get together."[105]

The U.S. Marine headquarters in Beirut had fallen victim to a terrorist truck bomb.[106] According to a flash message sent to Washington from Beirut :

> A large explosion at BLT 1/8 Hq Bldg collapsed the roof and leveled the building. Large numbers of dead and injured ... BLT Hq destroyed. Amplifying info to follow.[107]

Early reports estimated that more than 100 members of the Twenty-Fourth Marine Amphibious Unit (MAU) had been killed in the suicide attack.[108] After hearing this stunning news, Reagan called General Paul X. Kelley at 3:00 A.M. to discuss further the situation.[109] Once he had finished speaking with the Marine Commandant, the President spent two hours in conference with Shultz and McFarlane in the Eisenhower Cottage. "As dawn approached, the news from Beirut became grimmer and grimmer," Reagan later remembered.[110] At 6:30 A.M. the President left the Augusta compound by motorcade.[111] Given the extremely grave circumstances, Reagan could no longer remain in Georgia.[112]

Reagan departed for Washington with Shultz and McFarlane at 7:10 A.M.[113] Within an hour, Air Force One was making its final approach to Andrews Air Force Base.[114] Recalls George Shultz: "We were wheels down ... at 8:20 A.M. as word came in that the high-rise building housing the French contingent in the multinational force (MNF) also had been hit by a terrorist suicide bomber."[115]

From Andrews the President flew in Marine One to the White House, where his helicopter landed on the south lawn at 8:38 A.M. in darkness and pouring rain.[116] The grim weather reflected well the prevailing mood. While clasping his wife Nancy's hand in his left hand and an umbrella in his right, he made a brief statement to the press. The President spoke without notes, as the bareheaded McFarlane and Shultz stood behind him[117]:

> I know there are no words that can express our sorrow and grief over the loss of those splendid men and the injury to so many others. I know there are no words, also, that can ease the burden of grief for the families of those young men.
>
> Likewise, there are no words to properly express our outrage and, I think, the outrage of all Americans at the despicable act, following as it does on the one perpetrated several months ago, in the spring, that took the lives of scores of people at our Embassy in that same city, in Beirut.
>
> But I think we should all recognize that these deeds make so evident the bestial nature of those who assume power if they could have their way and drive us out of that area that we must be more determined than ever that they cannot take over that vital and strategic area of the Earth or, for that matter, any other part of the Earth.[118]

Ronald Reagan would spend much of the day in a series of meetings concerned both with Lebanon and Grenada. Among other things, he would have to decide whether the Beirut massacre should derail invasion plans.

From around 8:40 until 10:40 A.M., Reagan participated in the first of Sunday's two formal meetings of the National Security Planning Group (NSPG).[119] All of President Reagan's senior advisers were present: Vice President Bush; Secretary of Defense Weinberger; Secretary of State Shultz; National Security Adviser McFarlane; Admiral Poindexter; acting DCI McMahon; Chief of Staff James A. Baker III; presidential assistant Michael Deaver; and General Vessey.[120] As Reagan entered the White House Situation Room, he looked at his Secretary of Defense and said, "Remind me never to go away again. Look what happens."[121] The subject of the National Security Council meeting would be "Beirut, then Grenada."[122]

In the first hour or so, Reagan reviewed unrelenting bulletins from Lebanon. Reports of American casualties mounted steadily.[123] For the Marine Corps, the Beirut bombing would inflict their greatest single-day loss of life since the assault on Iwo Jima in 1945.[124] "Every time someone talked casualties, you could see that it took something out of [the President]," Michael Deaver would later recall. "His brow was never unfurrowed."[125]   Another White House aide would describe Reagan then as having been "controlled but furious."[126]

At length, the NSPG meeting turned to a consideration of Grenada.[127] Eagleburger, Motley, Ikle, Menges, and North were called into the Situation Room.[128]   The "Grenada group" gave Reagan an update on the military and political situation, including a status report on combat deployment and military planning. Presumably Reagan was now told that the Marines were steaming toward Grenada and that an Army airborne assault was being planned.

Then the President probed the various meeting participants, making certain that he had everyone's honest opinion about the contemplated American action. He now had carefully to weigh whether the Lebanon tragedy should affect the preliminary decision he had made Saturday.[129] An invasion of Grenada might well lead to more spilled American blood. Reportedly, President Reagan was inclined toward a resolute response: "If this was right yesterday, it's right today, and we shouldn't let the act of a couple of terrorists dissuade us from going ahead."[130]   Reagan apparently *did not* yet make a final decision to send in American troops, however.

At the end of the NSPG meeting, General Vessey asked for a private meeting with Reagan, Weinberger, Shultz, McFarlane, and McMahon.[131]   Accordingly, the Situation Room was emptied except for these six individuals. The JCS Chairman now cautioned about the risks that would be faced by the Special Forces on crucial pre-invasion missions. These operations, as we have seen, would include rescuing Sir Paul Scoon and determining landing sites for the Marines and Rangers.[132]

At 2:45 P.M. Sunday, Secretary Shultz met in his office with Rear Admiral Jonathan Howe, the State Department's Director of Political-Military Affairs.[133]   Here, Howe stressed that if the United States were to take forcible action in Grenada, it must do so without delay. Explained Howe to Shultz:

> Timing is important, and we are losing time. Some reconnaissance flights have been sent out. There are some advance CIA elements under way. But the Pentagon officers are still saying that if we invade, we have to do it right. They are reflecting Cap Weinberger's mood.[134]

Shultz believed that Weinberger's pleas for more preparation time and for more troops reflected the Secretary of Defense's desire to avoid a military operation: "I knew this was the counsel of no action at all."[135]

At 4:00 P.M., after a much-needed afternoon nap and a telephone conversation with Lebanese President Amin Gemayel,[136] Reagan reconvened the NSPG.[137] As in the morning session, the group focused first upon the situation in Lebanon, apparently considering the possibility of American retaliation.[138] At one point the President attempted to read aloud the letter of a father whose Marine son had been deployed in Lebanon, but Reagan was unable to finish it. He seemed then, thought Michael Deaver, a most "tired and unhappy man."[139]

Around 5:00 P.M., Eagleburger, Motley, Ikle, Menges, and North, who had been waiting next door in McFarlane's office, were again brought in for a one-hour meeting with Reagan and his top advisers. It was reportedly only now that serious attention was given to Grenada.[140] The discussion focused upon at least two themes: the possibility that American citizens would be held by the Grenadians; and the political risks of an invasion. Reagan's overriding concern seems now to have been over possible hostages. One administration official would recall, "The president and those around him thought it was risky to abort the operation. There was concern that news of it might leak out and that Americans would be seized before the Marines could land."[141] Given this potentially disastrous prospect, Reagan is said then to have lamented, "I'm no better off than Jimmy Carter."[142]

The President had also to weigh the political effects of a failed rescue effort: if the operation were unsuccessful, the Lebanon tragedy would only amplify the negative consequences. Reagan made clear that he recognized this unfortunate possibility but that he also felt an obligation both to the U.S. citizens in danger and to those Caribbean states that had sought American assistance.[143] When General Vessey asked if there were a firm decision to land U.S. troops, however, Reagan replied, "not yet."[144]

At some point during Sunday's deliberations, but probably during those that afternoon, Assistant Secretary Motley suggested to the President that Grenada's transition to democracy might be eased if the United States were to establish an embassy on the island and to appoint an ambassador to serve there. Motley urged that his deputy, Tony Gillespie, who was now on Barbados, be appointed and that the normally lengthy approval process be expedited. Seeing merit in the Assistant Secretary's recommendation, Reagan gave his assent.[145]

After the discussion of Grenada concluded around 6:00 P.M., North, Menges and several others waited outside the Situation Room for another hour while Reagan and the foreign policy cabinet had a final meeting about both Lebanon and Grenada. According to Menges' account, there was some speculation now by those outside about whether or not the Grenada mission would be undertaken given the changed circumstances. While Menges hoped "Urgent Fury" would proceed, a pessimistic Ollie North believed that it would be canceled in the name of retaliation in Lebanon, which would then also not happen. In North's opinion, the JCS "simply did not want to use U.S. military forces in limited combat operations."[146]

At 7:00 P.M., the outcome of the final NSPG deliberations was learned: the Grenada operation would take place as scheduled.[147] "[H]aving had the advice of all his advisers," Reagan had made what Shultz would later describe as a "tentative decision" shortly before 7:00 to proceed.[148] The President's determination seems to have been, in effect, a confirmation of his initial decision made early Saturday morning.[149] "The legitimacy of [the OECS] request, plus my own concern for our citizens, dictated my decision," Reagan would later explain in a televised address on October 27.[150]

That Sunday evening, several hours before an OECS written request for military assistance would be presented to American diplomats in Barbados, the President signed an NSDD authorizing the Grenada operation to take place no later than dawn, October 25.[151] This action did not constitute Reagan's ultimate invasion decision, however. As has already been noted, the administration "retained the ability to halt final implementation until the last moment."[152] If the situation on Grenada changed dramatically, or if, on the basis of his special mission to Barbados, Ambassador McNeil vigorously opposed American military action, "Urgent Fury" could apparently still have been canceled. Nevertheless, by Sunday night, the invasion decision seemed "almost set in concrete."[153]

At 10:00 P.M. Sunday, a CH-53 helicopter returned from Antigua to the Marine amphibious force in the Caribbean. Aboard the American aircraft were liaison officers from CINCLANT and subordinate commands. These officers brought additional intelligence information about Grenada and a draft operations order for the assault on the island:

Vice Admiral Joseph Metcalf III, the Commander, Second Fleet, would be in overall command of the Grenada operation, with a tactical designator of Commander, Task Force 120. He assigned to the amphibious force, now designated Task Force 124, the mission of seizing the Pearls airport and the port of Grenville, and of neutralizing any opposing forces in the area. Simultaneously, Army Rangers (Task Force 121) — together with elements of the 82nd Airborne Division (Task Force 123) — would secure points at the southern end of the island, including the nearly completed jet airfield under construction near Point Salines. A carrier battle group (Task Force 20.5) and Air Force elements would support the ground forces.[154]

Around midnight on October 23, less than thirty hours before the scheduled H-hour, the Marine battalion landing team and the squadron began planning for their assault on Grenada. At midnight, Lieutenant Colonel Smith, Commanding Officer of BLT 2/8, made a brief notation in his journal: "It's on."[155] Earlier that evening in Washington, Michael Deaver had admonished the President to "have a good night's rest tonight." Flashing a tired smile, Reagan had responded, "Are you kidding?"[156]

The McNeil Mission

The Ambassador is briefed

Around 7:00 A.M. Sunday morning, Frank McNeil was picked up at his hotel and escorted to the State Department by a young Foreign Service Officer on the Grenada Task Force. While en route to Foggy Bottom, McNeil was told that he had been summoned because of the dangerous situation that had developed on the island of Grenada: the Ambassador's earlier suspicions about the rationale behind State's Saturday afternoon telephone call were now confirmed.[157]

From around 8:00 until 9:00 A.M., while the President's helicopter was transporting Reagan, Shultz and McFarlane from Andrews to the White House, McNeil attended a RIG meeting chaired by Motley in the State Department's windowless "crisis room." Among the dozen or so others attending were George Crist, Oliver North, Michael Kozak, Richard Brown, and L. Craig Johnstone.[158] Here, McNeil was informed that due to the gravity of the OECS request, Reagan wanted another assessment of the Grenada situation before making a "go/no go" decision.[159] In a whimsical allusion to the "Mission Impossible" television series, Motley told McNeil: "Your mission, should you choose to accept it, will be to go to Barbados." McNeil was to probe the Caribbean leaders, to make certain of their commitment to invasion. "It's not every day that you get this sort of request," Motley observed.[160] McNeil was apparently also told now that the earliest the United States could invade would likely be Tuesday, October 25.[161]

After McNeil had given his assent to the proposed mission, the former Ambassador to Costa Rica received enumerated instructions and a list of essential points to be included in any formal OECS written request for assistance.[162] This latter document had been hastily prepared by Michael Kozak's legal team, apparently on Saturday afternoon.[163] McNeil examined it and told Motley that he believed the outline was unsatisfactory since it might be construed as a Washington-prepared document of invitation. Despite his reluctance, the President's Special Emissary ultimately decided to bring the list with him.[164]

For about a half hour after the RIG "crisis meeting," McNeil met with Eagleburger, Motley, Jonathan Howe, and perhaps a few other administration officials. The Ambassador reviewed his instructions and suggested other questions that he might ask the Caribbean leaders.[165] McNeil had been asked specifically to make "his own" independent evaluation of the situation. Eagleburger, who had just spoken by phone with Secretary Shultz at the White House, told McNeil that no final Grenada decision had yet been made and emphasized that McNeil should give no hint to the Caribbeans about his own recommendations. The tragedy in Beirut might derail an invasion.[166] McNeil would later write: "When I left I sensed that we would probably not intervene. The White House, shocked by the loss of 250 Marines in the Beirut bombing, feared the political consequences, and the Department of Defense was reluctant at the least, wanting more time to prepare."[167]

While Eagleburger and Motley sped to the White House for Sunday's first NSPG meeting, McNeil was rushed with General Crist to Andrews AFB where the two boarded an unmarked jet aircraft. With them in the Gulfstream were: Air Force Lieutenant Colonel Connelly, an assistant to General Crist; Larry Rossin, who would later participate in the attempt to rescue Sir Paul Scoon; and a member of the CIA.[168] As the aircraft took off around 10:15 A.M., McNeil agreed with Crist that the two would attempt to work harmoniously.[169]

During the five-hour flight to Barbados, which stopped once for fuel at Homestead AFB in Miami, McNeil reviewed his instructions with

General Crist. At length, McNeil developed a checklist of approximately twenty-eight points he wished to address in his imminent meeting in Bridgetown.[170] Around 5:00 P.M. Barbados time — about the same time that Reagan was reconvening the NSPG in Washington — the Americans arrived at Grantley Adams Airport and were greeted by Tony Gillespie.

McNeil stopped very briefly at the Sands Hotel, where he was met by Ambassador Bish, to drop off his bags. Unknown to McNeil then, he would not return to his accommodations until after 3:15 A.M. Monday morning.[171] He was next driven to Government House, which for many years had overlooked Carlisle Bay and which today was well protected by Barbadian police.[172]

A marathon meeting

Around 6:15 P.M., while Reagan and his advisers continued their Beirut/Grenada deliberations in the White House Situation Room, McNeil's marathon meeting with the Caribbean leaders began in the Cabinet Room of Government House.[173] Among those present for the four-hour meeting were: Prime Ministers Eugenia Charles, Tom Adams, John Compton, and Edward Seaga; Foreign Ministers Louis Tull and Neville Gallimore; Brigadier General Rudyard E. C. Lewis; and the Americans, General Crist, Tony Gillespie, Ambassador Bish and Kim Flower.[174]

After being introduced by Ambassador Bish, McNeil told those assembled that the President had not yet decided how the United States would respond to the OECS invitation. He then began to pose those questions which he had helped prepare that Sunday morning and afternoon.[175] Reportedly among them: Were the United States citizens on Grenada in genuine danger? Was resistance to the hardline faction growing on the island? Was a civil war on Grenada likely? In case of such a conflict, what was the probability that the communist forces would prevail? How would the Soviets and Cubans react in the event of a civil war?[176]

The Caribbean leadership told McNeil, whom Bish judged to be rather skeptical at first,[177] that the Americans on Grenada appeared vulnerable, especially the medical students. Moreover, they submitted, resistance on the island was growing and a bloody civil war seemed likely.[178] In that event, the Cubans and Soviets would probably become involved. Eventually, the West Indians feared, democracy would be at risk throughout the region.[179] In support of this last point, Eugenia Charles contended:

> Barbados and Jamaica, they're bigger than the other islands, but they still don't have much of a military force, not one ready to withstand air attacks and the army of Cuban advisers amassing in Grenada. The People's Revolutionary Army has access to an air strip more than 9,000 feet long, which the Cubans have been building for some time, clearly for military use. A thousand armed Cuban advisers are there to help them. That's what its all about: to point a dagger at the eastern Caribbean states.[180]

Ultimately, McNeil would conclude that the Caribbean leaders "were convinced in their own minds" that military action was necessary. He judged that "they had a good sense of what was happening on Grenada," better than U.S. intelligence had.[181]

At least an hour into the discussion, McNeil explained to the Caribbean leaders that if the United States were to act, it could not do so without a prior written request. McNeil deliberately had delayed introducing this point so as not to exaggerate the likelihood of American action. The leaders apparently had already been apprised of this requirement by Gillespie,[182] however, and asked McNeil about the list of required points he had brought with him from Washington. He replied that he did not think it very good and said he believed that they might compose a far better formal request.[183] After allowing them to peruse it, McNeil set the American document aside.[184] Barbadian Foreign Minister Louis Tull and Jamaican Foreign Minister Neville Gallimore were sent to Prime Minister's Adams' office, one floor below the Cabinet Room, to prepare their own invitation of American assistance. They would return in about forty minutes with a draft that the group quickly approved and sent out to be typed.[185] Meanwhile, Prime Minister Adams explained to McNeil and Gillespie in painstaking detail why he believed the Organization of Eastern Caribbean States specifically had authority in this matter and why it was acting in accordance with its charter.[186]

At length, Frank McNeil turned to a final concern of the State Department: How would the Grenadian people react to an invasion by the United States? Would the American restoration of order be well received or resented on the island?[187] The Caribbeans assured McNeil and his colleagues that there would be no "Yankee go home" signs.

During the October 19 demonstrations, they pointed out, pro-American and anticommunist signs had been very common. The English-speaking Grenadians, far from harboring anti-American sentiments, were in fact very pro-American.[188]

Throughout the lengthy meeting, in accordance with his explicit instructions, McNeil stressed that Washington had not yet made a decision. Indeed, as Eugenia Charles would later chide him, the President's special emissary had emphasized the point perhaps as many as five separate times.[189] Now, as his discussion with the Caribbeans came to an end, he and Tony Gillespie repeated that the leaders should not presume that the United States would join in the OECS collective action. The Americans pledged, however, that they would impress upon Washington the need for quick action one way or another.[190] Unknown to McNeil and Gillespie at the time, back in Washington Reagan had already made a "tentative" invasion decision.

After the meeting

At 10:00 P.M., immediately after their lengthy meeting had ended, Frank McNeil, Tony Gillespie and Kim Flower departed for the American Embassy. Meanwhile, at McNeil's suggestion, General Crist met with Caribbean military officials for approximately another two hours to discuss a "contingency plan" for invasion of Grenada. Like his diplomatic colleagues had done, the Marine General made clear that American planning for military action did not guarantee American participation, only American consideration.[191] Crist's objective was to ensure that in case of an invasion, Caribbean troops would quickly be introduced to the island, thus facilitating an early U.S. withdrawal.[192]

For the next hour or so, McNeil, Gillespie and Flower reviewed the most recent intelligence on the Grenada situation and presumably examined the RMC's diplomatic cable to the United States sent earlier that evening. They also spoke by telephone with Gary Chafin, who had flown with Gary Budeit to Grenada that Sunday afternoon.[193] Contrary to Peter Bourne's later suggestion that only about ten percent of the St. George's students wished to leave, Chafin reported that the majority of the American students were very much afraid and desirous of rescue.[194] After an initial assessment, and earlier phone calls from the State Department to which he deliberately did not respond, McNeil sent a preliminary cable to Washington.[195]

In the very brief cable, he concluded that the Revolutionary Military Council was convinced that the United States would invade Grenada that Sunday evening. "The Grenadians," the Ambassador wryly observed, "have put two and two together and come up with three-and-a-half."[196] The United States had two options, McNeil argued: either take military action quickly or present the RMC with a multifaceted ultimatum. If this second alternative were taken, McNeil believed, the RMC would not likely respond positively.[197]

Around 1:00 A.M., after General Crist's return to the embassy and further discussion, Gillespie and McNeil finally contacted Assistant Secretary Motley by secure telephone. McNeil reported that the OECS invitation had been formalized and then repeated what he had observed in his cable: the RMC was apparently convinced that the United States was about to invade Grenada. Moreover, the Grenadians seemed increasingly to view the American citizens on the island as pawns.[198] Accordingly, McNeil recommended that the United States take prompt military action to ensure surprise and minimize casualties. McNeil would later write:

> I recommended sending in the troops, so long as it was done quickly before surprise was lost. In so doing, I was mindful of Teheran, where colleagues had languished as hostages for so long. It is far easier to prevent a hostage situation than to deal with it once it is consummated, and I judged the danger to the students was growing. I also found the reasoning of the OECS leaders entirely persuasive as to the dangers to the neighboring small islands if the thugs who massacred Bishop and his followers kept power. But ... the make-or-break factor for me was the students.[199]

The Scoon invitation

Sometime after McNeil and Gillespie had spoken with Motley, perhaps around 2:00 A.M., Tom Adams called the American Embassy. Because Ambassador Bish was already asleep, Kim Flower took the call. The Barbadian Premier told Flower that Giles Bullard, the British High Commissioner, had conveyed to him some very important news: in a meeting at the Governor-General's residence that Sunday afternoon, Sir Paul Scoon had asked David Montgomery, the Deputy High Commissioner, to relay a request for external assistance.[200] Scoon would have sought outside help through more direct channels, Adams explained, but he had feared that he would have been killed had he done so.[201]

If Prime Minister Adams' report was an accurate one, then the United States had apparently just been invited to take action by the Grenadian Head of State.[202] Significantly, word of the Scoon invitation had been received by American authorities *after* Reagan's "tentative" decision to invade, *after* the OECS written request had been made, and even *after* McNeil's invasion recommendation. Flower promptly relayed word of Sir Paul Scoon's invitation to McNeil and Gillespie. McNeil, in turn, called Motley for the second time that early Monday morning.[203] Michael Kozak and his assistants, who would continue working through the night,[204] were quickly apprised of Adams' claim that Scoon had sought outside assistance.[205] Accordingly, Mary McLeod, the Assistant Legal Adviser for Politico-Military Affairs, began to examine in depth Grenadian constitutional law. In the event that the Adams' story were true, the legal status of the Governor-General had accurately to be ascertained.[206]

Assistant Secretary Motley, among other Reagan administration officials, was somewhat skeptical of the hawkish Adams' story. Although he could not be certain of its accuracy,[207] he would ultimately decide to "take the Prime Minister at his word." The invitation by the Grenadian Governor-General provided a "nice legal justification" for American action. Even without such an invitation, however, Motley would have favored an American invasion.[208] If the events of Sunday evening are any indication, so, too, would have most of the Reagan administration.

Final Preparations

Monday, October 24, was a day dominated by invasion preparation, not policy deliberation. President Reagan's NSDD signature on Sunday evening and McNeil's subsequent recommendations from Barbados seem virtually to have guaranteed that the United States would take action.[209] Now, the Reagan administration focused principally upon the political and military aspects of "Urgent Fury" and on informing the Caribbean, British and U.S. Congressional leaderships, but not the administration's spokespersons.

Less than a month before, Ronald Reagan had declared October 24 "United Nations Day."[210] With rhetorical flourish, the President had then proclaimed: "The United Nations remains today ... an institution uniquely endowed to promote international political, economic, social and technical cooperation."[211] Given the actual circumstances on October 24, 1983 — the U.N.'s thirty-eighth birthday — such presidential discourse might well have been viewed as ironic or even hypocritical. According to Allan Gerson, U.N. Ambassador Jeane Kirkpatrick's Legal Adviser, the Reagan administration had not given "a second's thought ... to bringing the crisis in Grenada to the United Nations."[212] Gerson noted in his 1991 memoir:

> Advance consultations would ... have telegraphed U.S. intentions without any offsetting gain. The U.S. medical students who were in a precarious position would have been further endangered. So, too, would Grenada's Governor-General, who was communicating with the United States in secret.[213]

With a bit of hyperbole, he concluded:

> Of course, in some vague sense, international law might have been declared the victor had the notice and consultation requirements of the UN and OAS Charters been complied with, but *no one in the administration thought in those terms*. The last American president to consider the ends of international law above national interests was President Dwight D. Eisenhower in the Suez Crisis of 1956.[214]

Monday in Norfolk

At 7:00 A.M., Admiral Wesley McDonald convened a final military commanders' conference in the upstairs briefing room of his CINCLANT headquarters in Norfolk, Virginia.[215] Seated at a lengthy table beside a map of Grenada were: Vice Admiral Joseph Metcalf; Major General H. Norman Schwarzkopf; and the commanders of the Army elements of Metcalf's task force, Major General Edward L. Trobaugh of the 82nd Airborne, and Major General Richard A. Sholtes of Special Operations. Also in attendance were Deputy Assistant Secretary of State L. Craig Johnstone and Commodore Jack N. Darby, the JCS Deputy Director for Plans and Policy. Both had been dispatched from Washington in a highly unusual coordination.[216]

The conference began with a detailed description of the planned Grenada operation, a "coup de main" or "one-punch knockout."[217] Next, briefers addressed a series of questions about the nature of the anticipated opposition on Grenada. General Schwarzkopf and his colleagues were assured then that there was no cause for worry: once the PRA recognized that American troops were involved in the operation, they would promptly surrender; the Grenadian antiaircraft gunners were poorly trained and did not represent a threat; and the Cuban workers would not fight. According to Schwarzkopf's memoir, the invasion plan

> called for the Rangers to drive to the Cuban compound and announce, "We are here to reinstall the legitimate government of Grenada. You will not be hurt. Please stay here while we get this thing over with."[218]

Major Generals Schwarzkopf and Sholtes were less sanguine than some of their colleagues. Schwarzkopf wondered to himself whether the Cubans might in fact fight. Sholtes, meanwhile, explicitly indicated his concern about the method of deployment for Ranger forces arriving at Grenada. Though they could parachute in if required, it would be preferable for the Ranger's transport planes simply to land at Point Salines runway. Since a Navy SEAL team had already been lost Sunday night in a failed attempt to assess that airfield's condition, Sholtes advocated a twenty-four-hour postponement of the invasion to improve intelligence. This proposal sparked a vigorous exchange of views. At length, Admiral McDonald interjected:

> I can't believe what I'm hearing around this table. All you're going to face is a bunch of Grenadians. They're going to fall apart the minute they see our combat power. Why are we making such a big deal of this?[219]

In the ensuing silence, State Department representative Craig Johnstone reportedly suggested that he would oppose a delay until October 26: "The Organization of Eastern Caribbean States, which asked us to intervene, is a shaky coalition at best. There's no telling how long it's going to support this thing."[220] With this assertion, McDonald was convinced that the operation must proceed on Tuesday,[221] although at Sholtes' instigation he shifted the "H-hour" from 2:00 A.M. until 4:00 A.M. to permit further reconnaissance efforts.

During the course of Monday's meeting at Norfolk, at least two other important issues were addressed. First, Johnstone expressed to the military what the political parameters of "Urgent Fury" would be, and how the mission's success or failure might be measured. He specifically explained why the rescue of Sir Paul Scoon was politically significant. Second, at the meeting's close, the military commanders discussed how the press would be treated during the operation. Recalls Schwarzkopf, "We agreed that we would open Grenada to reporters at five o'clock the next afternoon, because by then Grenada would be ours."[222]

Monday in Washington

That Monday in Washington, probably in the morning but perhaps the early afternoon, Admiral Poindexter convened another meeting of the Crisis Preplanning Group. Here, CPPG members reviewed the current situation on Grenada and operational plans. According to Menges, although the American students "remained surrounded, they were not under any tighter control." Hence, the planned rescue operation still appeared feasible.[223]

The President's day, meanwhile, was a busy one. "Nancy and I were in a state of grief, made almost speechless by the magnitude of the loss [of Marine lives]," Reagan later recalled. "But I had to go on with my schedule for the day."[224] Accordingly, the President met with: Arthur A. Hartman, U.S. Ambassador to the Soviet Union; President Gnassingbe Eyadema of Togo; several members of Congress in a series of photo sessions with their constituents; and a group of Republican Senators to discuss issues concerning women.[225] In addition, at some point during the day he made telephone calls to "Tip" O'Neill and Howard Baker to discuss the situation in Lebanon; he also received diplomatic credentials from Ambassador George Papoulias of Greece and Prince Bandar bin Sultan bin Abd al-Aziz Al Saud, Ambassador of Saudi Arabia.[226] At 1:07 P.M., Reagan spoke at a White House luncheon for regional editors and broadcasters in the State Dining Room. His remarks there on the Lebanon situation were followed by a brief "question-and-answer session."[227]

At noon Monday, Secretary of Defense Weinberger met with General Vessey at the Pentagon.[228] Here, Weinberger authorized the Chairman of the Joint Chiefs to use the 82nd Airborne Division as a backup in the event that U.S. forces encountered more opposition on Grenada than had been anticipated. The Secretary's last words to Vessey before the two shared a ride to the White House were: "Be sure we have enough strength."[229]

Between 2:15-3:30 P.M., President Reagan met in the Cabinet Room with Caspar Weinberger and the Joint Chiefs of Staff[230] in a final, technical planning meeting for the Grenada invasion.[231] The number of individuals participating was restricted because Weinberger and Vessey had decided that only the President and a few others should know the details of the military plans in advance.[232] "Throughout the day," Reagan observed later, "we [had] continued to worry about leaks that could endanger the students."[233] In his 1990 memoir, Weinberger would tersely summarize the Monday afternoon meeting: "The President polled each Chief of Staff and each told him the plan would work; but each said he was concerned about the lack of time to get intelligence, and to rehearse and practice several of the more difficult aspects of the operation."[234] At some point during the course of this discussion, General Vessey reaffirmed an earlier estimate that casualties would be light.[235] Based in part upon the assumptions that Grenadian resistance would be feeble and that the Cubans would not fight, the CINCLANT plan envisioned that "Urgent Fury" would be concluded by around 5:00 P.M. Tuesday.[236]

Information and disinformation

Also on Monday afternoon, McFarlane asked Menges to update the public briefing materials his staffer had prepared Saturday and to make certain that the President and his National Security Adviser had all the information needed to field questions from congressional leaders that Monday night and from the media the next morning.[237] Ironically, about the same time that day, the Reagan administration was already being pressed by the media on the Grenada situation.[238]

CBS White House correspondent Bill Plante came to Larry Speakes "very privately" and told the President's deputy press secretary that he had the makings of a big scoop: it appeared that U.S. forces were assembling in the Caribbean for an invasion of Grenada. Someone from CBS had noticed U.S. helicopters and other signs of military activity on Barbados. "I've got to know," Plante said. "It looks like something's coming down as early as tomorrow."[239] Speakes relayed Plante's query to Admiral Poindexter through Robert Sims, the National Security

Council's press officer. According to Speakes' memoir, Poindexter responded: "Preposterous! Knock it down hard!" In light of this straightforward instruction, Speakes complied, much to his later chagrin.[240] Plante transmitted Speakes' denial to his journalist colleagues in Washington and New York who in turn agreed not to pursue the invasion story.[241]

At 5:45 P.M. Monday, Vice Admiral Joseph Metcalf and his staff arrived on board the aircraft carrier *Guam* by helicopter to assume command of "Joint Task Force 120."[242] About fifteen minutes later, Reagan approved a cable to the eastern Caribbean leaders informing them that the United States would take joint military action with their forces. This presidential message was considered the "final order" to invade.[243]

Also around 6:00 P.M., the White House contacted London to report that President Reagan had "reached a conclusion" that military action was necessary.[244] Robert McFarlane had arranged for the communication. Earlier he had advised the President: "This is going to be something which may create misgivings among allies who never want you to do anything but support NATO, and any time you get very far off that course they begin to worry. So you ought to consult."[245] Though the notion of consultation was "not second nature" to him, Reagan agreed. The President had typically delegated such decisions to his staff members.[246]

Shortly after 6:00 P.M., White House Chief of Staff James Baker and Kenneth M. Duberstein, the President's Congressional liaison, began rounding up key Congressional leaders for a special Grenada briefing that same evening. The five who would be summoned to the White House were: House Speaker Tip O'Neill; Senate Majority Leader Howard Baker; House Majority Leader James C. Wright, Jr.; House Republican leader Robert H. Michel; and Senate Minority Leader Robert C. Byrd.[247]

At 6:45 P.M., O'Neill was in a meeting of a special House task force on Lebanon when his chief adviser, Kirk O'Donnell, called him outside. James Baker was down the hall, O'Donnell explained, and needed to talk privately with the Speaker of the House. Baker spoke directly, "There's a highly confidential meeting with the President at 8:00 tonight." O'Neill declined Baker's offer of Secret Service transport but promised that he would "show up" for the meeting as requested.[248] Meanwhile, the other four Congressional leaders were driven from Capitol Hill in White House limousines and informed that the imminent meeting was "so secret that they couldn't even call their wives and let them know they wouldn't be home for dinner."[249]

At 7:50 P.M. Monday, O'Neill entered the Old Executive Office Building and was taken to the White House basement where coffee was being served. While the rest of O'Neill's colleagues arrived, the President and his advisers continued discussions upstairs in the White House family sitting room.[250] Here, as a fire crackled in the fireplace, the Secretary of Defense reviewed the details of Tuesday morning's invasion plan, taking note of its risks as well as the military's hopes. He also reported that Navy SEAL forces had been dispatched once again to undertake pre-landing reconnaissance of Grenadian beaches. Though the SEALs were already under way, Weinberger explained, no reports had yet been received.[251]

When all five Congressional leaders had assembled, James Baker escorted them upstairs to Reagan's living quarters.[252] Besides the Congressional leadership, Shultz, Weinberger, McFarlane, Vessey, Deaver, Baker, Meese, Darman and Duberstein were present for the sitting room briefing.[253]

Reagan introduced the two-hour meeting[254] by telling the leaders of Congress, "I have a national security decision that I want to share with you."[255] He then announced that he had decided to launch an invasion of Grenada. According to Caspar Weinberger: "The President opened with a brief but thorough summary of the situation, emphasizing the risks to the American students, the evidence we had of growing Cuban involvement, the increasing madness of the regime presently in power in Grenada, as exemplified in the twenty-four-hour shoot-on-sight curfew, the risk of extensive and violent civil war there, and the knowledge we had had for a long time of both Soviet and Cuban involvement in the island itself, beyond the building of the new airfield." In addition, Reagan "emphasized the plight of our students and our fears they might all be held as hostages, or worse." Making note of the OECS request, he then concluded:

> I feel we have absolutely no alternative but to comply with this request.
> I think the risks of not moving are far greater than the risks of taking the action we have planned.[256]

The President then gave the floor to his new National Security Adviser, who provided a brief history of the island. Recalls O'Neill:

McFarlane ... said that there were six hundred Cubans in Grenada, building an airport, and that Cuba had several hundred armed troops there as well. He added that some of Grenada's neighbors were afraid the island was being used for training terrorists. But the most pressing reason we were going into Grenada was to protect approximately a thousand Americans, most of whom were medical students.[257]

After McFarlane had finished, Shultz, Weinberger, and General Vessey discussed some of the details of the operation.[258] The Congressional leaders were told that the invasion was already under way[259] and that the administration hoped to withdraw the Marines and Rangers from Grenada within five to seven days.[260] Reagan's aides would later observe that they had been "struck by the President's rapt interest" during the two-hour briefing. He had sat on the edge of his stiff-backed chair assisting General Vessey with the JCS Chairman's array of charts, and interjecting frequent comments.[261]

The reaction by the Congressional leadership to Reagan's decision to invade was mixed.[262] O'Neill seemed to some administration observers to "understand the reason for the action" and to support the President.[263] Such a perception ultimately proved mistaken, however.[264] Jim Wright "supported the need to take a stand against communist subversion" while Robert Byrd opposed the action and would say so publicly after it was officially announced. Of the two Republican leaders, Howard Baker thought the American action was "bad politics," an enormous political burden, but Robert Michel was "strongly supportive."[265]

Just before 9:00 P.M., President Reagan left the sitting room to receive a telephone call from Margaret Thatcher. He conversed with the British Prime Minister in his study, which opened off the Oval Office and in which a secure line was available.[266] Reagan later recalled their conversation:

> As soon as I heard her voice, I knew she was very angry. She said she had just learned about the impending operation ... and asked me in the strongest language to call off the operation. Grenada, she reminded me, was part of the British Commonwealth, and the United States had no business interfering in its affairs.[267]

Thatcher reportedly had other objections as well. According to one account:

The Commonwealth factor weighed with her, but what seemed to worry her more was the comparison with Afghanistan. How could we in the West condemn the Soviets convincingly if we seemed to be doing much the same sort of thing ourselves? Then there were the *legal considerations*. It was not for nothing that she had been trained as a lawyer. She was always uncomfortable if she had difficulty in justifying any action in terms of international law.[268]

Reagan remembers the explanation he offered to the British Prime Minister:

I told her about the request we'd received from the Organization of Eastern Caribbean States and said I had believed we had to act quickly and covertly because I feared any communication could result in a leak and spoil the advantage of surprise.[269]

His fear, the President explained, "was not that there would be a leak on her side but on his. Even the making of a telephone call," he suggested, "might have allowed something to get out in Washington at an earlier stage."[270] Thatcher was "very adamant and continued to insist that we cancel our landings on Grenada," Reagan recalled. Nevertheless, he recognized that he "couldn't tell her that [Urgent Fury] had already begun."[271]

The President returned to the sitting room upon the conclusion of his fifteen-minute trans-Atlantic call.[272] With "a rather rueful look on his face,"[273] he acknowledged that Thatcher had expressed misgivings about a lengthy U.S. involvement in Grenada and had told him that the invasion would be received badly by the allies. She had even suggested that the invasion might produce negative domestic political fallout as well. Michael Deaver recollects:

[President Reagan] clearly was unhappy that she was not as excited about this whole thing as he was. Finally he said to us, "But I told her we were going to go ahead anyway." It was too late. But he was troubled by that, you know.[274]

As the President's colleagues rose to the leave,[275] Reagan asked General Vessey, "What are you fellows going to do now?" The JCS Chair replied directly, "I'm going home and go to bed. You have approved our plan, and it is now in the hands of competent commanders and troops. There is nothing more we can do now." Responded Reagan, "Good, I'll do the same." Shortly thereafter, Reagan's advisers departed.

Along with General Vessey, Secretary Weinberger returned to the Pentagon to issue the final "execute order," to review once again the operational specifics of "Urgent Fury," and to receive any messages from the military forces that were now massing off Grenada. "Bad news was not long in coming," recalls Weinberger. "We knew at least one of the SEAL's rubber boats had foundered in very high seas after hitting a patrol boat, and we greatly feared at least two more of the SEALS were lost." Perhaps most troubling, "we had no real pre-landing intelligence."[276]

At about 11:30 P.M., Monday, there was a final NSC staff review in the White House Situation Room.[277] Joining McFarlane and Poindexter at the brief meeting were Menges, North, and Robert Sims, the NSC media liaison. Here, McFarlane related how the five Congressional leaders had reacted to the evening's Grenada briefing, and asked several of his staff to brief a few members of the House and Senate Foreign Relations committees. Top press officials at State and Defense had already been confidentially informed in Tony Motley's office after the Monday evening news broadcasts.[278]

Monday on Barbados

On Monday morning, after at most four hours of sleep, Ambassador McNeil went to Grantley Adams Airport to see off Edward Seaga.[279] For about an hour before the Jamaican Prime Minister's departure, McNeil, Gillespie, Adams and Seaga discussed the Grenada situation. Although McNeil repeated that no final decision had been made, he did concede that he had urged Washington to act immediately if it were to act at all. He added that he hoped word of a decision would be conveyed to the Caribbean leaders that same day.[280]

In time, McNeil and Gillespie returned to the Embassy where McNeil spoke again with Motley by phone. The Assistant Secretary now asked McNeil to pick up Prime Minister Charles on the nearby Caribbean island of Guadeloupe. At Ambassador McNeil's suggestion, the OECS chair would be present at President Reagan's Tuesday morning press conference. Milan Bish had already phoned to invite Charles to fly to Washington, without specifying the administration's intentions, and Charles had readily agreed.[281]

Shortly before his departure from Barbados, and shortly after Reagan's military planning meeting had ended, McNeil received final instructions from Tony Motley: unless word were sent to the contrary, the Caribbean leaders should be told at 6:00 P.M. that the United States would invade Grenada. The American invasion, it was now all but certain, would be undertaken Tuesday. Around 4:30 P.M., McNeil boarded his Gulfstream, carrying the written OECS invitation with him.[282]

After having landed on the Caribbean island of Guadeloupe, Ambassador McNeil met Eugenia Charles, who had been flown there from Dominica by the French.[283] Prime Minister Charles had understood that she was to be flown to Washington for the purpose of convincing President Reagan to launch a military mission.[284] In fact, McNeil told her at 6:05 P.M. as their plane was taking off for the United States, Reagan had already decided to invade. "That was quick," Charles exclaimed.[285]

After their lengthy flight, McNeil and Charles landed at Andrews AFB around 2:00 A.M. Tuesday morning.[286] From Andrews, McNeil drove Prime Minister Charles to the Madison Hotel in Washington, arriving there at approximately 2:30 A.M. From here he would pick her up in four and a half hours for a meeting with the President.[287]

Back on Barbados, Prime Minister Adams had been officially informed at 8:10 P.M. that the United States would participate in the Grenada intervention. Ambassador Milan Bish had arrived then at his house and had read aloud a letter of acceptance from Reagan.[288] Four hours later, at midnight, the U.S. Embassy in Bridgetown sent a commercial telex to General Austin, asserting that there was no legitimate government on Grenada and that U.S. citizens were in danger.[289]

October 24 on Grenada

On Monday, October 24, the situation on Grenada was far from routine, despite the end of the RMC's ninety-six hour "shoot-on-sight" curfew.[290] Although the RMC sought to encourage Grenadians to return to work, the group decided that the nightly 8:00 P.M.-5:00 A.M. curfew would be extended and that schools would stay closed for another week. Meanwhile, Alister Hughes and other RMC opponents remained in custody and Pearls airport virtually closed; indeed, only four small charter flights were able to leave Grenada. This lack of air traffic apparently reflected two factors. First, as has already been observed, the CARICOM states had voted Sunday to suspend all LIAT flights to Grenada. Only after the British and Canadians had applied diplomatic pressure did Vere Bird, the most strident opponent of any flight to Pearls, agree that an exception should be made on humanitarian grounds; this permission, however, came too late for a crew to be found.[291] Second, the RMC members, having "changed their tone" Monday, had demanded six hours advance notice for any evacuation flights and had warned that they could not guarantee the safety of foreigners on a ride from their residences to Pearls.[292]

Although the precise degree to which American citizens were in danger by Monday evening is ultimately debatable, the Reagan administration did not have the luxury of unharried, *post facto* deliberation.[293] As St. George's Medical School Vice Chancellor Geoffrey Bourne would later concede: "The whole situation with the students may have suddenly gone into reverse and the school have found itself in a hostage crisis. We had a volatile and highly dangerous situation ... which could have become disastrous at any minute."[294] Assistant Secretary Motley had a similar perception: given the State Department's responsibility for the lives of perhaps a thousand Americans on Grenada, even "eighty percent security would not have been good enough."[295] In any event, at 6:00 P.M. Monday — as McNeil and Charles were leaving Guadeloupe for Washington, as five Congressional leaders on Capitol Hill were being rounded up by Baker and Duberstein, and as the RMC on Grenada was fretting about its future — President Reagan made the final, irrevocable decision to launch "Urgent Fury."

D-Day in Washington

Tuesday began early for many within the Reagan administration.[296] The President himself was awake and phoning his aides by 6:30 A.M.[297] Already by 6:00 A.M., James Baker and Michael Deaver had been meeting in the White House dining room with the administration's four chief press liaisons: Larry Speakes, the President's deputy press secretary; Les Janka, Speakes' deputy for foreign affairs; David Gergen, the White House director of communications; and Robert Sims, the NSC's media representative.[298] Here, for the first time, Speakes, Janka and Gergen were formally notified that an invasion decision had been made. Baker began by characterizing the scope, timetable and objectives of the armed action, explaining that United States forces had already landed; then, the Chief of Staff set out how the press was to be handled. During the course of the breakfast briefing, Baker was asked whether the press would be permitted to cover the Grenada operation on location. He replied that military planners had not wished to bring reporters along and that the White House would not overrule them — a position that particularly alarmed Janka and Gergen.[299]

Larry Speakes was likewise displeased by the morning's revelations. Having been handed a packet of documents on Grenada about an inch thick, Speakes had been asked by Baker to make a press announcement within the hour.[300] He would later call October 25 his "low point as press spokesman." In Speakes' view, the Office of Press Secretary "should have been brought in at some point; Reagan and the rest of the Grenada planning group could have had the benefit of our advice, and we could have done a better job of explaining Reagan's reasons for invasion."[301] At 7:00 A.M., Speakes read a State Department-prepared statement to the Washington press corps: "The United States Government has decided to accede to an urgent plea from the Organization of Eastern Caribbean States ... to support and participate in a collective security effort to restore peace and order in Grenada."[302]

A half hour later, at 7:30 A.M., Reagan met with Eugenia Charles in his yellow Oval Office over juice and coffee.[303] Among those present for the twenty-eight minute discussion were Shultz, McFarlane, Weinberger, Meese, Deaver, McNeil, Motley and Menges. Prime Minister Charles began the morning conversation by thanking the President for deciding to help: year after year the Grenadian dictatorship had progressively worsened, and the faction that had overthrown Maurice Bishop was composed of the most hard-line, dangerous and pro-Moscow communists. Reagan replied that the United States and the states of the eastern Caribbean shared a common democratic heritage and a desire for peace. Describing the contents of his 9:00 A.M. public statement, President Reagan then extended his personal invitation to Charles to accompany him to the White House press room and to answer questions posed by the American media. The Prime Minister of Dominica promptly replied, "I would be pleased to appear with you, Mr. President."[304]

At 8:00 A.M., after her brief meeting with the President, Eugenia Charles was escorted by Constantine Menges to the White House dining room for breakfast with Ambassador McNeil and Deputy Secretary of State Kenneth Dam.[305] Here, Menges embarrassed his American colleagues by excoriating the State Department in front of the Prime Minister: it was Menges' long-held contention that State had often acted in ways contrary to the President's foreign policy objectives. While Charles was away, it was discovered — by McNeil, Menges, or perhaps by both — that the words "to restore democracy" had been deleted by the State Department from the President's prepared statement on American objectives, the statement that Reagan was to deliver in less than an hour. Such a deletion seemed inappropriate: McNeil had frequently stressed to the Caribbean leaders that if the United States were to become involved militarily, then Grenada would get a bona fide "democracy," not a return to Eric Gairy. Kenneth Dam agreed, and the words were restored to Reagan's announcement.

While Charles was being escorted to breakfast, Shultz, Weinberger, and the President's personal staff gathered around his desk to update him on the situation.[306] Shortly thereafter, the group walked to the White House cabinet room to brief the whole Congressional leadership on the Grenada action.[307] At 8:14 A.M., Reagan began the presentation, speaking for about ten minutes. The President then allowed Weinberger and McFarlane to provide details on the military operation that had begun only hours before. By 9:07 A.M., Reagan had moved to the press room where, with Eugenia Charles at his side, he made the startling announcement that the United States had invaded Grenada.

Notes

1. Menges, *Inside the NSC*, p. 79.
2. Lou Cannon's interview with Caspar Weinberger, March 29, 1990, cited in Cannon, *President Reagan*, p. 446.
3. Reagan, *An American Life*, p. 451.
4. Shultz, *Turmoil and Triumph*, pp. 334, 329.
5. "Shultz's News Conference," p. 70; Oberdorfer, "Reagan Sought," p. A21; Bennett, "Anatomy of a 'Go' Decision," p. 74.
6. Oberdorfer, "Reagan Sought," p. A21; Meese, *With Reagan*, p. 216.
7. See Woodward, *Veil*, p. 290; and Menges, *Inside the NSC*, p. 77. Although Clarridge is not mentioned explicitly by Menges, he is presumably the "operations officer from CIA" referred to by the author.
8. Tyler, "The Making of an Invasion," p. 14.
9. Francis X. Clines, "Days of Crisis for the President: Golf, a Tragedy and Secrecy," *New York Times*, October 26, 1983, p. A1.

10. For accounts of the meeting, see Bennett, "Anatomy of a 'Go' Decision," pp. 74-75; Menges, *Inside the NSC*, pp. 77-78; "Britain's Grenada Shut-out," *The Economist*, p. 32.

11. Menges, *Inside the NSC*, p. 77.

12. The Caribbean Community and Common Market or "CARICOM" was established by the Treaty of Chaguaramas in 1973. *United Nations Treaty Series*, Vol. 17, p. 947; *International Legal Materials*, Vol. 12, p. 1033. CARICOM is committed to the promotion of economic integration, the expansion of intra-regional functional cooperation and the coordination of regional foreign policy. Membership is comprised of all the states of the Commonwealth Caribbean region: Antigua and Barbuda; Barbados; Belize; Dominica; Grenada; Guyana; Jamaica; Montserrat; St. Kitts-Nevis; St. Lucia; St. Vincent; and Trinidad and Tobago. See Payne et al., *Revolution and Invasion*, p. 89.

13. Even before the OECS Heads of Government had finished their session, plans were being made for the CARICOM meeting. O'Shaughnessy argues that the "involvement of the large countries of the Commonwealth Caribbean in any legal action against the RMC would greatly strengthen its apparent justification. As far as international public opinion was concerned, the members of the OECS could hardly be expected to carry much weight." *Revolution, Invasion and Aftermath*, p. 160. The State Department does not appear, however, to have viewed a CARICOM invitation as legally significant since the organization was principally a commercial one. Author's interviews with Michael Kozak, November 3, 1988; Langhorne Motley, November 4, 1988.

14. Menges, *Inside the NSC*, p. 78.

15. Author's interview with Langhorne Motley, March 7, 1989. Motley's account challenges that offered by Menges in *Inside the NSC*, pp. 78-79.

16. Author's interview with Lawrence Eagleburger, March 15, 1993; Reynold A. Burrowes, *Revolution and Rescue in Grenada: An Account of the U.S.-Caribbean Invasion* (New York: Greenwood Press, 1988), p. 78.

17. Weinberger, *Fighting for Peace*, p. 112.

18. Menges, *Inside the NSC*, p. 78. See also Bennett, 'Anatomy of a 'Go' Decision," p. 75.

19. Author's interview with Langhorne Motley, March 7, 1989. See also Shultz, *Turmoil and Triumph*, pp. 332-334.

20. Magnuson, "D-Day in Grenada," p. 27.

21. One official would later recall, "I had a real fear that it could be a very bad situation: Desert One all over again." Cited by Magnuson, "D-Day in Grenada," p. 27.

22. Magnuson, "D-Day in Grenada," p. 27.

23. Oberdorfer, "Reagan Sought," p. A21.

24.   The contents of the NSDD are reported in Bennett, "Anatomy of a 'Go' Decision," p. 75. Oberdorfer also notes the three-fold objective of "Urgent Fury," including the elimination of Cuban "intervention" on Grenada and the prevention of its reestablishment. See "Reagan Sought," p. A1. Francis McNeil corroborated Oberdorfer's report in his interview with the author, August 11, 1988.

25.   Bennett, "Anatomy of a 'Go' Decision," pp. 74-75. Weinberger acknowledged in his memoir: "The President [on Saturday morning] also approved an expanded mission for us that included restoring a democratic government to Grenada." Weinberger, *Fighting for Peace*, p. 112.

26.   Author's interview with Lawrence Eagleburger, March 15, 1993.

27.   Menges, *Inside the NSC*, pp. 78; Woodward, *Veil*, p. 291; Cannon, *President Reagan*, p. 446.

28.   Davidson, *A Study in Politics*, p. 82.

29.   According to one SSG participant: "Everyone was gung-ho" for invasion. Magnuson, "D-Day in Grenada," p. 27. This characterization was probably somewhat exaggerated, however, in light of Defense Department concerns about intelligence and planning limitations.

30.   See "Britain's Grenada Shut-out," *The Economist*, p. 32. According to a recent account, Reagan "was not asked to sign a formal [invasion] order because Weinberger and Vessey wanted to wait for additional intelligence on the disposition of Cuban forces on the island." Cannon, *President Reagan*, p. 446. Eagleburger has observed that on Saturday, October 22, it was "very clear" that the United States would take military action. Author's interview with Lawrence Eagleburger, March 15, 1993.

31.   "Britain's Grenada Shut-out," *The Economist*, p. 32.

32.   Motley wanted to ensure that the Caribbean troops would be introduced early into Grenada. If not, he feared that they might not be brought in at all. Under such circumstances, the American post-invasion military presence would be undesirably prolonged. Author's interviews with Langhorne Motley, September 20, 1988; November 4, 1988.

33.   "Shultz's News Conference," p. 70.

34.   Author's interview with Langhorne Motley, March 7, 1989; Shultz, *Turmoil and Triumph*, p. 331.

35.   According to Eagleburger, "we mislead the British" because we "did not want to jeopardize operational security." Author's interview with Lawrence Eagleburger, March 15, 1993. See also, Payne et al., *Revolution and Invasion*, p. 151; "Britain's Grenada Shut-out," *The Economist*, pp. 32-34; and "Second Report," *Grenada*.

36.   See especially, Speakes, *Speaking Out*; and "Britain's Grenada Shut-out," *The Economist*, p. 32.

37.   Lehman, *Command of the Seas*, p. 297.

38. Menges, *Inside the NSC*, p. 78.

39. See Motley, "The Decision to Assist Grenada," p. 70; and Menges, *Inside the NSC*, p. 79. Emphasis mine.

40. See Cannon, *President Reagan*, p. 442; Reagan, *An American Life*, p. 452; Speakes, *Speaking Out*, p. 151; O'Shaughnessy, *Revolution, Invasion and Aftermath*, p. 162; Bennett, "Anatomy of a 'Go' Decision," p. 75; and Magnuson, "D-Day in Grenada," p. 28.

41. Shultz, *Turmoil and Triumph*, p. 330.

42. Reagan, *An American Life*, p. 452.

43. Reagan, *An American Life*, p. 452.

44. One of the President's aides was not actually "released." According to Reagan, "He said to the gunman, 'Gee, it's hot in here, don't you think a six-pack of beer would be good?' When the gunman agreed with that proposal, our man walked out of the pro shop on an errand to get the beer, never to return." *An American Life*, p. 452.

45. Walter Shapiro, "Testing Time: 'Reagan was Reagan,'" *Newsweek*, November 7, 1983, p. 82.

46. Author's interview with Francis McNeil, February 24, 1989.

47. Author's interview with Francis McNeil, February 24, 1989.

48. Lawrence G. Rossin's letter to the author, June 12, 1989.

49. Author's interview with Michael Kozak, November 3, 1988.

50. Author's interview with Michael Kozak, November 3, 1988.

51. Cited by Bennett, "Anatomy of a 'Go' Decision," p. 75.

52. Spector, *U.S. Marines in Grenada*, p. 8.

53. Lehman, *Command of the Seas*, p. 297.

54. Menges, *Inside the NSC*, p. 79.

55. Bradlee, *Guts and Glory*, p. 179. According to Menges, North spent the night before the Grenada invasion sleeping on the sofa in his office. *Inside the NSC*, p. 84.

56. In March, 1983, Major North was selected for promotion to Lieutenant Colonel. Gutman, *Banana Diplomacy*, p. 137. North actually received his promotion only a few weeks before McFarlane's appointment as National Security Adviser. Bradlee, *Guts and Glory*, p. 171.

57. Cited by Bradlee, *Guts and Glory*, p. 179.

58. Cited by Bradlee, *Guts and Glory*, pp. 179-180.

59. The PRA was described as numbering about 1,200 men, backed by a militia of 2,000 to 5,000 men and 300 to 400 armed police. Grenadian anti-aircraft batteries reportedly were equipped with Soviet-design 12.7mm and 37mm anti-aircraft guns with well-trained gunners. In addition, about 30 to 50 Cuban military advisers, and about 600 Cuban construction workers were believed to be on the island. Twenty-Second Marine Amphibious Division, "Operation Urgent Fury After Action Report, January 15, 1984," p. 6, cited by

Spector, *U.S. Marines in Grenada*, p. 3.

60. Colonel James P. Faulkner interview, November 13, 1983 (Oral History Collection, MCHC, Washington, D.C.), cited by Spector, *U.S. Marines in Grenada*, p. 3.

61. O'Shaughnessy, *Revolution, Invasion and Aftermath*, p. 162. See also Lewis, *The Jewel Despoiled*, pp. 94-97.

62. O'Shaughnessy, *Revolution, Invasion and Aftermath*, pp. 161-162.

63. Davidson, *A Study in Politics*, p. 82; and Payne et al., *Revolution and Intervention*, p. 151.

64. Reported in the *Trinidad Express*, November 1, 1983, p. 1.

65. O'Shaughnessy, *Revolution, Invasion, and Aftermath*, p. 163. See also "Address to the Nation on October 25, 1983 by his Excellency L.F.S. Burnham," in *Documents on the Invasion*, p. 63.

66. "Prime Minister George Chambers, Speech to the Trinidad and Tobago Parliament, October 26, 1983," cited by Davidson, *A Study in Politics*, p. 83; "Second Report," p. xiv; and O'Shaughnessy, *Revolution, Invasion and Aftermath*, pp. 162-163.

67. See Davidson, *A Study in Politics*, p. 83; and O'Shaughnessy, *Revolution, Invasion and Aftermath*, pp. 163-164.

68. Payne et al., *Revolution and Invasion*, p. 151; Davidson, *A Study in Politics*, p. 83.

69. Since the CARICOM Treaty required unanimity for a binding decision, it is arguable that a "decision" had not been made. Davidson, *A Study in Politics*, p. 83.

70. On the Sunday morning meeting, see Payne et al, *Revolution and Invasion*, pp. 151-152; Davidson, *A Study in Politics*, pp. 83-84; O'Shaughnessy, *Revolution, Invasion and Aftermath*, p. 164; and "Second Report," p. xiv.

71. Davidson, *A Study in Politics*, p. 84; Payne et al., *Revolution and Invasion*, pp. 152-153.

72. Any hope of assistance from Cuba was probably already dashed on October 20 when the Cuban Government released a statement harshly condemning the "atrocious acts" that had transpired on Grenada. O'Shaughnessy, *Revolution, Invasion and Aftermath*, pp. 149-150.

73. O'Shaughnessy, *Revolution, Invasion and Aftermath*, p. 150. At 9:00 PM Saturday, Cuba also sent a message to the United States through the Cuban Interests Section of the Swiss embassy in Havana. The message informed U.S. diplomats that Cuba was aware of American concerns for its citizens, that it was aware of U.S. naval forces approaching Grenada, and that it was concerned about its own nationals on the island. "Statement by the Cuban Party," in *Documents on the Invasion*, p. 47.

74. According to Kenneth Kurze, the "RMC saw value in letting [the] U.S. [representatives] see their citizens were not being harmed." Kenneth Kurze's letter to author, September 29, 1991.

75. U.S. State Department Cable No. 302385. According to Kenneth Kurze, either Hudson Austin or one of his staff visited St. George's Medical School and told Vice Chancellor Geoffrey Bourne that American embassy officers would be permitted to fly from Barbados to Grenada. Bourne in turn relayed this information to the U.S. Embassy in Bridgetown. Kenneth Kurze's letter to the author, September 29, 1991.

76. Bridgetown CANA report, 6:40 PM Grenada time, October 22, 1983. Transcript printed in *Unclassified FBIS - Latin America*, October 24, 1983, p. S18.

77. O'Shaughnessy, *Revolution, Invasion and Aftermath*, p. 160; Bourne, "Was the Invasion Unnecessary?" p. 1.

78. Jonathan Kwitny, *Endless Enemies: The Making of an Unfriendly World* (New York: Congdon & Weed, 1984), p. 412.

79. Kwitny, *Endless Enemies*, pp. 414-417.

80. Kenneth Kurze's letter to the author, September 6, 1991.

81. According to Motley, on October 22, "American officials were at last able to reach the island." Motley, "The Decision to Assist Grenada," p. 71. Bish implied that other visits may have been made by Americans between October 19 and 22. Author's interview with Milan Bish, October 26, 1988. At a minimum, one would expect the CIA or the military to have attempted to reconnoiter the island.

82. Author's interview with Kenneth Kurze, May 15, 1992; Kenneth Kurze's letter to the author, September 29, 1991.

83. Author's interview with Kenneth Kurze, May 15, 1992; Kenneth Kurze's letter to the author, September 29, 1991.

84. Kenneth Kurze's letter to the author, September 29, 1991.

85. Bridgetown CANA report, 7:30 PM Grenada time, October 23, 1983. Manuscript printed in *Unclassified FBIS - Latin America*, October 24, 1983, p. S10.

86. The inn is located slightly south of St. George's. Adkin, *The Battle for Grenada*, p. 100.

87. The U.S. diplomats had been instructed by the American Embassy in Bridgetown not to meet with Austin so as not to imply diplomatic recognition of the RMC. Kwitney, *Endless Enemies*, p. 412.

88. Author's interview with Kenneth Kurze, May 15, 1992.

89. Cited by Kwitny, *Endless Enemies*, p. 412.

90. Kenneth Kurze's letter to the author, October 8, 1992.

91. Kwitney, *Endless Enemies*, p. 414. Author's interviews with Milan Bish, September 26, 1988; and with Francis McNeil, November 11, 1988.

92. Kwitney, *Endless Enemies*, pp. 414-415; Adkin, *The Battle for Grenada*, p. 101.

93. Author's interview with Kenneth Kurze, May 15, 1992; Kenneth Kurze's letter to the author, October 8, 1992.

94. Motley reported that on Sunday, October 23, the "possibility of using a Cunard-line cruise ship then in the vicinity to evacuate Americans" was explored but that it was rejected when it became "apparent ... that conditions on the island [would] not permit evacuation by civilian carrier." Motley, "The Decision to Assist Grenada," p. 71. The Cunard liner *Countess*, which made one-week runs through the Caribbean islands between La Jolla, Venezuela and San Juan, Puerto Rico, was due to dock on Tuesday, October 25. Hendrick Smith, "Reagan Aide Says U.S. Invasion Forestalled Cuban Arms Buildup," *New York Times*, October 27, 1983, p. A21.

95. Kwitny, *Endless Enemies*, p. 413; Adkin, *The Battle for Grenada*, p. 101.

96. Sandford and Vigilante, *The Untold Story*, p. 8.

97. A U.S. intelligence report from Barbados on October 24 "raised the possibility that a hostage situation might develop as increasingly jittery Grenadian military leaders saw a peaceful evacuation of U.S. citizens as the prelude to an American invasion." Oberdorfer, "Reagan Sought," p. A1. This conclusion was shared by Francis McNeil and Linda Flohr. Author's interview with Francis McNeil, September 20, 1988; and Thomas Hammond's interview with Linda Flohr, November 9, 1989 - notes provided to author. Indeed, the intelligence report may well have been McNeil's. Tyler also alludes to "the expectation by the Grenadan military of imminent invasion." The RMC's fear "appears to have led U.S. officials to assume that the island's defenders might take hostages." See "The Making of an Invasion," p. A14.

98. U.S. State Department Cable No. 06572. Transcript of RFG broadcast printed in *Unclassified FBIS - Latin America*, October 24, 1983, p. S23.

99. "RMC note," UN Doc. S/PV .2487, cited by Davidson, *A Study in Politics*, p. 84. The diplomatic note is reprinted in full in appendix no. 6 of Gilmore, *Analysis and Documentation*, pp. 93-94. According to Tyler, at 2:00 AM Monday, a note from General Austin arrived at the U.S. Embassy in Barbados restating his guarantee for the safety of U.S. citizens and promising to return the country to a "fully constituted civilian government" in two weeks. See "The Making of an Invasion," p. 15.

100. On Monday morning, when the Scanplast staff discovered the Grenadian missives on their telex, they called the Foreign and Commonwealth's Caribbean and Atlantic Department and were told to "put them in an envelope," and to "leave them at the front door." Given the apparent lack of urgency, Scanplast decided to mail the materials. O'Shaughnessy, *Revolution, Invasion and Aftermath*, p. 152; Adkin, *The Battle for Grenada*, p. 102.

101. "Second Report," p xiv.

102. "Britain's Grenada Shut-out," *The Economist*, p. 33. Author's interview with Kenneth Kurze, May 15, 1992.

103. According to the Committee, both the timing and nature of Sir Paul's request "remain shrouded in mystery, and it is evidently the intention of the parties directly involved that the mystery should not be dispelled." See "Second Report," pp. xiv, xvi.

104. In his memoir, Reagan called October 23, 1983, "the saddest day of my presidency, perhaps the saddest day of my life." Reagan, *An American Life*, p. 437.

105. Lou Cannon's interview with Robert McFarlane, April 16, 1990, cited in Cannon, *President Reagan*, p. 442.

106. See Reagan, *An American Life*, pp. 452-3; Cannon, *President Reagan*, p. 440; Oberdorfer, "Reagan Sought," p. A21; Tyler, "The Making of an Invasion," p. 14; and Bennett, "Anatomy of a 'Go' Decision," p. 75. At 6:20 AM, a Mercedes truck laden with six tons of explosives penetrated American defenses at the Beirut airport before crashing into the Marine headquarters and detonating. Ultimately, 241 Americans were killed in the explosion. See Beth A. Salamanca, "Vehicle Bombs: Death on Wheels," in *Fighting Back: Winning the War Against Terrorism*, eds. Neil C. Livingstone and Terrell E. Arnold (Lexington, MA: Lexington Books, 1986), p. 44. FBI experts would later say that the Beirut explosion was the largest non-nuclear blast they had ever seen. Martin and Walcott, *Best Laid Plans*, p. 126.

107. Cited by Martin and Walcott, *Best Laid Plans*, p. 127.

108. Reagan, *An American Life*, p. 453; Bennett, "Anatomy of a 'Go' Decision," p. 75. The bombing also justified the decision to delay Shultz's Latin America trip. Oberdorfer, "Reagan Sought," p. A21.

109. Tyler, "The Making of an Invasion," p. 14.

110. Reagan, *An American Life*, p. 453.

111. Tyler, "The Making of an Invasion," p. 14.

112. "Shultz's News Conference," p. 70.

113. *Weekly Compilation of Presidential Documents* 19 (October 31, 1983): 1480.

114. Shultz, *Turmoil and Triumph*, p. 330; Magnuson, "D-Day in Grenada," p. 28; Isaacson, "Weighing the Proper Role," p. 48.

115. Shultz, *Turmoil and Triumph*, p. 330.

116. Isaacson, Weighing the Proper Role," p. 49; Tyler, "The Making of an Invasion," p. 14; Menges, *Inside the NSC*, p. 54. "Normally, [Reagan] would have been driven from Andrews Air Force base in such weather, but he was in a hurry to get back to the White House." Cannon, *President Reagan*, p. 443.

117. Cannon, *President Reagan*, p. 443.

118. *Weekly Compilation of Presidential Documents* 19 (October 31, 1983): 1480.

119. See "Shultz's News Conference, p. 70; and Bennett, "Anatomy of a 'Go' Decision," p. 75. The meeting probably lasted from 8:40-10:40 AM. Tyler, "The Making of an Invasion," p. 14.

120. Tyler, "The Making of an Invasion," p. 14; Menges, *Inside the NSC*, p. 80.

121. Weinberger, *Fighting for Peace*, p. 113.

122. Oberdorfer, "Reagan Sought," p. A21.

123. "Britain's Grenada Shut-out," *The Economist*, p. 32.

124. Martin and Walcott, *Best Laid Plans*, p. 126.

125. Cited by Shapiro, "Reagan Was Reagan," p. 80.

126. Cited by Bennett, "Anatomy of a 'Go' Decision," p. 75.

127. At some point during the meeting, Weinberger was sent upstairs to the White House's Roosevelt Room for a half-hour appearance on a CBS Sunday public affairs program. Weinberger, *Fighting for Peace*, p. 116-117; Tyler, "The Making of an Invasion," p. 14.

128. Author's interview with Lawrence Eagleburger, March 15, 1993.

129. Menges, *Inside the NSC*, p. 80.

130. Bennett, "Anatomy of a 'Go' Decision," p. 75. According to one senior adviser, Reagan "felt very strongly that this was the right thing to do and it should not be aborted because of what happened in Lebanon." Cited in Shapiro, "Reagan was Reagan," p. 82. Fred Ikle confirmed that there was a strong sentiment on Sunday that an act of terrorism should not alter a foreign policy decision that had already been made. Author's interview with Ikle, July 20, 1989. In his memoir, Weinberger recalled that at the Sunday morning meeting, Reagan "reaffirmed his determination to intervene in Grenada." Weinberger, *Fighting for Peace*, p. 113. According to one report, however, President Reagan "'momentarily ... considered abandoning the mission' after the Beirut bombing out of concern for additional American casualties." Cannon, *President Reagan*, p. 447, citing Douglas Brew, "D-Day in Grenada," *Time*, November 7, 1983.

131. Bennett, "Anatomy of a 'Go' Decision," pp. 75-6. Bennett reports that a CIA representative was present. Presumably, that representative was McMahon.

132. Bennett, "Anatomy of a 'Go' Decision," pp. 75-6.

133. Shultz, *Turmoil and Tragedy*, p. 331.

134. Shultz, *Turmoil and Tragedy*, p. 331.

135. Shultz, *Turmoil and Tragedy*, p. 331.

136. The call from Lebanon is reported in *Weekly Compilation of Presidential Documents* 19 (October 31, 1983): 1504.

137. "Shultz's News Conference," p. 70. The 72-year old President had had very little sleep the previous night and would average roughly five hours of sleep per day during the early part of the week. Shapiro, "Reagan Was Reagan," p. 80.

138. In the very early afternoon (Lebanon time), Howard Teicher had dictated a memo for McFarlane over a secure line from Beirut. Here, the NSC staffer recommended that the United States proceed immediately with plans to retaliate. Teicher argued that the United States "should hit targets associated with Syrian-sponsored terrorism in Lebanon." Cited by Martin and Walcott, *Best Laid Plans*, p. 132.

Menges reports that early Sunday morning the Middle Eastern NSC staff — with the help of State, Defense, and the CIA — began preparations for a possible American retaliation. He also suggests that the NSPG considered such an action in its Sunday afternoon meeting. *Inside the NSC*, pp. 54, 82.

On the Reagan administration's retaliation deliberations after the Beirut attack, see Martin and Walcott, *Best Laid Plans*, pp. 133-140; and Cannon, *President Reagan*, p. 451.

139. Lou Cannon's interview with Michael Deaver, October 24, 1983, cited in Cannon, *President Reagan*, p. 447.

140. "Britain's Grenada Shut-out," *The Economist*, p. 32.

141. Lou Cannon, "Strategic Airport, Hostage Fears Led to Move," *Washington Post*, October 26, 1983, p. A8.

142. "Britain's Grenada Shut-out," *The Economist*, p. 32. Motley does not recall Reagan having made such a statement. Author's interview with Langhorne Motley, March 7, 1989.

143. Bennett, "Anatomy of a 'Go' Decision," p. 76.

144. Oberdorfer, "Reagan Sought," p. A21.

145. Author's interviews with Langhorne Motley, September 20, 1988; March 7, 1989.

146. Menges, *Inside the NSC*, pp. 81-82.

147. Menges, *Inside the NSC*, pp. 81-82.

148. "Shultz's News Conference," p. 70.

149. "Britain's Grenada Shut-out," *The Economist*, p. 32. This interpretation was confirmed by Fred Ikle in an interview with the author, July 20, 1989.

150. "Address to the Nation," *Weekly Compilation of Presidential Documents* 19 (October 31, 1983): 1501.

151. Oberdorfer, "Reagan Sought," p. A21. Bennett reports that on Sunday evening McFarlane gave Reagan a "smooth copy" of the NSDD and the attached complete action plan. "Without hesitation, Reagan reache[d] into his pocket for a pen, sign[ed] the document and sa[id] one word: 'Go.'" Bennett, "Anatomy of a 'Go' Decision," p. 76. See also Adkin, *The Battle for Grenada*, p. 121; Lehman, *Command of the Seas*, p. 296; and Weinberger, *Fighting for Peace*,

p. 113.

152. Motley, "The Decision to Assist Grenada," p. 71.

153. Author's interview with Langhorne Motley, November 4, 1988.

154. Cited by Spector, *U.S. Marines in Grenada*, p. 5.

155. Lieutenant Colonel Ray L. Smith interview, November 8, 1983 (Oral History Collection, MCHC, Washington, D.C.), p. 8, cited by Spector, *U.S. Marines in Grenada*, p. 5.

156. Shapiro, "Reagan Was Reagan," p. 80.

157. Author's interview with Francis McNeil, November 11, 1988.

158. Author's interviews with Francis McNeil, November 11, 1988; February 24, 1989.

159. Author's interview with Francis McNeil, September 20, 1988. See also Sandford and Vigilante, *The Untold Story*, p. 6.

160. Author's interview with Francis McNeil, February 24, 1989. See also McNeil, *War and Peace in Central America*, p. 173.

161. Author's interview with Francis McNeil, February 24, 1989.

162. Author's interview with Francis McNeil, September 20, 1988; author's interview with Langhorne Motley, March 7, 1989; author's interview with Kim Flower, July 6, 1989.

163. Author's interview with Michael Kozak, November 3, 1988. Motley also acknowledged that an invitation draft was prepared in Washington by the State Department. Author's interview with Langhorne Motley, September 26, 1988.

164. Author's interview with Francis McNeil, February 24, 1989.

165. Author's interview with Francis McNeil, November 11, 1988.

166. Author's interview with Francis McNeil, February 24, 1989.

167. McNeil, *War and Peace in Central America*, p. 174.

168. Author's interview with Francis McNeil, February 24, 1989.

169. Author's interviews with Francis McNeil, September 20, 1988 and November 11, 1988. See also Sandford and Vigilante, *The Untold Story*, p. 6.

170. Author's interview with Francis McNeil, February 24, 1989.

171. Author's interview with Francis McNeil, February 24, 1989.

172. Author's interview with Kim Flower, July 6, 1989.

173. Author's interview with Kim Flower, July 6, 1989.

174. Author's interviews with Milan Bish, September 26, 1988; Francis McNeil, November 11, 1988; Kim Flower, July 6, 1989. See also McNeil, *War and Peace in Central America*, p. 174.

175. Author's interview with Francis McNeil, September 20, 1988. Author's interview with Milan Bish, September 26, 1988.

176. Sandford and Vigilante, *The Untold Story*, p. 6.

177. Author's interview with Milan Bish, September 26, 1988.

178. The pro-Soviet Coard might play an important role in such a war. The Caribbean leaders told McNeil that Coard was not dead, as the Americans had believed. Author's interview with Milan Bish, September 20, 1988.

179. Author's interview with Francis McNeil, September 20, 1988; Sandford and Vigilante, *The Untold Story*, p. 6.

180. Allan Gerson's interview of Eugenia Charles, March 21, 1987. Cited in Gerson, *The Kirkpatrick Mission*, pp. 221-222,

181. Author's interviews with Francis McNeil, August 11, 1988; February 24, 1989. Kenneth Dam later testified that McNeil "found these three Caribbean leaders unanimous -- and I repeat, unanimous -- in their conviction that the deteriorating conditions on Grenada were a threat to the entire region that required immediate and forceful action." See U.S. Congress, House of Representatives, Subcommittees on International Security and Scientific Affairs and on Western Hemisphere Affairs of the Committee on Foreign Affairs, *U.S. Military Actions in Grenada: Implications for U.S. Policy in the Eastern Caribbean*, 98th Cong., 1st sess., (hereafter cited as *U.S. Military Actions in Grenada*), p. 11.

182. Author's interview with Francis McNeil, February 24, 1989.

183. Author's interview with Francis McNeil, September 20, 1988.

184. McNeil recalled that he may even have torn up the document. Author's interview with Francis McNeil, February 24, 1989.

185. Author's interview with Milan Bish, September 26, 1988; author's interview with Francis McNeil, November 11, 1988; author's interview with Kim Flower, July 6, 1989.

The October 23, 1983 OECS invitation is reprinted in Gilmore, *Analysis and Documentation*, p. 100; and in the *New York Times*, October 26, 1983, p. 19. It is also cited in part in Motley, "The Decision to Assist Grenada," p. 72.

186. Sandford and Vigilante, *The Untold Story*, p. 7. McNeil confirmed that the Caribbean leaders had "talked in terms of law." Author's interview with Francis McNeil, August 11, 1988. According to Kozak, the Caribbean leaders "had good answers" when queried about the legality of the OECS invitation. Author's interview with Michael Kozak, November 3, 1988.

187. Author's interview with Francis McNeil, September 20, 1988. Sandford and Vigilante, *The Untold Story*, p. 7.

188. Author's interview with Francis McNeil, September 20, 1988; Sandford and Vigilante, *The Untold Story*, p. 7.

189. Author's interview with Francis McNeil, November 11, 1988.

190. Author's interview with Francis McNeil, September 20, 1988; Sandford and Vigilante, *The Untold Story*, p. 7.

191. Author's interview with Francis McNeil, November 11, 1988.

192. Author's interview with Langhorne Motley, November 4, 1988.

193. Kenneth Kurze's letter to the author, September 29, 1991.

194. Bourne's account is provided in his article, "Was the U.S. Invasion Necessary?" A different report was given in the author's interview with Francis McNeil, November 11, 1988. According to Motley, "conversations with Embassy officers indicated that more than 300 wished to leave the island." Motley, "The Decision to Assist Grenada," p. 71.

Gary Chafin also reported to McNeil, perhaps on Monday, that Colonel Pedro Tortolo, a Cuban expert of Grenada affairs, had arrived on Grenada from Cuba. Author's interview with Francis McNeil, February 24, 1989.

195. McNeil had been instructed to keep cables to a minimum for security reasons. Author's interview with Francis McNeil, February 24, 1989.

196. Motley would later jokingly refer to McNeil's missive as his "three-and-a-half cable." Author's interview with Francis McNeil, November 11, 1988.

197. Author's interview with Francis McNeil, February 24, 1989.

198. Author's interview with Francis McNeil, September 20, 1988.

199. McNeil, *War and Peace in Central America*, p. 174. After his Sunday return to Barbados from Grenada, Ken Kurze offered a similar recommendation: "If the United States Government was worried about the students being used/taken as 'hostages' (as I was), then [it should] take control of the island. A piecemeal deal with the RMC would *not* work. The RMC had no local support, was over its head, and would likely fall like a house of cards. It was, however, desperate to hang on to power and purify the Grenada revolution." Kurze wondered about Grenada's future: "Could the RMC survive once the populace was 'let out' after the lengthy curfew, or would there be a bloodbath?" Kenneth Kurze's letter to the author, September 29, 1991.

200. Author's interview with Milan Bish, August 24, 1988; author's interview with Kim Flower, July 6, 1989. These interview accounts tend to reinforce Scoon's statement made on October 31: "I think I decided [that an invasion was necessary] on Sunday the 23rd, late Sunday evening." Transcript of BBC-TV interview with the Grenadian Governor-General on "Panorama," October 31, 1983.

201. Author's interview with Francis McNeil, September 20, 1988.

202. Assistant Secretary Motley's Congressional testimony is not inconsistent with the account: "On October 24, Prime Minister Adams of Barbados informed us that he had received a confidential appeal from Governor-General Scoon for assistance to restore order on the island." Motley, "The Decision to Assist Grenada," p. 73.

203. Author's interviews with Francis McNeil, September 20, 1988; February 24, 1989.

204. Author's interview with Davis Robinson, September 21, 1988.

205. Author's interview with Michael Kozak, November 3, 1988.

206. Author's interview with Michael Kozak, November 3, 1988.

207. Author's interview with Langhorne Motley, November 4, 1988.

208. Author's interview with Langhorne Motley, September 20, 1988.

209. According to Michael Kozak, McNeil's recommendation "carried a lot of stroke." Author's interview with Kozak, November 3, 1988.

210. "United Nations Day, 1983 - Proclamation of September 27, 1983," *Weekly Compilation of Presidential Documents* 19 (October 3, 1983): 1344. Gerson mistakenly suggests the Reagan's proclamation of "United Nations Day" was actually made on October 24. Gerson, *The Kirkpatrick Mission*, p. 221.

211. Gerson, *The Kirkpatrick Mission*, p. 221.

212. Gerson, *The Kirkpatrick Mission*, p. 221.

213. Gerson, *The Kirkpatrick Mission*, p. 223.

214. Gerson, *The Kirkpatrick Mission*, p. 223. Emphasis added.

215. Spector, *U.S. Marines in Grenada*, p. 6; Schwarzkopf, *It Doesn't Take A Hero*, p. 246. According to Admiral Metcalf's account, the meeting began at 8:30 AM. Donn-Erik Marshall's interview with Joseph Metcalf, September 21, 1988, cited in Donn-Erik Marshall, "Urgent Fury: The U.S. Military Intervention in Grenada," University of Virginia, Department of History, Master's Thesis, 1989, p. 79.

216. Shultz, *Turmoil and Triumph*, p. 334; Oberdorfer, "Reagan Sought," p. A21.

217. Schwarzkopf, *It Doesn't Take A Hero*, p. 247.

218. Schwarzkopf, *It Doesn't Take A Hero*, p. 247.

219. Schwarzkopf, *It Doesn't Take A Hero*, p. 248.

220. Schwarzkopf, *It Doesn't Take A Hero*, p. 248.

221. Shultz confirms that Johnstone and Darby "turned around" reluctant military commanders at CINCLANT headquarters. *Turmoil and Triumph*, p. 334.

222. Schwarzkopf, *It Doesn't Take A Hero*, p. 248. Michael Deaver observed in his 1987 memoir: "Possibly the only successful ground action this country has taken since World War II was Grenada, or at least we perceive it as such. We got away with it by establishing special ground rules, by not letting the press in and justifying it later." Michael K. Deaver, *Behind the Scenes* (New York: William Morrow, 1987), p. 147.

223. Menges, *Inside the NSC*, p. 82.

224. Reagan, *An American Life*, p. 453.

225. *Weekly Compilation of Presidential Documents* 19 (October 31, 1983): 1504.

226. *Weekly Compilation of Presidential Documents* 19 (October 31, 1983): 1504.

227. "Remarks and a Question-and-Answer Session With Regional Editors and Broadcasters, October 24, 1983," *Weekly Compilation of Presidential Documents* 19 (October 31, 1983): 1482-1486.

228. Weinberger, *Fighting for Peace*, p. 113.

229. Weinberger, *Fighting for Peace*, p. 113.

230. "Shultz's News Conference," p. 70; Weinberger, *Fighting for Peace*, p. 113. The President's meeting with the JCS is also noted in *Weekly Compilation of Presidential Documents* 19 (October 31, 1983): 1504.

231. Reagan, *An American Life*, p. 454; Meese, *With Reagan*, pp. 217-218.

232. Menges, *Inside the NSC*, p. 82.

233. Reagan, *An American Life*, p. 454.

234. Weinberger, *Fighting for Peace*, p. 113.

235. Thomas M. DeFrank and John Walcott, "The Invasion Countdown," *Newsweek*, November 7, 1983, p. 75. According to Meese, Vessey also warned Reagan about a "potential public opinion downside ... because of what [had] happened to the Marines" in Beirut. Meese, *With Reagan*, p. 218.

236. Seymour Hersh's interview with General Schwarzkopf, PBS *Frontline* series, "Operation Urgent Fury." General Vessey noted on October 26, "we did not anticipate meeting Cuban fighting units." Philip Taubman, "Cuban Troops Called Surprise to US," *New York Times*, October 27, 1983, p. A20.

237. Menges, *Inside the NSC*, p. 83.

238. On the role of the press in the Grenada episode, see Mark Hertsgaard, *On Bended Knee: The Press and the Reagan Presidency* (New York: Farrar Straus Giroux, 1988), pp. 203-237.

239. Speakes, *Speaking Out*, pp. 152, 150.

240. Speakes, *Speaking Out*, p. 152; Hertsgaard, *On Bended Knee*, pp. 213-214.

241. Plante later recalled: "There wasn't much of a debate about it. There are unwritten rules concerning the qualifiers and statements made by White House spokesmen. And with that much of a knockdown, there wasn't much choice. Given the normal rules of the game, you have to assume they're not lying." Mark Hertsgaard's interview with Bill Plante, cited in Hertsgaard, *On Bended Knee*, p. 214.

242. Spector, *U.S. Marines in Grenada*, p. 6.

243. "Shultz's News Conference," p. 70. According to Cannon, Reagan "signed a formal order authorizing [the invasion] at 6:55 P.M., shortly before his meeting with the congressional leaders." *President Reagan*, pp. 447-448.

244. Around 2:15 PM (7:15 PM London time), Eagleburger had sent a message to Downing Street, intimating that "very serious consideration" was now being given to armed intervention. "Britain's Grenada Shut-out," *The Economist*, pp. 33-34. See also "Second Report," p. xv.

245. Geoffrey Smith's interview with Robert McFarlane, October 20, 1988, cited in Geoffrey Smith, *Reagan and Thatcher* (London: The Bodley Head, 1990), pp. 126-127.

246. Geoffrey Smith's interview with Robert McFarlane, October 20, 1988, cited in Smith, *Reagan and Thatcher*, p. 127.

247. DeFrank and Walcott, "The Invasion Countdown," p. 75; Speakes, *Speaking Out*, p. 153.

248. O'Neill, *Man of the House*, p. 364.

249. Speakes, *Speaking Out*, p. 153.

250. Weinberger, *Fighting for Peace*, p. 117.

251. According to Weinberger, "We did not get the reports of their actions until several hours later." Weinberger, *Fighting for Peace*, p. 118.

252. O'Neill, *Man of the House*, p. 365; Weinberger, *Fighting for Peace*, p. 117.

253. *Weekly Compilation of Presidential Documents* 19 (October 31, 1983): 1504-1505; Speakes, *Speaking Out*, p. 153.

254. Speakes, *Speaking Out*, p. 153.

255. DeFrank and Walcott, "The Invasion Countdown," p. 75.

256. Weinberger, *Fighting for Peace*, p. 118.

257. O'Neill, *Man of the House*, p. 365.

258. DeFrank and Walcott, "The Invasion Countdown," p. 75; Weinberger, *Fighting for Peace*, p. 118.

259. O'Neill, *Man of the House*, p. 365.

260. Jim Hoagland, "U.S. Invades Grenada," *Washington Post*, October 26, 1983, p. A1.

261. Shapiro, "Reagan was Reagan," p. 80.

262. Shultz, *Turmoil and Triumph*, p. 335.

263. "Speaker O'Neill seemed lost in though for a time, and then said, 'I can only say, Mr. President, God be with you, and good luck to us all.'" Weinberger, *Fighting for Peace*, p. 119. See also Meese, *With Reagan*, p. 217.

264. Menges, *Inside the NSC*, p. 83; Bennett, "Anatomy of a 'Go' Decision," p. 77. O'Neill would later explain: "The invasion was already under way, so even if we opposed it there was nothing any of us could do. I had some serious reservations, and I'm sure that my Democratic colleagues did as well, but I'll be damned if I was going to voice any criticism while our boys were out there." *Man of the House*, p. 365.

265. Menges, *Inside the NSC*, p. 83.

266. Smith, *Reagan and Thatcher*, p. 126.

267. Reagan, *An American Life*, p. 454. See also Shultz, *Turmoil and Triumph*, p. 335.

268. Smith, *Reagan and Thatcher*, p. 130. Emphasis added.

269. Reagan, *An American Life*, p. 454. See also Weinberger, *Fighting for Peace*, pp. 119-120.

270. Geoffrey Smith's interview with Ronald Reagan, July 17, 1989, cited in Smith, *Reagan and Thatcher*, p. 129. See also Reagan, *An American Life*, p. 451.

271. Reagan, *An American Life*, pp. 454-455.

272. Geoffrey Smith's interview with Michael Deaver, December 19, 1988, cited in Smith, *Reagan and Thatcher*, p. 126.

273. Weinberger, *Fighting for Peace*, p. 120.

274. Geoffrey Smith's interview with Michael Deaver, December 19, 1988, cited in Smith, *Reagan and Thatcher*, p. 126. McFarlane had a similar recollection: "[I]t was not a happy conversation. The President was very disappointed, not angry. His respect for her was too deep for him ever to become angry with her. But he was disappointed." Geoffrey Smith's interview with Robert McFarlane, January 10, 1990, cited in Smith, *Reagan and Thatcher*, p. 126.

275. This conversation is recounted in Weinberger, *Fighting for Peace*, p. 120.

276. Weinberger, *Fighting for Peace*, p. 120.

277. Menges, *Inside the NSC*, p. 83.

278. Shultz, *Turmoil and Triumph*, p. 333; Oberdorfer, "Reagan Sought," p. A21.

279. Author's interviews with Francis McNeil, November 11, 1988; February 24, 1988.

280. Author's interview with Francis McNeil, February 24, 1989.

281. It had earlier been suggested that one Caribbean leader should attend Reagan's press conference and Prime Minister Adams' name introduced as a possible choice. Adams believed he was too busy on Barbados to fly to Washington. Moreover, Eugenia Charles was the current OECS chair. Author's interview with Francis McNeil, February 24, 1989.

282. Kozak reported that McNeil carried the document with him. Author's interview with Michael Kozak, November 11, 1988.

283. McNeil's airplane was too large to land on Dominica. Since the Government of Dominica lacked its own airplane, the French transported Charles. Author's interview with Francis McNeil, September 20, 1988.

284. Reportedly, Charles "had come to tell President Reagan that 'it doesn't take much -- just a cell of twenty or so determined men, and they wouldn't have had any trouble finding recruits, to overthrow a state like Dominica.'" Allan Gerson's interview of Eugenia Charles, March 21, 1987. Cited by Gerson, *The Kirkpatrick Mission*, p. 221.

285. Author's interview with Francis McNeil, February 24, 1988.

286. Author's interview with Francis McNeil, September 20, 1988; Shultz, *Turmoil and Triumph*, p. 336.

287. Author's interview with Francis McNeil, September 20, 1988.

288. Burgess, "Rescue Bishop," p. A10.

289. See Tyler, "The Making of an Invasion," p. 15; and Gwertzman, "Steps to the Invasion," p. 20.

290. For accounts of Grenada on the day before its invasion, see O'Shaughnessy, *Revolution, Invasion and Aftermath*, pp. 167-168; Schoenhals and Melanson, *Revolution and Intervention*, p. 144; Hendrick Smith, "Ex-U.S. Official Cites Ease in Leaving Grenada Day before Invasion," *New York Times*, October 29, 1983, p. A7; Kwitney, *Endless Enemies*, pp. 416-417; and Adkin, *The Battle for Grenada*, p. 102.

291. O'Shaughnessy, *Revolution, Invasion and Aftermath*, p. 168.

292. Schoenhals and Melanson, *Revolution and Intervention*, p. 144.

293. According to Representative Thomas Foley, chairman of the Congressional delegation that visited Grenada after its invasion: the President did not have the luxury of waiting a week to see how things developed before making a decision. "Waiting a week was a decision." William S. Broomfield, "The President Couldn't Wait," *Washington Post*, November 14, 1983, p. A17.

294. Geoffrey Bourne in *U.S. Military Actions in Grenada*, p. 196.

295. Author's interview with Langhorne Motley, September 20, 1988.

296. Some time early on Tuesday, the State Department cabled Havana and Moscow to assure them the U.S. action was not aimed at them or their people on Grenada. Oberdorfer, "Reagan Sought," p. A21. The information was delayed so that "Cuba and the Soviet Union [could] not interfere with the success of the operation." Motley, "The Decision to Assist Grenada," p. 71.

297. Clines, "Days of Crisis," p. A22.

298. Hertsgaard, *On Bended Knee*, p. 215; Speakes, *Speaking Out*, p. 153.

299. Hertsgaard, *On Bended Knee*, pp. 215-216.

300. Speakes, *Speaking Out*, p. 153.

301. Speakes, *Speaking Out*, p. 155. Emphasis mine.

302. Cited in Speakes, *Speaking Out*, p. 160.

303. For accounts of the October 25 meeting, see Bennett, "Anatomy of a 'Go' Decision," p. 77; Woodward, *Veil*, p. 291; Menges, *Inside the NSC*, pp. 85-86; and Weinberger, *Fighting for Peace*, pp. 121-122. This account also draws upon the author's interview with Francis McNeil, September 20, 1988.

304. Menges, *Inside the NSC*, p. 86.

305. Menges, *Inside the NSC*, p. 86; Author's interview with Francis McNeil, September 20, 1988.

306. Bennett, "Anatomy of a 'Go' Decision," p. 77.

307. Bennett, "Anatomy of a 'Go' Decision," p. 77.

6

Law After the Invasion Announcement

*You can't be serious.... The whole world knows that
[protection of nationals is] not what the operation was really
about. If it was, it would have been much more limited,
without the need for OECS involvement. If protection of
nationals is what we were truly interested in, we would have
done an Entebbe-style rescue. Here U.S. national security
interests in the region were involved. We didn't want another
Cuba or Nicaragua in the Caribbean, especially one led by
the likes of the group that killed Maurice Bishop. And we had
reason to act: the OECS states felt threatened. Isn't that why
we did what we did? If so, why not say it?[1]*
— Allan Gerson to Michael Kozak,
October 26, 1983

The story of international law's role in the *decision* to invade Grenada
ends on the morning of October 25, 1983 — with the closing words of
the President's White House press conference. By then, the administration's die had been cast. Operation "Urgent Fury" had begun and
Ronald Reagan had publicly acknowledged U.S. participation in the
collective operation. Already, Pearls Airport had been secured and
American servicemen had perished. Though by Tuesday morning, the
military option had been selected and executed, international legal
considerations continued to have a bearing on administration policy.
Specifically, in the next several days, law would influence the *articulation* of American policy. It is upon this justificatory function of law that
Chapter Six will focus, concentrating in particular on the post-invasion

dialogue between the State Department in Washington and the United States Mission to the United Nations (USUN) in New York. Within the Reagan administration, it will be shown, markedly different approaches to legal justification were favored.

Law at the USUN

Listening Tuesday morning to the "squawk box" in his New York office was Allan Gerson, Legal Adviser to USUN.[2] As President Reagan's news conference with Eugenia Charles was transmitted from the State Department, Gerson learned for the first time of the administration's decision to use armed force in Grenada.[3] "At the U.S. Mission," he later recalled, "we prepared ourselves for an onslaught of condemnation across the street [in the U.N. Headquarters] as news of the invasion was announced."[4] Gerson was not the only administration legal authority to have been excluded from the decisionmaking loop. Attorney General William French Smith, for example, had been briefed about "Urgent Fury" only shortly before it had been launched when Constantine Menges and Robert Kimmitt, the National Security Council's Legal Counsel, had come to Smith's Justice Department office.[5] Indeed, as we have seen, only a select few lawyers were privy to the Reagan administration's Grenada deliberations.

The next day, in the early afternoon of Wednesday, October 26, U.N. Ambassador Jeane Kirkpatrick sought the counsel of her legal adviser:

> Allan, we're scheduled to speak tomorrow .... I'd like to deliver a major address. I'd like you to make the strongest case possible in international law on behalf of the Grenada operation.[6]

Gerson had assumed until then that Kirkpatrick's speech would be "big on facts and little on the law" — that it would be consistent with the line of argument already suggested in earlier White House statements. He asked his superior about her intended scope:

> Do you wish ... to go beyond what the President said at the news briefing? He's already spelled out our legal defense: protection of the lives of U.S. nationals, forestalling further chaos and anarchy, and the restoration of conditions of law and order on the island.[7]

Gerson then proffered his assessment of the legal "case" thus far advanced by the Reagan administration:

> It's not a defense in any doctrinal sense of international law, but apparently it's the case the White House, and presumably the State Department, want to make. They haven't come out with any legal defense. Do you want me to go beyond that?[8]

Kirkpatrick told Gerson that it did not matter to her if the State Department had not made a doctrinal legal argument. She wanted her aide to prepare one that could be incorporated into her speech to be delivered the next day.[9]

Gerson knew now that a long evening awaited him. First, he canceled a planned dinner engagement. Then, he telephoned Michael Kozak, the State Department's Deputy Legal Adviser in Washington, to brief Kozak on USUN activities and to solicit Kozak's legal input.[10]

Prior to his call to Foggy Bottom, Gerson had judged that the American action might be justified as an act of anticipatory "collective self-defense." Though Grenada had not launched an "armed attack" *per se* against the other OECS states, he believed that the eastern Caribbean microstates had "valid legal grounds for acting *before* the men and women responsible for the killing of Prime Minister Maurice Bishop could consolidate their control of Grenada with the help of 1,000 or more Cuban advisers on the island."[11] Within this context, Kirkpatrick's legal adviser supposed, "we would argue that the United States assistance [had been] based on concern for the safety of the region and for the stability of the Western Hemisphere, as well as an interest in serving the safety of American medical students left stranded on the island."[12]

"You can't say that," responded Kozak to Gerson's proposed argument. Grenada had posed to the other OECS states no imminent threat of "armed attack." Accordingly, to invoke an anticipatory self-defense argument here would be seriously to damage Article 51's limitation on the permissible recourse to self-defense.[13] Recalled Gerson:

> [Michael Kozak's] primary concern seemed to be the effect [my suggested] interpretation would have on other states who might then claim an expanded notion of self-defense to justify their own preemptive military adventures. Were the United States, he warned, to endorse self-

defense as a rationale for the Grenada operation, it would be enlarging an exception to the UN Charter's prohibition on the use of force to the point that armies could march through it.[14]

In a 1988 interview, Michael Kozak foreshadowed Gerson's 1991 memoir account. In its process of developing the administration's case for Grenada, Kozak then observed, "L"'s biggest concern had been to avoid creating a legal rationale for "another Afghanistan."[15]

Allan Gerson was himself rather skeptical of Kozak's view. An aggressive state, Gerson argued, need not rely upon an expanded self-defense definition in order to undertake whatever armed action it judged to be consistent with its national interest. Moreover, the former Justice Department prosecutor contended, Reagan had already implicitly supported the "self-defense" argument by his allusions to the Cuban role in the Grenada takeover.[16]

Gerson's views notwithstanding, the State Department strongly opposed the "self-defense" rationale, fearing such an argument would send the wrong international message. Hence, Gerson was "instructed" to limit the USUN's legal justification to "protection of nationals" grounds.[17] According to Gerson's memoir account, he indignantly retorted:

> You can't be serious.... The whole world knows that that's not what the operation was really about. If it was, it would have been much more limited, without the need for OECS involvement. If protection of nationals is what we were truly interested in, we would have done an Entebbe-style rescue. Here U.S. national security interests in the region were involved. We didn't want another Cuba or Nicaragua in the Caribbean, especially one led by the likes of the group that killed Maurice Bishop. And we had reason to act: the OECS states felt threatened. Isn't that why we did what we did? If so, why not say it?[18]

Kozak replied that State did not want the U.S. legal case tied to grounds of checking Soviet or Cuban influence in the western hemisphere. The Deputy Legal Adviser therefore proposed that he and Gerson exchange drafts of their arguments and that they then develop a final one.[19]

To facilitate Gerson's efforts, Kozak over the next several hours transmitted facsimiles of relevant information from Foggy Bottom to the U.N. Mission in New York.[20] Among the materials Gerson could draw upon were the following: a chronology of recent events; public justificatory statements by some of the Caribbean leadership;[21] Sir Paul Scoon's request for assistance;[22] and Mary McLeod's assessment[23] of the legal status of that request. Gerson recalls having been urged then not to make any reference yet to Scoon's request, however.[24] In his memoir, Gerson suggests that by Wednesday evening, October 26, no public revelation of Sir Paul Scoon's request could safely have been made by the United States. Such a disclosure then or on Thursday, he intimates, would only have endangered Scoon's life because the Grenadian Governor-General remained on Grenada "in hiding." Accordingly, "[w]e could inform the UN Secretary-General privately of this development, but were asked not to make it public."[25]

For two reasons, Gerson's account of the Scoon request is somewhat problematic. First, as has been recounted in Chapter Two, Sir Paul had been not been "hiding" on Grenada, but rather had been under virtual house arrest in his Government House residence in St. George's. Second, Scoon had been rescued by Marine units on *Wednesday morning*, October 26, and thereafter flown by helicopter to the safety of the USS *Guam*. Hence, by Wednesday evening there should have been no reason for the United States not to refer to Scoon's letter. In fact, Kirkpatrick's October 27 address to the Security Council would make a brief allusion to Sir Paul's request, the first such reference by the Reagan administration.[26]

As Gerson contemplated late Wednesday evening how he would structure a legal defense of American actions, he came to believe that a sound one "would have to rest not on a single argument — like individual and collective self-defense — but on the cumulative weight of several arguments — which, if taken individually, might be insufficient to make our case."[27] He would employ, therefore, a "kitchen sink" approach.[28] Tossed into that "sink" would be three arguments: protection of nationals; restoration of conditions of law and order; and an end to anarchy.[29]

Thursday, October 27

By around 2:00 A.M. Thursday morning, a draft had been completed of the portion of Ambassador Kirkpatrick's address that would set out the legal rationale for "Urgent Fury." Her speech to the U.N. Security Council would stress "the facts, not the law."[30] Kozak urged that Kirkpatrick accentuate the "unique combination of circumstances" that the Grenada case had offered. Such an emphasis, maintained Kozak, would signal that the administration did not consider the Grenada operation precedent-setting for future uses of armed force by the United States — whether against Nicaragua, Cuba, or any other sovereign state.[31] That impression, Gerson countered, was probably *not* the one Reagan himself wished to communicate.[32]

Early on Thursday morning, Deputy Secretary of State Kenneth Dam telephoned Ambassador Kirkpatrick from Washington.[33] Dam, a former University of Chicago law professor, was calling on behalf of his boss. The Secretary of State, declared Dam, wanted Kirkpatrick's Security Council address to underscore that "the U.S. operation in Grenada was based on a unique combination of circumstances, that it was a reaction to very particular and compelling circumstances." It was George Shultz's wish, Dam reported, that Ambassador Kirkpatrick "avoid any reference to self-defense as a legal justification."[34] Either Shultz or Dam, it now seems likely, had been briefed Thursday by Kozak on USUN's predilection for a self-defense argument.

To a certain limited extent, Kirkpatrick's October 27 address to the Security Council would reflect her conversation that morning with Kenneth Dam. She "pencilled in,"[35] for example, modifications to her prepared text that reflected State's desire to underscore the "unique" character of the Grenada case. Nevertheless, her speech did not eschew the self-defense argument. Indeed, she argued that the OECS states had been "spurred to action" because Bishop's murderers "could reasonably be expected to wield [Grenada's] awesome power against its neighbors." When asked for assistance, explained Kirkpatrick, "the United States, whose own nationals and vital interests were independently affected, joined the effort to restore minimal conditions of law and order in Grenada and eliminate the threat posed to the security of the entire region."[36]

Ambassador Kirkpatrick and the State Department

Ambassador Kirkpatrick's argument before the United Nations, as Chapter 3 has emphasized, was fundamentally informed by a contextual approach to international law. The U.N. Charter's prohibitions against the use of force, she declared, were "contextual, not absolute." Hence, they provided "ample justification for the use of force in pursuit of other values also inscribed in the Charter — freedom, democracy, peace."[37] Here, Kirkpatrick appeared to follow the "policy-oriented" jurisprudence advocated by Myres McDougal and her Columbia University mentor, Harold Lasswell — *not* the more conventional legal approach preferred by the State Department.

As depicted in the rhetoric of Jeane Kirkpatrick, as well as that of Ronald Reagan,[38] Grenada represented an unambiguous case of United States support for "freedom" and "democracy."[39] To a certain limited degree, therefore, the American action in Grenada would prefigure the "Reagan Doctrine."[40] Allan Gerson recalls in his memoir that "for many in the State Department, President Reagan's unabashed assertion of the American *right* to aid freedom fighters — what came to be known as the Reagan Doctrine — was cause for embarrassment." Hence,

> [State's] insistence that "self-defense" not be relied on to justify the American intervention in Grenada took on new significance. At stake was not some obscure point of international law. The issue was whether Grenada would stand for the reassertion of American power in the Western hemisphere.

Concludes Gerson:

> Kirkpatrick saw nothing wrong with putting Nicaragua's Daniel Ortega on notice about the capabilities of U.S. power and the limits of U.S. patience. She assumed that was what the President wanted. But few in the State Department sought the accolade of being shock troops for the Reagan Doctrine.[41]

Michael Kozak was equally candid in a 1988 interview. Noted then the former Deputy Legal Adviser of the State Department: Ambassador Kirkpatrick "talked policy, not law."[42]

Notes

1.   Gerson, *The Kirkpatrick Mission*, p. 227.
2.   This account of Gerson's role draws heavily upon his memoir, *The Kirkpatrick Mission*, pp. 222-233; and to a lesser degree, upon author's interviews with Gerson, November 4, 1988; and with Michael Kozak, November 3, 1988.
3.   Author's interview with Allan Gerson, November 4, 1988.
4.   Gerson, *The Kirkpatrick Mission*, p. 223.
5.   Menges, *Inside the NSC*, p. 82.

6. Gerson, *The Kirkpatrick Mission*, p. 225. According to Gerson's account, Ambassador Kirkpatrick's speech was scheduled for "Thursday morning." Though her Security Council address may have been so scheduled, it was actually delivered around 7:00 PM Thursday evening.

7. Gerson, *The Kirkpatrick Mission*, p. 225.

8. Gerson, *The Kirkpatrick Mission*, p. 225.

9. Gerson, *The Kirkpatrick Mission*, p. 225.

10. Author's interview with Allan Gerson, November 4, 1988; Gerson, *The Kirkpatrick Mission*, p. 225; author's interview with Michael Kozak, November 3, 1988.

11. Gerson, *The Kirkpatrick Mission*, p. 226. Emphasis added.

12. Gerson, *The Kirkpatrick Mission*, p. 226.

13. Gerson, *The Kirkpatrick Mission*, p. 226; author's interview with Allan Gerson, November 4, 1988; author's interview with Michael Kozak, November 3, 1988.

14. Gerson, *The Kirkpatrick Mission*, p. 226; author's interview with Allan Gerson, November 4, 1988.

15. Author's interview with Michael Kozak, November 3, 1988.

16. Gerson, *The Kirkpatrick Mission*, pp. 226-227.

17. Gerson, *The Kirkpatrick Mission*, p. 227.

18. Gerson, *The Kirkpatrick Mission*, p. 227.

19. Gerson, *The Kirkpatrick Mission*, p. 227.

20. Gerson, *The Kirkpatrick Mission*, p. 227.

21. Kirkpatrick's October 27 speech before the Security Council would explicitly refer to public statements by Prime Ministers Seaga of Jamaica and Adams of Barbados.

22. As noted in Chapter 5, word of Sir Paul Scoon's request had been received in Washington early on Monday morning, October 24. His letter of request, as reported in Chapter 2, was formally received by Lawrence Rossin on the morning of October 26. That letter may well have been drafted by the State Department and delivered to Scoon for his signature by Rossin. See Alan George, "Did Washington Ghost-Write Scoon's Appeal?" *New Statesman*, November 11, 1983, p. 5; and Larry Black, *Toronto Globe and Mail*, November 2, 1983, p. 2.

23. Author's interview with Michael Kozak, November 3, 1988.

24. Gerson, *The Kirkpatrick Mission*, p. 227; author's interview with Allan Gerson, November 4, 1988.

25. Gerson, *The Kirkpatrick Mission*, p. 227.

26. "That the coup leaders had no arguable claim to being the responsible government was, indeed, made clear by their own declarations, the failure of other states to recognize them as the legitimate government, and by the fact that *the Governor-General of Grenada, the sole remaining symbol of governmental*

authority on the island, invited OECS action." See Chapter 3 and "Ambassador Kirkpatrick's Statement, UN Security Council, October 27, 1983," *Department of State Bulletin* 83 (December 1983): 76.

27. Gerson, *The Kirkpatrick Mission*, pp. 227-228.

28. Author's interview with Allan Gerson, November 4, 1988.

29. Gerson, *The Kirkpatrick Mission*, p. 228.

30. Gerson, *The Kirkpatrick Mission*, p. 228.

31. Gerson, *The Kirkpatrick Mission*, pp. 228, 231; author's interview with Michael Kozak, November 3, 1988; author's interview with Allan Gerson, November 4, 1988.

32. Gerson, *The Kirkpatrick Mission*, p. 228.

33. Gerson, *The Kirkpatrick Mission*, p. 228.

34. Gerson, *The Kirkpatrick Mission*, p. 228.

35. Gerson, *The Kirkpatrick Mission*, p. 228.

36. "Ambassador Kirkpatrick's Statement, UN Security Council, October 27, 1983," p. 76.

37. "Ambassador Kirkpatrick's Statement, UN Security Council, October 27, 1983," p. 74.

38. See, for example, Reagan's "Address to the Nation, October 27, 1983," *Weekly Compilation of Presidential Documents* 19 (October 31, 1983): 1497-1502.

39. On the pro-democratic efforts of the Reagan administration in Latin America, see Thomas Carothers, *In the Name of Democracy: U.S. Policy Toward Latin America in the Reagan Years* (Berkeley: University of California Press, 1991).

40. According to Edwin Meese, "For the first time ever, a country that had been drawn into the communist orbit had been liberated by force of arms, and by American willingness to assist forces of freedom." Hence, "Grenada gave us a sampling of what was increasingly known as the Reagan Doctrine." Meese, *With Reagan*, p. 222.

41. Gerson, *The Kirkpatrick Mission*, p. 232.

42. Author's interview with Michael Kozak, November 3, 1988.

7

Thirteen Days in October, Again

[L]aw was one of the critical forces molding decision.[1]
— Abram Chayes on John F. Kennedy's
Cuban missile crisis decisionmaking

[I]t seems as though the President thinks he is a law unto himself ....[2]
— Abram Chayes on Ronald Reagan's
Grenada invasion decisionmaking

In the middle of October 1962, the Kennedy administration spent thirteen anxious days considering whether to use military force in response to menacing communist activities on a Caribbean island.[3] By an ironic twist of fate, twenty-one years later, the Reagan administration devoted thirteen mid-October days to much the same thing.[4] In 1983, however, the island in question was Grenada, not Cuba, and the immediate threat to Americans was posed not by Soviet intermediate-range nuclear missiles, but by the uncertain conditions that followed a hardline Marxist coup within an existing Marxist government. Once again, after extended debate in secret high-level meetings, the President authorized the use of military force. And as in 1962, the administration euphemistically characterized its use of force, except now the American action was dubbed a "rescue mission," not a "quarantine." Finally, like Kennedy's naval blockade of Cuba, Reagan's combined-service invasion of Grenada was legally controversial but politically successful: the U.S. action proved a setback for Soviet strategic interests, but some charged, one for international legality as well.[5]

Among the more prominent critics of President Reagan's decision to launch "Urgent Fury" was Abram Chayes, a professor of law at Harvard University who had served as State Department Legal Adviser from 1961 to 1964. During the Cuban missile crisis, international law had been "one of the *critical forces* molding opinion," Chayes argued in a 1974 work.[6]   During October of 1983, however, international law had apparently played no such role. Professor Chayes remarked on the day of the Grenada invasion: "[I]t seems as though the President thinks he is a law unto himself."[7]

Was Chayes' criticism of the Reagan administration well grounded? To what degree did international law actually play a role in the "thirteen-day" decision to invade Grenada?   How satisfactory was the legal justification ultimately tendered by the administration?   And what more general "lessons" may be gleaned from the Grenada episode about international law and its policy-relevance?

To answer these questions, this chapter will first set out the three legal principles cited by the State Department Legal Adviser's Office to justify action by the United States. Then, using these three principles as reference points, it will offer a general assessment of "how" international legal considerations affected the shaping of policy, but not precisely "how much" they did so.   To measure law's influence with any great accuracy would be, as Professor Chayes and other scholars have argued, virtually impossible.[8]   Having evaluated law's influence, this chapter will next briefly reconsider whether the *jus ad bellum* principles invoked by "L" actually justified the American invasion of Grenada.   Finally, it will set out the broader implications of the "Urgent Fury" story for contemporary international law and foreign policy decisionmaking.

Three Plausible Legal Principles

It is impossible now to determine with certainty what legal principles, if any, the Reagan administration thought would legitimately justify the various American actions undertaken in "Urgent Fury."   Indeed, at least one administration decisionmaker judged that the U.S. operation could *not* be justified under international law.[9]   Nevertheless, Davis Robinson's letter to Edward Gordon, the administration's best legal "case," suggests which principles the State Department Legal Adviser's Office believed might *plausibly* justify the Grenada invasion.

Robinson's letter of February 10, 1984 was actually drafted by Deputy Legal Adviser Michael Kozak.[10] Robinson deemed the letter a better legal defense of Reagan's Grenada invasion than the defenses that had earlier been advanced in support of Kennedy's Cuba quarantine and of Johnson's Dominican Republic intervention.[11] Robinson and Kozak were concerned that the State Department's rendition of the *jus ad bellum* not be considered illegitimate since "the way in which States articulate[d] and interpret[ed] principles of international law [was] perhaps even more important" than factual debates. One could quibble about facts, Kozak would later observe, but it was important that there be "nothing new in international law."[12]

Too facile an appeal to law, the Legal Adviser's Office recognized, might well come back to haunt the United States. "L" was particularly mindful that it not create a justification for "another Afghanistan."[13] Accordingly, Robinson's letter deliberately eschewed appeals to "humanitarian intervention" and to "new interpretations of Article 2(4)." Instead, it invoked three "well-established legal principles" to defend American actions in Grenada: (1) the "protection of nationals;" (2) "collective action under Article 52 of the U.N. Charter;" and (3) "the request of lawful authority." But what influence did these three "principles" actually exert on Reagan administration decisionmaking?

(1) Protection of nationals

What role did protection of nationals play in the Reagan administration's invasion decision? Many post-invasion observers have disparaged the administration's assertion that it had feared for the safety of U.S. citizens. Indeed, even USUN Legal Adviser Allan Gerson has argued that protection of nationals was "not what the [Grenada] operation was really about."[14] Despite such perceptions, a reconstruction of the Grenada decisionmaking process demonstrates that at least some U.S. Government officials were genuinely concerned that American nationals might be harmed or taken hostage — if also that Grenada might become "another Cuba" and threaten its eastern Caribbean neighbors.

In October of 1983, memories of the Iran hostage crisis were still fresh: no one in the administration need then have been reminded that Jimmy Carter's inability to effect the release of American hostages had greatly facilitated Ronald Reagan's electoral victory. Might Americans again be taken hostage? This frightful specter was raised frequently during administration deliberations, apparently first by Undersecretary of State Lawrence Eagleburger in a cabinet-level meeting on October 20.[15] Nor could the State Department ignore the sound of telephones ringing as the anxious parents of American medical students on Grenada called to inquire about the welfare of their offspring. "Who was going to write an insurance policy on those [American] kids?" wondered Tony Motley, the Assistant Secretary of State for Inter-American Affairs.[16] In determining the proper course for U.S. policy, he would later suggest, "eighty percent security [for the students] would not have been good enough."[17] George Shultz would recall his Grenada discussions with Motley: "We both had the searing memory of Tehran and the sixty-six Americans seized from our embassy on November 4, 1979, and held hostage for well over a year."[18]

On Thursday, October 13, and Friday, October 14, the Reagan administration's first meetings to consider the Grenada situation appear to have concentrated principally on the welfare of U.S. citizens. Discord within the Grenadian government might mean trouble, Motley's Restricted Interagency Group recognized. It might also have important geopolitical implications.

On Monday, October 17, two days before Bishop's death, Tony Motley urged that serious thought be given to planning a "noncombatant evacuation operation," despite Vice Admiral Moreau's reluctance. All across Grenada on Saturday, protestors had demanded Bishop's release, and real trouble seemed now to be brewing on Grenada. Moreover, elsewhere in the Caribbean, the leaders of several island states had begun Saturday to discuss the possibility of taking collaborative military action. Given these circumstances, President Reagan ordered Monday evening that "NEO" planning proceed. Reagan's October 17 decision was made after a briefing by his just-appointed National Security Adviser, Robert McFarlane.

On the afternoon of October 19, "Bloody Wednesday," Maurice Bishop and scores of other Grenadians perished in the gruesome aftermath of an unsuccessful attempt to return Bishop to power. Back in Washington that same afternoon, a majority of the RIG members resolved that serious planning for a "nonpermissive evacuation" — a military invasion — was necessary. Whether the Restricted Interagency Group knew during its meeting what brutality had just taken place on Grenada is uncertain. Nevertheless, by October 19 Assistant Secretary Motley and his colleagues had become even more concerned about the welfare of the Americans on Grenada. They must also have recognized that the unstable conditions on the island presented attractive opportunities: to remove a Marxist regime disliked both by Grenada's neighbors and Washington; and to expel Cuban and Soviet influence. Despite these prospects, the safety of U.S. citizens on Grenada remained the central preoccupation. Such concern would surely have been warranted given the manifest limitations then of American intelligence on the Grenada situation. As John Lehman has tersely observed: "Grenada pointed out that we have the worst human intelligence network of any major power. We simply had no one on the scene in Grenada, even after several years of visible Communist penetration."[19]

In the four days after "Bloody Wednesday," the State Department sought unsuccessfully to find a peaceful way to ensure the safety of Americans on Grenada. In part, State's failure may actually have stemmed from actions taken by the OECS and by Washington. General Hudson Austin's Revolutionary Military Council appears at first to have deliberately pursued a policy of accommodation. Such a conciliatory approach would seem then to have been only prudent. Why would Austin and his colleagues seek to provide the United States with a convenient pretext for invasion, or even to alienate St. George's Medical School, a major source of Grenadian revenue? As word of Friday's OECS discussions in Bridgetown and of the diversion of a U.S. flotilla reached Grenada, however, the Council became convinced that invasion was imminent. Because of this fear, it changed its strategy and began to stall. Leon Cornwall's diplomatic intransigence on Sunday, October 23, in turn reinforced American fears that the medical students might be viewed as "pawns."

So believed Ambassador Frank McNeil when he urged very early on Monday morning, October 24, that action be taken:

> I recommended sending in the troops, so long as it was done quickly before surprise was lost. In so doing, I was mindful of Teheran, where colleagues had languished as hostages for so long. It is far easier to prevent a hostage situation than to deal with it once it is consummated, and I judged the danger to the students was growing. .... [T]he make-or-break factor for me was the students.[20]

Given its timing, McNeil's invasion recommendation probably had little or no influence on Reagan's invasion decision. Nevertheless, the Ambassador's assessment of the dangers posed to Americans on Grenada should not be taken lightly. A respected professional diplomat and a political moderate, McNeil was no cheerleader for activist foreign policy *per se*. Indeed, his critique of Assistant Secretary of State Elliot Abrams' Central American "fantasy" in 1984-1986 lead to McNeil's forced resignation from the State Department.[21] Consequently, Frank McNeil's memoir account cannot merely be dismissed as "special pleading" for the Reagan administration.

By its decision to divert naval forces toward Grenada, the Reagan administration may unintentionally have endangered U.S. citizens. This point is certainly open to scholarly debate. Also arguable is the degree to which the administration's prodemocracy, anticommunist policy in Latin American influenced deliberations. Clearly, fears of "another Cuba" in the Caribbean shaped the views of some policymakers.[22] Nevertheless, the record of the Grenada decisionmaking process confirms that at least some U.S. Government officials were authentically concerned about the welfare of U.S. citizens.[23] To suggest otherwise, as some critics have done, is to impute to every Reagan administration decisionmaker either a cavalier disregard for life or Machiavellian motives in the extreme.

The report of William S. Broomfield, member of a bipartisan congressional fact-finding mission that traveled to Grenada after the invasion, reinforces a more benign interpretation of administration intent:

> [I]t is clear from what the embassy officials told the delegation that every attempt was made to extract the students prior to the intervention, but those attempts were met by a persistently hardening opposition on the part of the revolutionaries. The State Department was prepared to bring in a commercial cruise ship, Pan American aircraft, military aircraft, charter aircraft, civilian boats, and military boats to get the students out, but all of these avenues were rejected by Revolutionary Military Council official Leon Cornwall.[24]

The U.S. government had pursued diplomatic measures, but these had proved ultimately unfruitful. Representative Thomas Foley, chair of the congressional delegation to Grenada, argued that the President did not have the luxury of waiting a week before deciding what course to undertake: "Waiting a week," he concluded, "was a decision."[25] Even the Vice Chancellor of St. George's Medical School, Geoffrey Bourne, came to recognize the potential dangers that had been faced by his student body on Grenada. An early critic of the Reagan administration's invasion decision, Bourne would later concede during a congressional

like the weight and consequence of anticommunist ideology or Reagan's desire to restore American hegemony or the Vietnam Syndrome's persistence within Defense Department are, and must remain, unknowable. This work accepts the fundamental premise, then, that the effects of subjective factors on decisionmaking can be observed and sometimes even isolated, but that they cannot be precisely quantified.

A careful review of the Reagan administration's deliberations readily supports the conclusion that international legal considerations were not determinative of policy. Sir Paul Scoon's invitation, for example, could not have exerted any significant influence upon Reagan's invasion decision given the timing of its receipt by the American Embassy. Moreover, the President's essential decision to act was reached Sunday evening — even before Ambassador McNeil's receipt of a formal written invitation from the OECS. If law had been a critical factor in administration deliberations, one might expect Reagan's determination to launch "Urgent Fury" to have followed, not preceded, these two legally significant invitations. Certainly, at least three prominent participants have intimated that legal considerations did *not* play a significant role in final administration deliberations.[37] That United States citizens might be in danger and that the OECS had made a verbal request for military assistance appear to have been deemed by Reagan administration decisionmakers sufficient cause for American action.[38]

To suggest that law was not determinative of policy is not to suggest that law played no role in administration deliberations, however. In fact, law seems to have played two different roles in the Grenada decision-making process: first, it acted briefly as a restraint on administration action; and second, it served more prominently as a justification for action.

As we have seen, the lack of an OECS invitation on Thursday, October 20, postponed at least for a time the administration's ultimate decision to take forcible action. Whether an OECS failure to request U.S. help would have prevented the Reagan administration from launching "Urgent Fury" is disputable. However, the Reagan administration would likely have taken some sort of action even lacking a formal request for military assistance: American students seemed genuinely in danger, and the opportunities to restore democracy to Grenada and to expel Cuban influence from the island were surely tempting ones.

International law's role as a justification for action was far more pronounced than its role as a restraint on action. Relatively early in the decisionmaking process, on October 21, Motley apprehended that an inadequate legal defense might well compromise the administration's justification exercise. That Friday, he decided to approve James Michel's suggestion to bring in the lawyers. The Assistant Secretary recognized that a plausible legal rationale would simplify matters later if the American military were to launch a full-scale invasion of Grenada. Because he "didn't want nine thousand years of [post-invasion] Security Council debate," he directed his principal deputy to convene a group of attorneys to consider the various legal implications of an American invasion.

Motley and Michel, the former Deputy Legal Adviser and senior State Department attorney, had appreciated that an inadequate legal defense might well compromise the administration's justification exercise. Not all those within the Reagan administration had shared this perspective, however. According to one State Department official, Undersecretary Lawrence Eagleburger opposed the introduction of the Legal Adviser's office into the decisionmaking process for fear that the security of "Urgent Fury" might be compromised.[39]

Because "L" was brought in, Michael Kozak would later explain, "we were able to influence events to improve [the administration's] subsequent justification."[40] Specifically, the necessity of rescuing Sir Paul Scoon could be amplified. Moreover, introducing the lawyers at least three days before D-Day permitted them some time, if not as much as might have been desired, to prepare and to coordinate a legal defense. According to Kozak, who directed that defense, it is "better to include law in the [foreign policy] process, even if it is not conclusive."[41]

Concern for legal advocacy was also evidenced by the administration's actions surrounding the OECS invitation. Once word of the OECS verbal invitation was received very early on Saturday morning, October 22, policy discussions were held until some time after dawn. Only five hours or so later, the Special Situations Group decided to dispatch a special emissary to Barbados to secure a written invitation and that he would carry with him an invitation outline previously drafted by "L" in Washington. Such behavior well supports Scott Davidson's conclusion that "whatever role is attributed to law, it will never be absent ... from the complex of decisionmaking."[42]

Nor did international law's role in bureaucratic politics end once the final Grenada decision had been reached. Indeed, even after Reagan's public invasion announcement, legal questions continued to command governmental attention and to provoke a measure of interdepartmental controversy. As we have seen, those principally responsible for legal justification at the State Department and the U.S. Mission to the United Nations, Michael Kozak and Allan Gerson, advocated fundamentally different rationales for Operation "Urgent Fury."

In preparing Ambassador Kirkpatrick's legal argument for her October 27 address to the Security Council, for example, Allan Gerson believed that the American use of force might be justified principally as an anticipatory "collective self-defense" action. Though Grenada had not launched an "armed attack" as such, he judged that the eastern Caribbean states had legitimate legal grounds for acting before those responsible for Bishop's murder could consolidate their control. Within this context, he supposed, the United States could maintain that its military assistance had been grounded "on concern for the safety of the region and for the stability of the Western Hemisphere, as well as an interest in serving the safety of American medical students left stranded on the island."[43]

In his late-night telephone conversation with Gerson, Michael Kozak objected strongly to the proposed anticipatory self-defense argument. Grenada had posed to the other OECS states no imminent threat of "armed attack." Hence, to invoke an anticipatory self-defense argument here would be seriously to damage Article 51's limitation on the permissible recourse to self-defense. If the United States were to endorse a self-defense rationale, Kozak feared, it would extend an exception to the U.N. Charter's prohibition on the use of force to the point that armies could march through it. And any such future armies might not be those of the United States and its allies.

Kozak advised Gerson to limit the USUN's legal justification to "protection of nationals" grounds. According to Gerson's own account, he responded:

> You can't be serious.... The whole world knows that that's not what the operation was really about. If it was, it would have been much more limited, without the need for OECS involvement.[44]

The Deputy Legal Adviser replied that the State Department did not wish the U.S. legal case tied to grounds of checking Soviet or Cuban influence in the western hemisphere. At length, the telephone debate concluded, though to neither side's complete satisfaction.

George Shultz was sufficiently concerned about the content of Jeane Kirkpatrick's imminent Security Council speech that he directed his deputy, Kenneth Dam, to contact the ambassador on Thursday morning, October 27. Dam explained then to Kirkpatrick that Shultz wanted her address that day to underscore that "the U.S. operation in Grenada was based on a unique combination of circumstances, that it was a reaction to very particular and compelling circumstances." Moreover, the Secretary wished her to "avoid any reference to self-defense as a legal justification."[45] Either Shultz or Dam must earlier have been briefed by Michael Kozak about USUN's predilection for a self-defense rationale, and have shared Kozak's concern that the U.S. legal justification be narrowly drawn.

That Thursday evening in New York, Kirkpatrick would comply with the letter, if not the spirit, of Secretary Shultz's directive. Although she altered her prepared text to emphasize the "unique" character of the Grenada case, her speech did not altogether eschew the self-defense argument. Indeed, she submitted that the OECS microstates had been "spurred to action" because Bishop's murderers "could reasonably be expected to wield [Grenada's] awesome power against its neighbors." When asked for assistance, explained Ambassador Kirkpatrick, "the United States, whose own nationals and vital interests were independently affected, joined the effort to restore minimal conditions of law and order in Grenada and eliminate the threat posed to the security of the entire region."[46] The content of this speech, however accurately it reflected the administration's policy thinking, could little have pleased Foggy Bottom. Noted Michael Kozak tersely in a 1988 interview: "[Ambassador Kirkpatrick] talked policy, not law."[47]

The Legality of "Urgent Fury"

In keeping with its principal objectives, this study has carefully traced the Reagan administration's "Urgent Fury" deliberations and has established what role international law actually played in decisionmaking: law did not determine the outcome, but it did influence the policy process — both before *and* after the invasion decision was made. Although its primary tasks have been accomplished, this work would nevertheless be remiss if it did not offer at least a very concise reassessment of the lawfulness of the Grenada invasion in light of the previously unpublished information it has revealed. To this end, the American use of force will be judged here in terms of the three "well-established legal

principles" set out in the administration's best legal defense, Davis Robinson's letter of February 1984. The validity of each claim will be briefly evaluated in turn: (1) the request of the Governor-General; (2) the OECS decision to take collective action; and (3) protection of American nationals.

(1) The request of the Governor-General

Sir Paul Scoon's request for outside assistance could at most have exerted negligible influence upon President Reagan's final decision to launch "Urgent Fury." Given the time that word of the Governor-General's invitation was received by the American Embassy in Bridgetown, his plea was simply too late to have been "an important factor" influencing Washington deliberations, as Robinson's letter wrongly implies. Indeed, President Reagan *never* mentioned Scoon's request in any of his public explanations for his invasion decision — not even in his most prominent justificatory speech of October 27, delivered after Scoon had been rescued. Nor is any mention whatsoever made of the Grenadian Governor-General or his request in Reagan's 1990 memoir account of the invasion decision.[48]

Once word of Scoon's invitation was received, the Reagan administration may indeed have regarded it "as entitled to great legal and moral weight," as Robinson's letter asserts. Moreover, the Legal Adviser's Office probably did rely "heavily upon this request from the time [the office was] apprised of it." However, "L" did not receive the report of Scoon's request "on October 23," as Robinson's letter mistakenly suggests, but rather, on October 24. This error does not appear to have been a deliberate attempt to misrepresent the facts; rather, it seems merely to reflect that the Legal Adviser's Office was told of Scoon's invitation not long after midnight on Sunday, October 23,[49] and that Scoon's invitation was actually extended on the afternoon of October 23.

But regardless of how and when the United States received it, did Scoon's invitation constitute a *lawful basis* for American recourse to armed force? Robinson's letter submits that "the request of lawful authority is a well-established basis for providing military assistance, whether the requesting state is seeking assistance in the exercise of its inherent right of self defense as recognized in Article 51 of the U.N. Charter, or for other lawful purposes, such as maintenance of internal order." In support of this contention, the letter cites Sir Hersh Lauterpacht's edition of Oppenheim's *International Law*. The claim made by

Lauterpacht that an "invitation of a lawful authority" justifies intervention has certainly been advanced by a number of publicists. Nevertheless, it is far from universally accepted.

Even if one accepts the premise that "invitation by lawful authority" renders intervention permissible, one must still question whether Governor-General Scoon represented a bona fide "lawful authority." Robinson's letter concedes that determining who constitutes the "lawful authority" is sometimes difficult in a situation of factional strife; however, it contends that such was not the case in Grenada: "Under both the Constitution of Grenada as well as the law and practice of the British Commonwealth, the Governor-General possessed a necessary residuum of power to restore order" when "confronted by the breakdown of government in his nation." Scoon was "a recognized head of state of longstanding tenure." To support this view, the State Department Legal Adviser's Office cites authorities less venerable than Sir Hersh Lauterpacht: a 1964 book by Stanley de Smith, *The New Commonwealth and its Constitutions*; and articles from *The Guardian* and *The Economist*.

These sources notwithstanding, Scoon does not appear to have been constitutionally-authorized to invite foreign military forces. The Governor-General had enjoyed certain broad executive powers under the 1967 Constitution,[50] which Grenada formally adopted in 1974 upon gaining its independence from Great Britain.[51] These powers might arguably have validated an invitation of outside intervention until March of 1979. Then, however, the People's Revolutionary Government of Maurice Bishop suspended the 1967 Constitution,[52] proclaiming instead a series of "People's Laws." The second law vested "all executive and legislative power" in the PRG, while the third relegated the Governor-General's personality to that of being merely the Queen's "representative," with the capacity to "perform such functions as the [PRG] may from time to time advise." Having been delegated only limited minor powers of removal and appointment, the office of Governor-General was in October 1983 constitutionally regarded as principally advisory and ceremonial.[53] In view of these circumstances, the argument offered by Christopher Joyner is persuasive:

> Whether Governor-General Scoon in fact "remained the sole source of governmental legitimacy" on Grenada after October 24, 1983 is both arguable and unclear. That he alone possessed sufficient legal and constitutional authority at that time to legitimate an official invitation for the U.S. and OECS military forces to intervene also seems polemical.

What appears beyond dispute is simply that the Governor-General did issue a private appeal for action and that his personal safety may have been in jeopardy. Yet, though hardly inconsequential, these considerations in and of themselves fall short of legally validating external military intervention into the domestic affairs of a sovereign state.[54]

Scoon's invitation, it seems clear, did not constitute a lawful basis for the American use of force.

(2) The OECS decision to take collective action

According to Robinson's letter, the October 21 OECS decision to take collection action provided "further legal support for the U.S. action." The letter advances three basic arguments in support of this claim. First, it contends that the organization's action fell "within Article 52 of the U.N. Charter." Second, it asserts that because the OECS was acting in response to Scoon's request, "the limits of what action a regional organization may properly take absent such a request were not tested in this case." The OECS member states "were doing no more collectively than they could lawfully do individually." Third, Robinson's letter maintains that the "decision [of the OECS] to take military action on Grenada was reached by the heads of government of the OECS nations, who ... have plenary authority under Article 6 of that Treaty."

One may perhaps accept the first premise of Robinson's letter that the OECS was a legitimate "regional arrangement" under Article 52. To concede this point is to grant little of legal consequence *per se*. However, the second and third premises — that the OECS *was not acting* "under its own initiative," and that the OECS *was acting* with "the invitation of the lawful authorities of the State," that is, with the invitation of Sir Paul Scoon — are simply not supported by the facts.

Almost a week before Sir Paul Scoon's invitation of assistance, Tom Adams, John Compton, and Eugenia Charles had approached the United States about collaborative military action. Moreover, the OECS verbal request of American assistance was made on Friday, October 21, two days before Scoon's Sunday afternoon request. Even the OECS written request was drafted approximately four hours before the American receipt of Sir Paul's invitation. Given the time of its drafting, the OECS written request naturally mentions *nothing* about Sir Paul Scoon's request. Almost certainly, the OECS was unaware of Scoon's request when the foreign ministers of two non-OECS states drafted the OECS written invitation. Hence, the argument advanced in Robinson's letter to Gordon fails on factual grounds: the OECS had been intent on military action long before Sir Paul Scoon met with David Montgomery; the regional arrangement was not acting, as the letter wrongly implies, in response to Scoon's plea. The Governor-General's invitation, which was of dubious legal effect anyway, was *post facto*.

But did the OECS have *independent* authority to take military action, and accordingly, to issue invitations of military assistance to the United States, Barbados, and Jamaica? Absent Scoon's invitation, could the OECS as "regional arrangement" lawfully have used force under the circumstances presented by the Grenada situation? Robinson's letter concedes that the issue of "the proper scope of competence of regional organizations to act to restore internal order in a member state" is one of great "import for the development of international law," one that "requires careful analysis in circumstances where an organization acts on its own initiative." Since, as has been shown, the OECS had acted on its own initiative, the questions of the organization's legal capacity to use force and to invite military assistance are relevant ones.

A reconstruction of the events of October 13-25 indicates that the decisionmakers in Washington and Bridgetown believed that the OECS possessed — at least plausibly so — the independent legal authority both to use force and to invite forcible assistance. That the organization in fact had such independent legal authority is highly questionable, however. There are three circumstances under which a regional arrangement may use force in a manner consistent with the U.N. Charter: (1) it may engage in "collective self-defense," in accord with Article 51; (2) it may take "enforcement action" after Security Council authorization, in accord with Article 53; or (3) arguably, it may act after the invitation of a lawful authority. When the OECS voted to take action on Friday, October 21, it lacked both Security Council endorsement and lawful invitation. Accordingly, the only claim remaining would have been anticipatory self-defense, the legal ground favored by Allan Gerson. Yet such a claim lacked plausibility. What *immediate* threat to the OECS states could Grenada have posed when, according to the OECS's own statement on the situation,[55] "law and order [had to be restored] in the country?" To be sure, a Grenada under Marxist leadership might eventually have threatened the microstates of the eastern Caribbean. Nevertheless, in the days immediately following October 19, 1983, such a threat was scarcely "imminent."

decisionmaking process. The President had planned to appoint Baker, a moderate pragmatist, at the beginning of the Grenada deliberations. When confronted by robust opposition from William Clark, Ed Meese, William Casey, and Caspar Weinberger, however, he "reversed [himself] and scrap[ped] the change." Reagan would describe his October 1983 decision to appoint Robert McFarlane instead of Baker as "a turning point for my administration, although at the time I had no idea how significant it would prove to be."[69]

Because foreign policy choices are made and publicly articulated by individuals within government bureaucracies, not by unitary states, several basic principles should inform the study of international law and its political efficacy. First, legal scholars should accustom themselves to looking more regularly inside the "black box" that constitutes the government's decisionmaking process.[70] Unfortunately, the predominant contemporary international legal approach of "positivism" concentrates almost exclusively on *state* practice and *state* consent.[71] While positivism's statist preoccupation simplifies the task of legal analysis, it necessarily obscures international law's essential nature. Hedley Bull has captured well that nature:

> [T]o the extent that rules of international law actually influence behavior in international politics, they are part of social reality. In this sense the view of the Yale international lawyers [i.e., the Lasswell-McDougal jurisprudential school] and others that law is "a social process" is a correct one. It may be conceded, furthermore, that the actual social process of legal decisionmaking, in the international as in the municipal setting, is not a "pure" process of the application of existing legal rules, but reflects the influence of a variety of factors "extraneous" to legal rules themselves, such as the social, moral and political outlook of judges, legal advisers and legal scholars.[72]

In conducting their analyses, students of international law must become less ready to impute "motives" to states and more willing to explore the idiosyncratic influences exerted by individuals upon government policymaking.

Second, scholars should appreciate that comprehensive and nuanced studies of law's policy-relevance can typically not be accomplished either briefly or contemporaneously.[73] Such investigations require careful reconstructions of often byzantine policy processes. They demand, moreover, the accumulation of credible evidence of individual decisionmakers' actions and viewpoints — materials that generally become available to researchers only after the passage of years and governments. Terse, on-the-spot assessments of state action can certainly be undertaken by international lawyers and political scientists, but analyses of this kind should explicitly acknowledge their provisional characters.[74]

Third, scholars should accept the inherent limitations of any inquiry into the human sources of international political action. Professor Henkin has written:

> [I]t is never possible to say how much law weighed among the forces that restrained action. The evidence is usually not available, and, at bottom, conclusive evidence cannot exist, for if indeed one had access to all the records, if the actors told all, one could not be confident that one had reached the springs of official behavior.[75]

Though such a conclusion is rather pessimistic, it serves as a healthy corrective for any who might assume that the normative influences upon foreign policy decisions can be fairly readily isolated and distinguished. No study of international law's impact on policy and policymakers, however well-devised and well-executed, can ever yield a genuinely "complete" picture.

Nor, indeed, can a truly "objective" portrait ever be rendered. As Michael Reisman conceded in the introduction to his edited 1988 work, *International Incidents: The Law That Counts in World Politics*:

> Most of the incidents in this volume were prepared by young North American students in a seminar conducted by North American scholars. Every effort was made to be scrupulous in the description of the events and the facts. Yet, without question, factors such as nationality, culture, class, race or ethnicity, interest group, and exposure to crisis influenced the choice of events, their description, and their appraisal.[76]

Similarly, in his 1978 account of law's role in the U.N. Operation in the Congo, Georges Abi-Saab observed: "there remains [in the process of scholarly analysis] an element of subjectivity deriving from conscious or unconscious factors such as one's initial perception and understanding of the standards of legality, one's evaluation of factual situations which may be highly complex and dynamic, and one's own background, ideology, and sympathy with, or antipathy to, causes and persons involved in a situation."[77] Individual scholars cannot expunge completely the effects of personal bias from their investigations of the behavior and motives of individual actors.

The significance of language

This study has systematically employed neither quantitative nor interpretive methods of textual analysis.[78] Nevertheless, it has bolstered a fundamental methodological premise common to various "discourse" approaches: a close examination of language patterns can help to reveal underlying perceptions and motives.[79] International legal scholars have traditionally recognized that "words matter" and that language should be carefully scrutinized in order to divine subjective intentions; international political scientists, however, have too frequently dismissed as epiphenomenal the public statements of government officials. By neglecting the verbal record, however, scholars have denied themselves a potentially useful research supplement.

In the Grenada episode, many Reagan administration decisionmakers took seriously the task of publicly explaining American actions, sometimes fretting over the use of a single word or phrase. Less than an hour before Reagan's televised invasion announcement, for example, administration officials discovered that the words "to restore democracy" had been deleted by the State Department from the President's prepared statement. Such a deletion seemed inappropriate: Ambassador Frank McNeil had frequently stressed to the Caribbean leaders that if the United States were to become involved militarily, then Grenada would get a bona fide "democracy," not a return to Eric Gairy. Kenneth Dam agreed with McNeil, and the words were promptly restored to Reagan's declaration.

Two days after Operation "Urgent Fury" had begun, Kenneth Dam telephoned Ambassador Kirkpatrick in New York.[80] Dam told Kirkpatrick then that Secretary Shultz wished her Security Council address to emphasize that the U.S. action in Grenada had been "based on a unique combination of circumstances." Moreover, Kirkpatrick should eschew "any reference to self-defense as a legal justification."[81] To a certain limited extent, Ambassador Kirkpatrick's speech would reflect her morning discussion with Dam. Though she did not altogether eliminate allusions to "self-defense," Kirkpatrick "pencilled in" modifications to her prepared text to underscore the "unique" nature of the Grenada case.[82]

Four months after the invasion, Michael Kozak drafted Davis Robinson's letter to Professor Edward Gordon. Here, among other arguments, Kozak explicitly repudiated the notion that U.S. forces had undertaken a "humanitarian intervention." The United States had not asserted "a broad new doctrine of 'humanitarian intervention.'" Instead, it had relied upon "the narrower, well-established ground of protection of U.S. nationals." This explicit dismissal of a "humanitarian intervention" rationale constituted a deliberate attempt to distinguish the U.S. legal case from arguments expressed earlier by Reagan administration officials. Ambassador William Middendorf, it will be recalled, had submitted on October 26 that the United States had been motivated by "a particularly humanitarian concern,"[83] while a November 3 White House statement had claimed that the Grenada action had been "taken for humanitarian reasons."[84]

Although Reagan administration personnel disagreed markedly over international legal and policy matters, officials of various political stripes apprehended that the "words" of U.S. public justification had to be carefully chosen. Even Allan Gerson, a legal skeptic, readily acknowledged the significance of justificatory language. He observed in his memoir:

> [O]ur job at the U.S. Mission was to present the facts and the best legal rationales on behalf of our government. What we said in our speeches might not affect the voting patterns of other countries at the United Nations, but it could establish precedent and guidelines for use by American ambassadors around the world.[85]

The Grenada case well illustrated this principle, Gerson suggested: "How we chose to characterize the Grenada operation — whether as a fluke, as an isolated incident in U.S. foreign relations reflecting no more than the reaction to one set of unique circumstances, or whether we chose to cast the matter in larger terms as part of the pattern and strategy of U.S. foreign policy — would help determine U.S. foreign policy." Concluded Gerson: "Our explanations in New York would give the world notice on how the administration perceived the Grenada operation, and whether other 'Grenadas' might be in store for the future."[86]

Because governments at times pay close attention to their public discourse, international relations scholars should consider doing so as well. Valuable insights may well be gleaned. Chapter Three's scrutiny of the "Grenada rationale," for example, suggested a number of conclusions about the Reagan administration, *inter alia*: its personnel held divergent legal and policy views; its attitude toward international law was rather indifferent; it considered the international legal aspects of the Grenada operation sometime on or before October 23; and its decisionmaking was informed by the goal of eliminating Soviet and Cuban influence from Grenada. These accurate interpretations presupposed no knowledge of the decisionmaking process *per se*; they were adduced solely from an analysis of the content and evolution of twelve public statements made by President Reagan and six different administration officials over a four-month period.

Though the careful study of public governmental statements can prove illuminating, textual analysis has inherent limitations. First, it requires "texts," preferably numerous texts, so that language patterns and arguments can be traced. In the Grenada case, a wide array of materials from a variety of official government sources was accessible: letters, speeches, and congressional testimony. Often, however, such a substantial verbal record is unavailable. Governments may simply remain silent on particular issues or offer scanty public commentary. Under these circumstances, analysis of public discourse is either impossible or unlikely to be productive.

Second, it is not clear that all governments — whether American or otherwise — are equally concerned about the language of their public statements or about the political and legal implications of those statements. It may be true, for example, that the governments of liberal democratic states are more likely to trouble themselves about formal explanation than those of non-liberal states. Nor has it been established that the concern of any given government for public justification remains constant from issue area to issue area. Surely, more study of governmental attitudes towards public discourse is warranted.

Third, official government statements do not necessarily reveal all "the facts." Indeed, one would expect politically-sensitive information regularly to be omitted. Secretary Shultz's October 25 Grenada press conference typified this phenomenon.[87] Here, he noted simply that on Saturday morning, October 22, "a message [had come] in from Bridgetown in Barbados." The "information in the cable basically gave the OECS states' analysis of the situation and stated their very strong feeling that they must do something about it on Grenada and their feeling that they were not able to do it on their own, and so they asked if we would help them." Shultz's account could reasonably be construed to mean that the Bridgetown message had been sent by the Caribbean states themselves. In fact, the cable had been drafted by American officials on Barbados who had earlier attended Friday's OECS deliberations. Shultz only noted blandly that there had been "various discussions during the course of Friday," October 21. He neglected to report that exchanges between United States diplomats and Caribbean leaders about the possibility of taking forcible action in Grenada had been taking place since Saturday, October 15 — four days before Maurice Bishop's murder. Secretary Shultz's statement misleadingly implied that Caribbean leaders had first indicated their desire for U.S. military assistance on October 22. His selective rendition of the facts helped to sketch, along with other official government statements, a suggestive but ultimately incomplete picture of Reagan administration motives.

The significance of context

A third broad conclusion reinforced by a reconstruction of the Reagan administration's Grenada decisionmaking process is that "context matters."[88] Foreign policy decisionmaking does not take place within a vacuum. Rather, it typically reflects a constellation of factors external to decisionmakers and to law. Although this phenomenon has been regularly acknowledged, international legal scholars have too often insufficiently appreciated it.[89] As Professor Bowie has rightly cautioned, however, "the legal aspects" of policymaking "cannot be treated in isolation." They are merely "one dimension of a complex and tangled" process.[90]

In the Grenada case, two contextual factors are particularly noteworthy. First, the invasion decisionmaking and its legal dimensions cannot be viewed in isolation from the Beirut massacre of Sunday, October 23. When word of that devastating terrorist attack reached the United States, it obliged Reagan to return immediately from Augusta to Washington and prompted two lengthy National Security Planning Group meetings devoted to "Lebanon and Grenada." Wondered administration policymakers then: Might the Middle East tragedy circumscribe U.S. policy options in the eastern Caribbean?

Before the first NSPG meeting convened Sunday morning, Lawrence Eagleburger told Frank McNeil that no final Grenada decision had been made and that the bloodshed in Beirut might derail an invasion.[91] McNeil would later write: "When I left [Washington for Barbados] I sensed that we would probably not intervene. The White House, shocked by the loss of 250 Marines in the Beirut bombing, feared the political consequences, and the Department of Defense was reluctant at the least, wanting more time to prepare."[92] Others within the administration shared McNeil's perception. As Sunday's second NSPG meeting continued, for example, those outside the Situation Room speculated about whether the Grenada mission would still be launched. Though Constantine Menges hoped that it would, Oliver North believed that the operation would be canceled in the name of retaliation in Lebanon, which would then also not be executed. North judged that the Joint Chiefs "simply did not want to use U.S. military forces in limited combat operations."[93]

Reagan, himself, had been profoundly shaken by the slaughter of the Marines. Indeed, he would subsequently describe October 23 as "the saddest day of my presidency, perhaps the saddest day of my life."[94] The President's grief had been apparent to all his advisers. During Sunday afternoon's NSPG meeting, for example, Reagan had been so moved that he could not finish reading aloud the letter of a father whose Marine son had been dispatched to Lebanon.[95] Michael Deaver had been keenly aware of the President's emotional state: "Every time someone talked casualties, you could see that it took something out of him. His brow was never unfurrowed."[96] Despite Ronald Reagan's personal anguish, however, his preliminary decision Saturday morning to launch Operation "Urgent Fury" was not overturned — events in Lebanon neither stymied nor inspired the Grenada invasion. "If this was right yesterday, it's right today," the President would ultimately conclude, "and we shouldn't let the act of a couple of terrorists dissuade us from going ahead."[97] Indeed, Lawrence Eagleburger has observed, the events in Beirut only amplified the necessity to "demonstrate American resolve."[98]

Though Reagan was compelled to make discrete decisions regarding Grenada and Lebanon, the two policy areas were nevertheless linked. Even before the Beirut tragedy, Caspar Weinberger has conceded, the administration's Grenada decisionmaking process was "greatly complicated by events in Lebanon." The "Urgent Fury" deliberations then were:

> ... all taking place as a kind of sideshow, or at least as a very important, but separate and simultaneous, activity added to those other problems that then required our daily and active attention. Lebanon and the future of our forces there required virtually continuous meetings at this time with the President, the State Department and the National Security Council

(NSC). At the same time, of course, rumors had begun to spread in the press that we were thinking about some kind of intervention in Grenada.[99]

Reflecting on the relationship between the Beirut massacre and the Grenada situation, Weinberger concluded in his memoir: "[O]ne could not and cannot isolate particular crises or events in the constantly shifting history of security issues."[100]   In his October 27 televised address, Ronald Reagan underscored the interrelated nature of foreign policy. With a measure of rhetorical embellishment, he submitted that the "events in Lebanon and Grenada, though oceans apart," were "closely related."[101]

A second contextual factor conspicuously affecting the Grenada decisionmaking process, and the invasion decision *per se*, was the Reagan administration's broader Latin America policy.[102]   Though the precise relationship between that prodemocracy, anticommunist policy and Operation "Urgent Fury" can never be assayed, some connection was nevertheless manifest.   Jeane Kirkpatrick, for example, used the occasion of the Grenada action to fire a "warning shot" at Nicaragua's Sandinista regime.   She argued in Security Council debate that the U.N. Charter's *jus ad bellum* provisions offered "ample justification for the use of force in pursuit" of "freedom, democracy, [and] peace." With the Grenada operation, the United States had helped "eliminate the threat to the security of the entire region," a "combination of brutal men with awesome might .... amassed with Cuban and Soviet backing."[103]   Such trenchant language could scarcely have been ignored in Managua,[104] and Kirkpatrick "saw nothing wrong with putting Nicaragua's Daniel Ortega on notice about the capabilities of U.S. power and the limits of U.S. patience."[105]

President Reagan's televised October 27 address likewise savored of his administration's prodemocracy, anticommunist ideology.   Here, he submitted that U.S. forces had discovered on Grenada "a complete base with weapons and communications equipment, which [made] it clear a Cuban occupation of the island had been planned." Grenada had been "a Soviet-Cuban colony, being readied as a major military bastion to export terror and undermine democracy," Reagan averred, and the United States had "got there just in time."[106]

The President's activist sentiments were shared by at least some members of Tony Motley's Restricted Interagency Group.   That Inter-American policy body, it will be recalled, both initiated the Reagan administration's Grenada deliberations *and* its plan to mine covertly Nicaraguan harbors — within a period of only a few months in 1983.[107]

Undersecretary of State Eagleburger also viewed the Grenada situation through red-tinted lenses. In a 1993 interview, he conceded that fears of "another Cuba" were "clearly involved" in the administration's invasion decision and that in 1983 he had personally believed that the threat of expanded Cuban power had constituted the "principal reason" for taking action. An American use of force, he had then judged, would both expel communist influence from Grenada and exert an important "demonstration effect." To some degree, Eagleburger acknowledged, the genuine predicament of the American students on Grenada had provided "an excuse" for launching an invasion; however, had the political upheaval of "Bloody Wednesday" and its aftermath not taken place, the United States would likely never have undertaken "Urgent Fury."[108]

Perhaps the best evidence of the link between the Reagan administration's invasion decision and its broader Latin America policy aims is provided by the text of the "Grenada" National Security Decision Directive (NSDD). Before U.S. forces could be committed to combat, President Reagan was required to sign that formal authorizing document. Though the Grenada NSDD has not been declassified, its contents have nevertheless been revealed in the press and confirmed by former administration officials.[109] Among other provisions, the presidential directive explicitly articulated three U.S. policy goals served by the Grenada intervention: the protection of American citizens; the restoration of democratic government to Grenada; and the elimination of current and future Cuban intervention on the island. The second and third objectives reflected core Reagan administration values.

Notes

1. Abram Chayes, *The Cuban Missile Crisis: International Crises and the Role of Law* (New York: Oxford University Press, 1974), p. 6.

2. Cited by Stuart Taylor, Jr., "Legality of Grenada Action Disputed," *New York Times*, October 26, 1983, p. A19.

3. For a study using the thirteen days motif, see Robert F. Kennedy, *Thirteen Days: A Memoir of the Cuban Missile Crisis* (New York: W. W. Norton & Company, 1968). The recent declassification of correspondence between Kennedy and Khrushchev suggests, however, "that the missile crisis

lasted more than the '13 days' memorialized in Robert Kennedy's book." Peter Kornbluh and Sheryl Walter, "History Held Hostage: 30 Years Later, We're Still Learning the Secrets of the Cuban Missile Crisis," *Washington Post*, October 11, 1992, p. C2.

4.   For a comparison of the American interventions in the Dominican Republic and Grenada, see Isaak I. Dore, "The U.S. Invasion of Grenada," pp. 173-189.

5.   A prominent critic of the invasion, Davidson concedes that "it is difficult to avoid the conclusion that the US and her allies prospered politically from Grenada." *A Study in Politics*, p. 176.

6.   Chayes, *The Cuban Missile Crisis*, p. 6. Emphasis mine. Chayes' legal defense of U.S. actions during the crisis was published in "Law and the Quarantine of Cuba," *Foreign Affairs* 41 (1962-63): 550-557.

7.   Cited by Taylor, "Legality of Grenada Action Disputed," p. A19. In an Opinion Editorial debate with Professor Eugene Rostow of Yale, Chayes elaborated his opposition. See Chayes, "Grenada Was Illegally Invaded," *New York Times*, November 15, 1983, p. A35. Moore attacks Chayes's legal analysis of Grenada as inconsistent with his analysis of the Cuban missile crisis. See Moore, *Law and the Grenada Mission*, pp. 67.

8.   Chayes, *The Cuban Missile Crisis*, p. 5. See also Abi-Saab, *The United Nations Operation in the Congo 1960-1964*; Bowie, *Suez 1956*; Davidson, *A Study in Politics*; Ehrlich, *Cyprus 1958-1967*; Forsythe, *The Politics of International Law*; and Louis Henkin, "Comment," in Ehrlich, *Cyprus 1958-1967*, pp. 128-133.

9.   In a background interview with the author, one participant in the Grenada decisionmaking process conceded that she/he had judged that the contemplated operation would be illegal, and had indicated her/his belief to other Reagan administration decisionmakers.

10.   Author's interview with Michael Kozak, November 3, 1988.

11.   Author's interview with Davis Robinson, September 21, 1988.

12.   Author's interview with Michael Kozak, November 3, 1988.

13.   Author's interview with Michael Kozak, November 3, 1988.

14.   Gerson, *The Kirkpatrick Mission*, p. 227.

15.   O'Shaughnessy, *Grenada: Revolution, Invasion and Aftermath*, p. 154.

16.   Author's interviews with Langhorne Motley, September 20, 1988; November 4, 1988.

17.   Author's interview with Langhorne Motley, September 20, 1988. See also Shultz, *Turmoil and Triumph*, p. 328.

18.   Shultz, *Turmoil and Triumph*, p. 328.

19.   Lehman, *Command of the Seas*, p. 300. For an account of the *opera bouffe* quality of U.S. intelligence on Grenada, see Nita M. Renfrew and Peter Blauner, "Ollie's Army," *New York*, December 7, 1987, pp. 101-134.

20. McNeil, *War and Peace in Central America*, p. 174.

21. See Walter LaFeber's review of McNeil's *War and Peace in Central America* in *Political Science Quarterly* 104 (Fall 1989): 532-533.

22. Author's interview with Lawrence Eagleburger, March 15, 1993.

23. In his 1992 critique of the Reagan presidency, Lou Cannon concluded on the basis of interviews with all the principal Grenada decisionmakers: "There is no doubt that Reagan was genuinely worried about the plight of the Americans on Grenada, especially the eight hundred students at the St. George's School of Medicine. Considering the violence and anarchy that then prevailed on the island," Cannon submits, "it is not surprising that Reagan's advisers reached the conclusion that Americans were endangered." Concludes Cannon: "The specter of the Iranian hostage crisis haunted the Reagan administration." Cannon, *President Reagan*, p. 446.

24. William S. Broomfield, "The President Couldn't Wait," *Washington Post*, November 14, 1983, p. A17.

25. Broomfield, "The President Couldn't Wait," p. A17.

26. Testimony of Geoffrey Bourne in U.S. Congress, House of Representatives, Subcommittees on International Security and Scientific Affairs and on Western Hemisphere Affairs of the Committee on Foreign Affairs, *U.S. Military Actions in Grenada: Implications for U.S. Policy in the Eastern Caribbean*, 98th Congress, 1st Session, 1983, p. 196.

27. Woodward, *Veil*, p. 290.

28. *The Economist*, "Britain's Grenada Shut-out," p. 32.

29. Author's interview with Francis McNeil, February 24, 1989.

30. Reagan, *An American Life*, p. 450-451.

31. Bennett, "Anatomy of a 'Go' Decision," p. 75; Oberdorfer, "Reagan Sought," p. A1; Weinberger, *Fighting for Peace*, p. 112; author's interview with Francis McNeil, August 11, 1988.

32. According to Kozak, the Scoon invitation "heightened the necessity" that he be rescued. Author's interview with Michael Kozak, November 3, 1988.

33. Alan George, "Did Washington Ghost-Write Scoon's Appeal?" *New Statesman*, November 11, 1983, p. 5. See also Larry Black, *Toronto Globe and Mail*, November 2, 1983, p. 2, cited by Quigley, "Stranger than Fiction," pp. 334-335.

34. Chayes, *The Cuban Missile Crisis*, p. 4. See also Roger Fisher's "Foreword" to Chayes' work, p. v.

35. Chayes, *The Cuban Missile Crisis*, p. 5.

36. Many other analyses of international law's efficacy have been informed by the same premise. Davidson, for example, has submitted: "Political expediency, short-term advantage, domestic influences are all part of the complex brew of foreign affairs." *A Study in Politics*, p. 176. Similarly, Forsythe has contended that "it is impossible to say exactly how much"

opposition to the Reagan administration's Nicaragua policy "was based on the international legal premise that forceful intervention against a sovereign state was impermissible." *The Politics of International Law*, p. 142. Professor Levi, meanwhile, has argued that international law "performs a number of roles and exists in various contexts. Its efficacy varies with the particular part it is given in a a particular context. And it is usually not possible to determine whether any given result was due to the law itself or the context which it applied." Werner Levi, *Law and Politics in the International Society* (Beverly Hills, CA: Sage, 1976), p. 163. See also Abi-Saab, *The United Nations Operation in the Congo 1960-1964*; Bowie, *Suez 1956*; and Ehrlich, *Cyprus 1958-1967*.

37. Author's background interview with State Department official; author's interview with Fred Ikle, July 20, 1989; author's interview with Lawrence Eagleburger, March 15, 1993. Speaking ironically, Eagleburger noted that international law was "not at the top of the agenda."

38. For Reagan's own view see *An American Life*, pp. 449-458.

39. Author's background interview with State Department official. In a 1993 interview, Eagleburger acknowledged his concerns regarding the security of the Grenada operation and argued that international legal considerations should not have affected administration deliberations. Author's interview with Lawrence Eagleburger, March 15, 1993.

40. Author's interview with Michael Kozak, November 3, 1988.

41. Author's interview with Michael Kozak, November 3, 1988. Reflecting on the relationship between foreign policy decisionmaking and law, Kozak candidly admitted, "You do what you have to do, and then you look for a [legal] justification."

42. Davidson, *A Study in Politics*, p. 177. Of international law, Professor Forsythe has similarly written: "Sometimes its impact is greater, sometimes less, but never entirely absent." *The Politics of International Law*, p. 141.

43. Gerson, *The Kirkpatrick Mission*, p. 226.

44. Gerson, *The Kirkpatrick Mission*, p. 227.

45. Gerson, *The Kirkpatrick Mission*, p. 228.

46. "Ambassador Kirkpatrick's Statement, UN Security Council, October 27, 1983," p. 76.

47. Author's interview with Michael Kozak, November 3, 1988.

48. Reagan, *An American Life*, pp. 449-458.

49. This interpretation was reinforced by the author's interviews with Davis Robinson, September 21, 1988; and with Michael Kozak, November 3, 1988. Both noted that "L" had been working through the night.

50. Albert Blaustein and John O'Leary, "Grenada," in *Constitutions of the Countries of the World*, vol. 1, eds. Albert P. Blaustein and Gisbert H. Flanz (Dobbs Ferry, New York: Oceana Publications, 1974), p. 1.

51. "The Grenada Constitution Order, 1973, No. 2155 (1973)," in operation February 7, 1974, reprinted in Blaustein and O'Leary, "Grenada," p. 1.

52. "People's Law No. 1, March 13, 1979," reprinted in Albert P. Blaustein and Steven Holt, "Grenada," in *Constitutions of the Countries of the World*, vol. 6, eds. Albert P. Blaustein and Gisbert H. Flanz (Dobbs Ferry, New York: Oceana Publications, 1983), p. 18.

53. See Blaustein and Holt, "Grenada," pp. 9, 18, 26, 30, 51, 54, and 58.

54. Joyner, "Reflections on the Lawfulness of Invasion," p. 139.

55. "Statement on the Grenada Situation From the OECS Secretariat," reprinted in Moore, Appendix 2, *The Grenada Mission*, p. 90.

56. Arend and Beck, *International Law and the Use of Force*, pp. 60-65.

57. See Arend and Beck, *International Law and the Use of Force*, pp. 93-111.

58. Bennett, "Anatomy of a 'Go' Decision," pp. 74-75.

59. In attempting to derive broad "lessons," a single case study such as this confronts inherent limitations. As Professor Davidson has rightly cautioned, "it is difficult, and perhaps unwise, to attempt to draw universally applicable conclusions" from a single case study. Davidson, *A Study in Politics*, p. 176. See also Robert R. Bowie, *Suez 1956* (New York: Oxford University Press, 1974), p. 98.

60. See especially Graham T. Allison's seminal study, *Essence of Decision: Explaining the Cuban Missile Crisis* (Boston: Little Brown 1971). See also Chayes, *The Cuban Missile Crisis*, pp. 4-5, 101; Forsythe, *The Politics of International Law*, pp. 2, 149-150; and Edwin Hoyt, "Comment," in Ehrlich, *Cyprus*, pp. 134-141.

61. The "bureaucratic politics" dimensions of Reagan administration decisionmaking were well-illustrated by Caspar Weinberger and George Shultz in their memoirs. See Weinberger, *Fighting for Peace*, p. 159; and Shultz, *Turmoil and Triumph*, pp. 323-345.

62. Gerson, *The Kirkpatrick Mission*, p. 4.

63. For discussions of "liberal theory" and of democracy's relationship to international law, see Anne-Marie Slaughter Burley, "International Law and International Relations Theory: A Dual Agenda," *American Journal of International Law* 87 (April 1993): 205-239; Anne-Marie Burley, "Law Among Liberal States: Liberal Internationalism and the Act of State Doctrine," *Columbia Law Review* 92 (December 1992): 1907-1996; Gregory H. Fox, "The Right to Political Participation in International Law," *Yale Journal of International Law* 17 (1992): 539-607; Thomas M. Franck, "The Emerging Right to Democratic Governance," *American Journal of International Law* 86 (January 1992): 46-91; and Theodor Meron, "Democracy and the Rule of Law," *World Affairs* 153 (Summer 1990): 23-27.

64. For a broad legal assessment of Reagan administration policy, see Stuart S. Malawer, "Reagan's Law and Foreign Policy, 1981-1987: The 'Reagan Corollary' of International Law," *Harvard International Law Journal* 29 (Winter 1988): 85-109.

65. Gerson, *The Kirkpatrick Mission*, p. 223.

66. Weinberger, *Fighting for Peace*, p. 159.

67. Shultz, *Turmoil and Triumph*, p. 345.

68. Gerson, *The Kirkpatrick Mission*, p. 223. Author's emphasis.

69. Reagan, *An American Life*, p. 448.

70. Burley, "International Law and International Relations Theory: A Dual Agenda," p. 227; Forsythe, The Politics of International Law, pp. 149-150; Chayes, *The Cuban Missile Crisis*, p. 101. See also Stephan Haggard and Beth A. Simmons, "Theories of International Regimes," *International Organization* 41 (Summer 1987): 491-517.

71. The international legal concept of "positivism" must be distinguished here from the social scientific one. International legal "positivism" is a state-centric approach to international law that developed in the latter part of the eighteenth century. It holds that states are bound only by that to which they have given their sovereign consent. Gerhard von Glahn, *Law Among Nations* (New York, NY: Macmillan, 1992), pp. 29-30, 33-34.

Social scientific "positivism," by contrast, holds that "knowledge comes from empirical testing of propositions or hypotheses against evidence or facts." Paul R. Viotti and Mark V. Kauppi, *International Relations Theory: Realism, Pluralism, Globalism* (New York, NY: Macmillan, 1993), p. 591. In this sense, much of contemporary international relations scholarship can be characterized as "positivist."

72. Bull, *The Anarchical Society*, p. 128. See also Burley, "International Law and International Relations Theory," pp. 227, 235.

73. Professor Forsythe has tersely observed that "we cannot write a definitive history of any issue in a short treatment." Forsythe, *The Politics of International Law*, p. 6.

74. Scott Davidson, for example, acknowledged in his Grenada study: "Unfortunately, there is, at present, very little direct information on the actual decisionmaking processes of the intervening states other than relatively exiguous references in post-intervention statements and it is therefore necessary to attempt to infer from references to legal norms within those statements the importance which was attached to the law in reaching decisions. Reconstruction is thus likely to be a hazardous process." Because "the evidence is clearly incomplete and the full details of the decisionmaking process with all its variable inputs will not emerge for some time," Davidson conceded, his was only "an interim assessment." Davidson, *A Study in Politics*, pp. 159, 151.

75. Henkin, "Comment," p. 129.

76. W. Michael Reisman, "International Incidents: Introduction to a New Genre in the Study of International Law," in W. Michael Reisman and Andrew R. Willard, *International Incidents: The Law That Counts in World Politics* (Princeton: Princeton University Press, 1988), p. 21. See also Andrew R. Willard, "Incidents: An Essay in Method," in Reisman and Willard, eds., *International Incidents*, pp. 27-29.

77. Abi-Saab, *The United Nations Operation in the Congo*, pp. 195-196.

78. Examples of discourse analysis relevant to the Grenada episode include: David S. Birdsell, "Ronald Reagan on Lebanon and Grenada," *The Quarterly Journal of Speech* 73 (August 1987): 267-279; Denise M. Bostdorff, "The Presidency and Promoted Crisis: Reagan, Grenada, and Issue Management," *Presidential Studies Quarterly* 21 (Fall 1991): 737-750; William F. Lewis, "Telling America's Story: Narrative Form and the Reagan Presidency," *The Quarterly Journal of Speech* 73 (August 1987): 280-302; and Jan Servaes, "European Press Coverage of the Grenada Crisis," *Journal of Communication* 41 (Autumn 1991): 28-41.

79. For discussion and application of "interpretivist" or "reflective" approaches in international relations, see Robert Keohane, "International Institutions: Two Approaches," *International Studies Quarterly* 32 (December 1988): 379-396; Friedrich Kratochwil and John Ruggie, "International Organization: A State of the Art on the Art of the State," *International Organization* 40 (Autumn 1986): 753-775; Richard Ashley and R.B.J. Walker, "Speaking the Language of Exile: Dissident Thought in International Studies," *International Studies Quarterly* 34 (September 1990): 259-268; Alexander Wendt, "Anarchy is What States Make of It: The Social Construction of Power Politics," *International Organization* 46 (Spring 1992): 391-425; and Audie Klotz, "Reclaiming the Interpretive Study of Norms in International Relations: Epistemological, Methodological and Practical Implications," unpublished manuscript provided to author.

On interpretivism within social science generally, see David R. Hilley, James F. Bohman and Richard Shusterman, eds., *The Interpretive Turn: Philosophy, Science and Culture* (Ithaca, NY: Cornell University Press, 1991); Paul Rabinow and William Sullivan, eds., *Interpretive Social Science: A Reader* (Berkeley, CA: University of California Press, 1979) and *Interpretive Social Science: A Second Look* (Berkeley, CA: University of California Press, 1987); Jeffrey C. Alexander and Steven Seidman, eds., *Culture and Society* (Cambridge: Cambridge University Press, 1990); and Sandra Harding, *Whose Science? Whose Knowledge?* (Ithaca, NY: Cornell University Press, 1991).

80. Gerson, *The Kirkpatrick Mission*, p. 228.

81. Gerson, *The Kirkpatrick Mission*, p. 228.

82. Gerson, *The Kirkpatrick Mission*, p. 228.

83. "Ambassador Middendorf's Statement, OAS, Permanent Council, October 26, 1983," p. 73.

84. "White House Statement, November 3, 1983," p. 78.

85. Gerson, *The Kirkpatrick Mission*, p. 225.

86. Gerson, *The Kirkpatrick Mission*, p. 225.

87. "Secretary Shultz's News Conference," pp. 69-70.

88. Professor Davidson, for example, has observed: "The role which law plays in international relations depends upon the context in which it is placed." Davidson, *A Study in Politics*, p. 159.

89. The self-consciously contextual Lasswell-McDougal jurisprudence is one notable exception. See Burley, "International Law and International Relations Theory," pp. 209-211.

90. Bowie, *Suez*, p. ix.

91. Author's interview with Francis McNeil, February 24, 1989.

92. McNeil, *War and Peace in Central America*, p. 174.

93. Menges, *Inside the NSC*, pp. 81-82.

94. Reagan, *An American Life*, pp. 437, 453.

95. Lou Cannon's interview with Michael Deaver, October 24, 1983, cited in Cannon, *President Reagan*, p. 447.

96. Cited by Shapiro, "Reagan Was Reagan," p. 80.

97. Bennett, "Anatomy of a 'Go' Decision," p. 75.

98. Author's interview with Lawrence Eagleburger, March 15, 1993.

99. Weinberger, *Fighting for Peace*, pp. 109-110.

100. Weinberger, *Fighting for Peace*, p. 115.

101. "Address to the Nation," *Weekly Compilation of Presidential Documents* 19 (October 31, 1983): 1501.

102. See, for example, Carouthers, *In the Name of Democracy*, pp. 77-116; Gutman, *Banana Diplomacy*; Meese, *With Reagan*, pp. 222-227; and Schoultz, *National Security and United States Policy Towards Latin America*.

103. "Ambassador Kirkpatrick's Statement, UN Security Council, October 27, 1983," *Department of State Bulletin* 83 (December 1983): 74-76.

104. Gelb, "Shultz, With Tough Line, Is Now Key Voice in Crisis," p. A15.

105. Gerson, *The Kirkpatrick Mission*, p. 232.

106. "Address to the Nation," *Weekly Compilation of Presidential Documents* 19 (October 31, 1983): 1497-1502.

107. See Gutman, *Banana Diplomacy*, pp. 194-198; Woodward, *Veil*; and Bradlee, *Guts and Glory*, p. 169.

108. Author's interview with Lawrence Eagleburger, March 15, 1993.

109. Bennett, "Anatomy of a 'Go' Decision," p. 75; Oberdorfer, "Reagan Sought," p. A1; Weinberger, *Fighting for Peace*, p. 112; author's interview with Francis McNeil, August 11, 1988.

Appendix
Dramatis Personae - October 1983

I. UNITED STATES GOVERNMENT

White House

Ronald W. Reagan - President
George H. Bush - Vice President; chair of Special Situations Group (SSG)
James A. Baker III - White House Chief of Staff
Michael K. Deaver - Presidential Assistant
Edwin Meese III - White House Counsellor
David Gergen - White House Director of Communications
Larry M. Speakes - President's Deputy Press Secretary
Kenneth M. Duberstein - President's Congressional Liaison
Francis J. McNeil - President's Special Emissary

National Security Council Staff

William P. Clark - President's National Security Adviser; resigned October 13
Robert C. "Bud" McFarlane - President's National Security Adviser; appointed
    October 17
Vice Admiral John M. Poindexter - President's Deputy National Security
    Adviser; chair of Crisis Preplanning Group (CPPG)
Constantine C. Menges - President's National Security Assistant for Latin
    American Affairs
Lieutenant Colonel Oliver L. North - Deputy Director of Political-Military
    Affairs; Restricted Interagency Group (RIG) member
Robert B. Sims - Media Liaison

Diplomatic Representatives to International Organizations

Jeane J. Kirkpatrick - Ambassador to the United Nations
Allan Gerson - Legal Adviser to the U.S. Mission to the United Nations
William J. Middendorf, Jr. - Ambassador to the O.A.S.

U.S. Embassy - Bridgetown, Barbados

Milan D. Bish - Ambassador to Barbados
Ludlow "Kim" Flower - Deputy Chief of Mission
Kenneth A. Kurze - Foreign Service Officer
Linda Flohr - Foreign Service Officer
James Budeit - Consul General
Gary Chafin - Consular Officer
Lieutenant Colonel Lawrence Reiman - Defense Attache

State Department

George P. Shultz - Secretary of State
Kenneth W. Dam - Deputy Secretary
Lawrence S. Eagleburger - Undersecretary for Political Affairs
William Montgomery - Executive Assistant to the Undersecretary for Political
    Affairs
Langhorne A. "Tony" Motley - Assistant Secretary for Inter-American Affairs;
    chair of Restricted Interagency Group (RIG)
James H. Michel - Principal Deputy Assistant Secretary for Inter-American
    Affairs
Charles A. "Tony" Gillespie - Deputy Assistant Secretary for Inter-American
    Affairs
L. Craig Johnstone - Deputy Assistant Secretary for Inter-American Affairs
Rear Admiral Jonathan Trumbull Howe - Director of Political-Military Affairs
Davis R. Robinson - Legal Adviser
Michael G. Kozak - Deputy Legal Adviser
K. Scott Gudgeon - Assistant Legal Adviser for Inter-American Affairs
Mary E. McLeod - Assistant Legal Adviser for Political-Military Affairs
Lawrence G. Rossin - Foreign Service Officer, participated in Scoon rescue
    attempt

Central Intelligence Agency

William J. Casey - Director of Central Intelligence
John N. McMahon - Acting Director of Central Intelligence
Duane R. "Dewey" Clarridge - Latin America Division Chief of the Directorate
    of Operations; Restricted Interagency Group (RIG) member

Defense Department

Caspar W. Weinberger - Secretary of Defense
Fred C. Ikle - Undersecretary for Policy
Nestor D. Sanchez - Deputy Assistant Secretary for Inter-American Affairs; Restricted Interagency Group (RIG) member
John F. Lehman, Jr. - Secretary of the Navy
General John W. "Jack" Vessey - Chairman of the Joint Chiefs of Staff
Vice Admiral Arthur S. Moreau, Jr. - Assistant to the Chairman of the Joint Chiefs; Restricted Interagency Group (RIG) member
Commodore Jack N. Darby - Deputy Director for Plans and Policy, Joint Chiefs of Staff
General Paul X. Kelley - Commandant, Marine Corps
Admiral Wesley McDonald - Commander-in-Chief, Atlantic
Vice Admiral Joseph Metcalf III - commander of "Joint Task Force 120"
Major General H. Norman Schwarzkopf - deputy commander of "Joint Task Force 120"
Major General Richard A. Scholtes - commander of Special Operations forces
Major General Edward L. Trobaugh - commander of 82nd Airborne forces
Captain Carl Erie - commodore of Marine amphibious task force
Major General George Crist - participant in McNeil mission to Barbados

II. BRITISH GOVERNMENT

Margaret H. Thatcher - Prime Minister
Sir Geoffrey Howe - Foreign Secretary
Giles Bullard - High Commissioner in Barbados
David Montgomery - Deputy High Commissioner in Barbados
John Kelly - British representative, Grenada

III. THE OECS

Vaughan Lewis - OECS director general
(Mary) Eugenia Charles - Prime Minister of Dominica; current OECS chair
Vere Bird, Sr. - Prime Minister, Antigua and Barbuda
Lester Bird - Deputy Prime Minister and Foreign Minister, Antigua and Barbuda
John Osbourne - Chief Minister of Montserrat
Kennedy Simmonds - Prime Minister of St. Kitts-Nevis
John Compton - Prime Minister of St. Lucia
R. Milton Cato - Prime Minister of St. Vincent and the Grenadines

IV. GRENADA

Sir Paul Scoon - Governor-General
Maurice Bishop - Prime Minister, murdered on October 19
Bernard Coard - Deputy Prime Minister, New Jewel Movement's chief
    theoretician, plotted coup against Bishop
Sir Eric Gairy - former Prime Minister, ousted in 1979 coup
Dessima Williams - Ambassador to the Organization of American States

Bishop supporters

Norris Bain - PRG Minister of Housing, murdered on October 19
Jacqueline Creft - PRG Minister of Education and Bishop's pregnant mistress
Major Einstein Louison - former PRA Chief of Staff
George Louison - former PRG Minister of Agriculture and Bishop's strongest
    ally, purged from NJM
Vincent Noel - participated in ill-fated Bishop rescue attempt
Lynden Ramdhanny - PRG Minister of Tourism
Unison Whiteman - PRG Foreign Minister

Coard supporters

General Hudson Austin - head of PRA, proclaimed formation of Revolutionary
    Military Council
Major Leon "Bogo" Cornwall - negotiated with U.S. diplomats
Major Christopher Stroud - commander of Fort Rupert
Lieutenant Colonel Ewart "Headache" Layne - directed counter-Bishop operation
Lieutenant Lester "Goat" Redhead - participated in Bishop's murder
Lieutenant Iman Abdullah - participated in murder of Bishop and colleagues

V. OTHER CARIBBEAN STATES

Tom Adams - Prime Minister of Barbados
Bernard "Bree" St. John - Deputy Prime Minister of Barbados
Louis Tull - Foreign Minister of Barbados
Brigadier General Rudyard Lewis - commander of Barbadian Defence Force
Edward Seaga - Prime Minister of Jamaica
Neville Gallimore - Foreign Minister of Jamaica
Forbes Burnham - President of Guyana
George Chambers - Prime Minister of Trinidad and Tobago
Sir Lynden Pindling - Prime Minister of the Bahamas
George Price - Prime Minister of Belize

Bibliography

I. INTERVIEWS

A. Author's interviews/correspondence

Bish, Milan D. Former U.S. Ambassador to Barbados. Telephone interviews conducted on August 24, 1988; September 26, 1988; October 20, 1988; and October 26, 1988.

Eagleburger, Lawrence S. Former Undersecretary of State for Political Affairs. In-person interview conducted on March 15, 1993.

Flower, Ludlow. Former Deputy Chief of Mission, U.S. Embassy, Barbados. Telephone interview conducted on July 6, 1989.

Gerson, Allan. Former Legal Adviser to the U.S. Mission to the United Nations. Telephone interview conducted on November 4, 1988.

Gudgeon, K. Scott. Former State Department Assistant Legal Adviser for Inter-American Affairs. Letters to author dated November 15, 1988; April 28, 1989.

Ikle, Fred. Former Undersecretary of Defense for Policy. In-person interview conducted on July 20, 1989.

Johnstone, L. Craig. Former Principal Deputy Assistant Secretary of State for Inter-American Affairs. Background interview.

Kozak, Michael G. Former State Department Deputy Legal Adviser. In-person interview conducted November 3, 1988.

Kurze, Kenneth A. Retired U.S. Foreign Service Officer. Letters to the author dated September 29, 1991; October 8, 1992. Telephone interview conducted on May 15, 1992.

McFarlane, Robert C. Former National Security Adviser. Background letter to author.

McNeil, Francis J. Former Special Emissary of the President. Telephone interviews conducted on August 11, 1988; November 11, 1988; and February 24, 1989. In-person interview conducted on September 20, 1988.

Menges, Constantine C. Former Latin America Adviser, National Security Council. In-person interview conducted on September 21, 1988.

Motley, Langhorne A. Former Assistant Secretary of State for Inter-American Affairs. In-person interviews conducted on September 20, 1988; November 4, 1988. Telephone interview conducted on March 7, 1988.

Robinson, Davis. Former State Department Legal Adviser. In-person interview conducted on September 21, 1988.

Rossin, Lawrence G. Foreign Service Officer. Letters to author dated March 20, 1989; June 12, 1989.

B.   Other interviews

Lind, William S. Former Senate aide and President of the Military Reform Institute. Interviewed by Seymour Hersh in "Operation Urgent Fury," a PBS "Frontline" report broadcast on February 2, 1988.

Motley, Langhorne A. Interviewed by Seymour Hersh in "Operation Urgent Fury," a PBS "Frontline" report broadcast on February 2, 1988.

Schwarzkopf, Major General H. Norman. Interviewed by Seymour Hersh in "Operation Urgent Fury," a PBS "Front Line" report broadcast on February 2, 1988.

Louison, George. Interview conducted by International Press correspondent Mohammed Oliver, International Press, April 14, 1984.

II.   U.S. GOVERNMENT DOCUMENTS

A.   Weekly Compilation of Presidential Documents

"Address Before the Permanent Council of the Organization of American States, February 24, 1982." *Weekly Compilation of Presidential Documents* 18 (March 1, 1982): 217-223.

"Remarks at Bridgetown, Barbados, April 8, 1982." *Weekly Compilation of Presidential Documents* 18 (April 19, 1982): 463.

"Central America and El Salvador, March 10, 1983." *Weekly Compilation of Presidential Documents* 19 (March 14, 1983): 376-382.

"National Security: Address to the Nation, March 23, 1983." *Weekly Compilation of Presidential Documents* 19 (March 28, 1983): 445.

"Radio Address to the Nation, October 22, 1983," *Weekly Compilation of Presidential Documents* 19 (October 31, 1983): 1479-1480.

"Remarks and a Question-and-Answer Session With Regional Editors and Broadcasters, October 24, 1983." *Weekly Compilation of Presidential Documents* 19 (October 31, 1983): 1482-1486.

"Address to the Nation, October 27, 1983." *Weekly Compilation of Presidential Documents* 19 (October 31, 1983): 1497-1502.

"Remarks to Citizens, February 20, 1986." *Weekly Compilation of Presidential Documents* 22 (February 24, 1986): 248-251.

B.   Department of State Bulletin

"President's Remarks, October 25, 1983." *Department of State Bulletin* 83 (December 1983): 67.

"OECS Statement, October 25, 1983." *Department of State Bulletin* 83 (December 1983): 67-68.

"Secretary Shultz's News Conference, October 25, 1983." *Department of State Bulletin* 83 (December 1983): 69-72.

"Ambassador Middendorf's Statement, OAS, Permanent Council, October 26, 1983." *Department of State Bulletin* 83 (December 1983): 72-73.

"Ambassador Kirkpatrick's Statement, UN Security Council, October 27, 1983." *Department of State Bulletin* 83 (December 1983): 74-76.

"Ambassador Kirkpatrick's Statement, UN General Assembly, November 2, 1983." *Department of State Bulletin* 83 (December 1983): 76-77.

"White House Statement, November 3, 1983." *Department of State Bulletin* 83 (December 1983): 78.

"President's Remarks and Question-And-Answer Session (Excerpts), November 3, 1983." *Department of State Bulletin* 83 (December 1983): 78-79.

"Deputy Secretary Dam's Remarks, Louisville, November 4, 1983." *Department of State Bulletin* 83 (December 1983): 79-82.

Langhorne A. Motley, "The Decision to Assist Grenada." *Department of State Bulletin* 84 (March 1984): 70-73.

C. Foreign Broadcast Information Service

"Bridgetown CANA report by Albert Brandford, 8:30 PM Grenada time, October 19, 1983." *Unclassified FBIS - Latin America*, October 24, 1983, p. S2.

"Bridgetown CANA report, 6:40 PM Grenada time, October 22, 1983." *Unclassified FBIS - Latin America*, October 24, 1983, p. S18.

"St. George's Domestic Service, 6:10 PM Grenada time, October 23, 1983." *Unclassified FBIS - Latin America*, October 24, 1983, p. S23.

"Bridgetown CANA report, 7:30 PM Grenada time, October 23, 1983." *Unclassified FBIS - Latin America*, October 24, 1983, p. S10.

D. Other U.S. Government Documents

U.S. Army. Office of Public Affairs. Consolidated List, Grenada casualties, June 1984.

U.S. Congress. House of Representatives. Committee on Foreign Affairs, Subcommittee on Inter-American Affairs. *United States Policy toward Grenada*, 97th Congress, 2nd session, 1982.

U.S. Congress. House of Representatives. Subcommittees on International Security and Scientific Affairs and on Western Hemisphere Affairs of the Committee on Foreign Affairs. *U.S. Military Actions in Grenada: Implications for U.S. Policy in the Eastern Caribbean*, 98th Congress, 1st session, 1983.

U.S. Congress. Senate. Committee on Foreign Relations. *The Situation in Grenada*, 98th Congress, 1st session, 1983.

U.S. Department of State. Bureau of Public Affairs. "Caribbean Basin Initiative, February 24, 1982," Current Policy No. 370.

U.S. Department of State. Bureau of Public Affairs. "Background Notes: Grenada," March 1980.

U.S. Department of State and Department of Defense. "Grenada: A Preliminary Report." December 16, 1983.

U.S. Department of State and Department of Defense. *Grenada Documents: An Overview and Selection*, 3 vols. September 24, 1984. Edited by Michael Ledeen and Herbert Romerstein.

III. OTHER DOCUMENTS/PAMPHLETS

American Foreign Service Association. *Duty & Danger: The American Foreign Service In Action*. Washington, D.C.: American Foreign Service Association, 1988.

Documents on the Invasion of Grenada, Caribbean Monthly Bulletin. October 1983, Supplement No. 1, Item XX, pp. 87-88.

Embassy of Grenada. "Proceedings of Aid Donors Meeting Held in Brussels at ACP House, 1981." *International Airport Project — Grenada*.

Great Britain. Parliament. House of Commons. Foreign Affairs Committee, Fifth Report. *Caribbean and Central America*. Session 1981-1982.

Great Britain. Parliament. House of Commons. Foreign Affairs Committee, Second Report. *Grenada*. Session 1983-1984.

Lind, William S. *Report to the Congressional Military Reform Caucus: The Grenada Operation*. Washington, D.C.: Military Reform Institute, 1984.

IV. MEMOIR ACCOUNTS

Deaver, Michael K. *Behind the Scenes*. New York: William Morrow, 1987.

Meese, Edwin, III. *With Reagan: The Inside Story*. Washington, D.C.: Regnery Gateway, 1992.

Gerson, Allan. *The Kirkpatrick Mission: Diplomacy Without Apology. America at the United Nations 1981-1985*. New York: The Free Press, 1991.

Lehman, John F., Jr. *Command of the Seas*. New York: Charles Scribner's Sons, 1988.

McNeil, Frank. *War and Peace In Central America: Reality and Illusion*. New York: Charles Scribner's Sons, 1988.

Menges, Constantine C. *Inside the National Security Council: The True Story of the Making and Unmaking of Reagan's Foreign Policy*. New York: Simon and Schuster, 1988.

O'Neill, Thomas P. *Man of the House.* New York: Random House, 1987.

Reagan, Ronald W. *An American Life: The Autobiography.* New York: Simon and Schuster, 1990.

Schwarzkopf, H. Norman, with Peter Petre. *General H. Norman Schwarzkopf: The Autobiography: It Doesn't Take A Hero.* New York: Linda Grey Bantam Books, 1992.

Shultz, George P. *Turmoil and Triumph: My Years as Secretary of State.* New York: Charles Scribner's Sons, 1993.

Speakes, Larry. *Speaking Out.* New York: Charles Scribner's Sons, 1988.

Weinberger, Caspar W. *Fighting for Peace: Seven Critical Years in the Pentagon.* New York: Warner Books, 1990.

V.   BOOKS ON INTERNATIONAL LAW

Abi-Saab, Georges. *The United Nations In the Congo 1960-1964.* New York: Oxford University Press, 1979.

Akehurst, Michael. *A Modern Introduction to International Law.* 5th ed. London: Allen and Unwin, 1985.

Arend, Anthony Clark, and Robert J. Beck. *International Law and the Use of Force: Beyond the U.N. Charter Paradigm.* London: Routledge, 1993.

Blaustein, Albert P., and Gisbert H. Flanz, eds. *Constitutions of the Countries of the World.* Dobbs Ferry, New York: Oceana Publications, 1974.

Bowett, Derek. *Self-Defense in International Law.* Manchester: Manchester University Press, 1958.

Bowie, Robert R. *Suez 1956.* New York: Oxford University Press, 1974.

Boyle, Francis A. *The Future of International Law and American Foreign Policy.* Ardsley-on-Hudson, NY: Transnational Publishers, 1989.

____. *World Politics and International Law.* Durham, NC: Duke University Press, 1985.

Brierly, J.L. *The Law of Nations.* Oxford: Oxford University Press, 1963.

Brownlie, Ian. *International Law and the Use of Force by States.* Oxford: Clarendon Press, 1963.

Bull, Hedley. *The Anarchical Society: A Study of Order in World Politics.* New York: Columbia University Press, 1977.

Chayes, Abram. *The Cuban Missile Crisis: International Crises and the Role of Law.* New York: Oxford University Press, 1974.

Claude, Inis L., Jr. *Power and International Relations.* New York: Random House, 1962.

Coplin, William D. *The Functions of International Law.* Chicago: Rand McNally, 1966.

Davidson, Scott. *Grenada: A Study in Politics and the Limits of International Law.* Aldershot: Avebury, 1987.

Deutsch, Karl W., and Stanley Hoffmann, eds. *The Relevance of International Law: Essays in Honor of Leo Gross*. Cambridge: Shenman Publishing Co., 1971.

de Smith, Stanley A. *The New Commonwealth and its Constitutions*. London: Stevens, 1964.

Dore, Isaak I. *International Law and the Superpowers: Normative Order in a Divided World*. New Brunswick, NY: Rutgers University Press, 1984.

Ehrlich, Thomas. *Cyprus 1958-1967*. New York: Oxford University Press, 1974.

Erickson, Richard J. *Legitimate Use of Military Force Against State-Sponsored International Terrorism*. Maxwell Air Force Base, AL: Air University Press, 1989.

Fisher, Roger. *Improving Compliance With International Law*. Charlottesville: University of Virginia Press, 1981.

____. *Points of Choice*. New York: Oxford University Press, 1978.

Forsythe, David P. *The Politics of International Law: U.S. Foreign Policy Reconsidered*. Boulder, Colo.: Lynne Rienner, 1990.

Gilmore, William C. *The Grenada Intervention: Analysis and Documentation*. London: Mansell, 1984.

Goodrich, Leland, Edvard Hambro, and Anne Patricia Simons. *The Charter of the United Nations*. 3rd ed. New York: Columbia University Press, 1969.

Gould, Wesley L., and Michael Markun, eds. *International Law and the Social Sciences*. Princeton: Princeton University Press, 1970.

Grotius, Hugo. *De Jure Belli Ac Pacis*. Edited by James B. Scott. Volume Two. *The Translation*. Translated by Francis W. Kelsey et al. Oxford: Clarendon Press, 1925.

Henkin, Louis. *How Nations Behave: Law and Foreign Policy*. New York: Columbia University Press, 1979.

Henkin, Louis, et al. *Right v. Might: International Law and the Use of Force*. New York and London: Council on Foreign Relations Press, 1989.

Hoyt, Edwin G. *Law and Force in American Foreign Policy*. Lanham, MD: University Press of America, 1985.

Jessup, Philip C. *A Modern Law of Nations*. New York: Macmillan, 1958.

Johnson, James T. *Just War Tradition and the Restraint of War*. Princeton: Princeton University Press, 1981.

Kaplan, Morton A., and Nicholas Katzenbach. *The Political Foundations of International Law*. New York: Wiley, 1961.

Levi, Werner. *Law and Politics in the International Society*. Beverly Hills, CA: Sage, 1976.

McDougal, Myres S., and Florentino P. Feliciano. *Law and Minimum World Public Order*. New Haven, Conn.: Yale University Press, 1961.

McNair, Arnold Duncan. *The Law of Treaties*. Oxford: Clarendon Press,1961.

Moore, John Norton. *Law and the Grenada Mission*. Charlottesville, VA: Center for Law and National Security, 1984.

O'Brien, William V. *U.S. Military Intervention: Law and Morality*. Washington Papers, No. 68. Beverly Hills, Calif.: Sage/Center for Strategic and International Studies, Georgetown University, 1979.

____. *The Conduct of Just and Limited War*. New York: Praeger, 1981.

Oppenheim, L. *International Law: A Treatise*. Vol. 1. *Peace*. 5th ed. Edited by Hersh Lauterpacht. London: Longman, 1955.

Reisman, W. Michael, and Andrew R. Willard, eds., *International Incidents: The Law That Counts in World Politics*. Princeton: Princeton University Press, 1988.

Ronzitti, Natalino. *Rescuing Nationals Abroad through Military Coercion and Intervention on Grounds of Humanity*. Dordrecht: Martinus Nijhoff, 1985.

Sheinman, Lawrence, and David Wilkinson, eds. *International Law and Political Crisis: An Analytical Casebook*. Boston: Little Brown, 1968.

Tesón, Fernando R. *Humanitarian Intervention: An Inquiry into Law and Morality*. Dobbs Ferry, NY: Transnational Publishers, 1988.

Thomas, Ann Van Wynen, and A. J. Thomas, Jr. *Non-Intervention: The Law and Its Import in the Americas*. Dallas: Southern Methodist University Press, 1956.

Von Glahn, Gerhard. *Law Among Nations*. New York, NY: Macmillan, 1992.

VI. BOOKS ON THE REAGAN ADMINISTRATION

Bradlee, Ben, Jr. *Guts and Glory: The Rise and Fall of Oliver North*. New York: Donald I. Fine, Inc., 1988.

Cannon, Lou. *President Reagan: The Role of a Lifetime*. New York: Simon & Schuster, 1992.

Carothers, Thomas. *In the Name of Democracy: U.S. Policy Toward Latin America in the Reagan Years*. Berkeley: University of California Press, 1991.

Emerson, Steven. *Secret Warriors: Inside the Covert Military Operations of the Reagan Era*. New York: G.P. Putnam's Sons, 1988.

Gutman, Roy. *Banana Diplomacy: The Making of American Foreign Policy in Nicaragua, 1981-1987*. New York: Simon and Schuster, 1988.

Hertsgaard, Mark. *On Bended Knee: The Press and the Reagan Presidency*. New York: Farrar Straus Giroux, 1988.

Martin, David C., and John Walcott. *Best Laid Plans: The Inside Story of America's War Against Terrorism*. New York: Harper & Row, 1988.

Smith, Geoffrey. *Reagan and Thatcher*. London: The Bodley Head, 1990.

Smith, Hedrick. *The Power Game: How Washington Works*. New York: Random House, 1988.

Woodward, Bob. *Veil: The Secret Wars of the CIA*. New York: Simon & Schuster, 1987.

VII. BOOKS ON NATIONAL SECURITY AND FOREIGN POLICY

Gabriel, Richard A. *Military Incompetence*. New York: Hill & Wang, 1985.

Hartmann, Frederick H., and Robert L. Wendzel. *Defending American Security*. Washington, D.C.: Pergammon-Brassey, 1988.

Kennedy, Robert F. *Thirteen Days: A Memoir of the Cuban Missile Crisis*. New York: W. W. Norton & Company, 1968.

Kissinger, Henry A. *White House Years*. Boston: Little Brown, 1979.

Kwitney, Jonathan. *Endless Enemies: The Making of an Unfriendly World*. New York: Congdon & Weed, 1984.

Livingstone, Neil C., and Terrell E. Arnold, eds. *Fighting Back: Winning the War Against Terrorism*. Lexington, MA: Lexington Books, 1986.

Luttwak, Edward. *The Pentagon and the Art of War*. New York: Simon and Schuster, 1985.

Schoultz, Lars. *National Security and United States Policy Towards Latin America*. Princeton: Princeton University Press, 1987.

Sick, Gary. *All Fall Down*. New York: Viking Penguin, 1985.

Viotti, Paul R., and Mark V. Kauppi. *International Relations Theory: Realism, Pluralism, Globalism*. New York, NY: Macmillan, 1993.

VIII. BOOKS ON GRENADA AND THE CARIBBEAN

Adkin, Mark. *Urgent Fury: The Battle for Grenada*. Lexington, Mass.: D.C. Heath and Company, 1989.

Bishop, Maurice. *Selected Speeches, 1979-81*. Havana: Casade las Americas, 1982.

Burrowes, Reynold A. *Revolution and Rescue in Grenada: An Account of the U.S.-Caribbean Invasion*. New York: Greenwood Press, 1988.

Dujmovic, Nicholas. *The Grenada Documents: Window on Totalitarianism*. Washington, D.C.: Pergammon-Brassey's, 1988.

Dunn, Peter M., and Bruce W. Watson, eds. *American Intervention in Grenada: The Implications of Operation Urgent Fury*. Boulder, Colo.: Westview Press, 1985.

EPICA Task Force. *Grenada: The Peaceful Revolution*. Washington, D.C.: EPICA Task Force, 1982.

Heine, Jorge and Leslie Manigat, eds. *The Caribbean and World Politics: Cross Currents and Cleavages*. New York: Holmes & Meier, 1988.

Latin American Bureau. *Grenada: Whose Freedom?* London: Latin American Bureau, 1984.

Lewis, Gordon K. *Grenada: The Jewel Despoiled.* Baltimore: Johns Hopkins, 1987.

MacDonald, Scott B., Harald M. Sandstrom, and Paul B. Goodwin, Jr., eds. *The Caribbean After Grenada: Revolution, Conflict, and Democracy.* New York: Praeger, 1988.

Marcus, Bruce, and Michael Taber, eds. *Maurice Bishop Speaks: The Grenada Revolution, 1979-83.* New York: Pathfinder Press, 1983.

O'Shaughnessy, Hugh. *Grenada: Revolution, Invasion and Aftermath.* London: Hamilton Hamish, 1984.

Payne, Anthony, et al. *Grenada: Revolution and Invasion.* New York: St.Martin's Press, 1984.

Sandford, Gregory. *The New Jewel Movement: Grenada's Revolution.* Washington, D.C.: Foreign Service Institute, 1985.

Sandford, Gregory, and Richard Vigilante. *Grenada: The Untold Story.* New York: Madison Books, 1984.

Seabury, Paul, and Walter A. McDougall, eds. *The Grenada Papers.* San Francisco: Institute for Contemporary Studies, 1984.

Searle, Chris. *Grenada: The Struggle Against Destabilization.* London: Writers and Readers Publishing, 1983.

Schoenhals, Kai, and Richard A. Melanson. *Revolution and Intervention in Grenada: The New Jewel Movement, the United States, and the Caribbean.* Boulder, Colo.: Westview Press, 1985.

Spector, Ronald H. *U.S. Marines in Grenada.* Washington, D.C.: History and Museums Division Headquarters, 1987.

Valenta, Jiri, and Herbert J. Ellison, eds. *Grenada and Soviet/Cuban Policy: Internal Crisis and U.S./OECS Intervention.* Boulder, Colo.: Westview Press, 1986.

IX. LAW JOURNAL ARTICLES

Arend, Anthony Clark. "International Law and the Recourse to Force: A Shift in Paradigms." *Stanford Journal of International Law* 27 (1990): 1-47.

Badr, Gamal M. "The Exculpatory Effect of Self-Defence in State Responsibility." *Georgia Journal of International and Comparative Law* 10 (1980): 1-28.

Boyle, Francis A. Boyle, et al. "International Lawlessness in Grenada," *American Journal of International Law* 78 (January 1984): 172-175.

Burley, Anne-Marie Slaughter. "International Law and International Relations Theory: A Dual Agenda." *American Journal of International Law* 87 (April 1993): 205-239.

Burley, Anne-Marie. "Law Among Liberal States: Liberal Internationalism and the Act of State Doctrine." *Columbia Law Review* 92 (December 1992): 1907-1996.

Dieguez, Richard P. "The Grenada Invasion: 'Illegal' in Form, Sound as Policy." *New York University Journal of International Law and Politics* 16 (Summer 1984): 1167-1203.

Dore, Isaak I. "The US Invasion of Grenada: Resurrection of the 'Johnson Doctrine?'" *Stanford Journal of International Law* 20 (Spring 1984): 173-189.

Doswald-Beck, L. "The Legality of the U.S. Intervention in Grenada." *Netherlands International Law Review* 31 (1984): 355-377.

Fox, Gregory H. "The Right to Political Participation in International Law." *Yale Journal of International Law* 17 (1992): 539-607.

Franck, Thomas M. "The Emerging Right to Democratic Governance." *American Journal of International Law* 86 (January 1992): 46-91

Fraser, H. Aubrey. "Grenada: The Sovereignty of the People." *West Indian Law Journal* 7 (October 1983): 205-291.

Gordon, Edward, et al. "International Law and the United States Action in Grenada." *International Law* 18 (1984): 331-419.

Henkin, Louis. "Force, Intervention and Neutrality in Contemporary International Law." *Proceedings of the American Society of International Law* (1963): 147-173.

Iacewicz, Andrzej. "The Concept of Force in the United Nations Charter." *Polish Yearbook of International Law* 9 (1977-1978): 137-159.

Joyner, Christopher. "Reflections on the Lawfulness of Invasion." *American Journal of International Law* 78 (January 1984): 131-144.

Karas, Jon M., and Jerald M. Goodman. "The United States Action in Grenada: An Exercise in Realpolitik." *University of Miami Inter-American Law Review* 16 (Spring 1984): 53-108.

Levitin, Michael J. "The Law of Force and the Force of Law: Grenada, the Falklands, and Humanitarian Intervention." *Harvard International Law Journal* 27 (Spring 1986): 621-657.

Malawer, Stuart S. "Reagan's Law and Foreign Policy, 1981-1987: The 'Reagan Corollary' of International Law." *Harvard International Law Journal* 29 (Winter 1988): 85-109.

Moore, John Norton. "Grenada and the International Double Standard." *American Journal of International Law* 78 (January 1984): 145-168.

____. "The Secret War in Central America and the Future of World Order." *American Journal of International Law* 80 (January 1986): 43-127.

Mosler, Hermann. "The International Society as a Legal Community." *Recueil des Cours* 140 (1974-IV): 11-320.

Nanda, Ved P. "The United States Intervention in Grenada — Impact on World Order." *California Western International Law Journal* 14 (Summer 1984): 395-424.

Quigley, John. "The United States Invasion of Grenada: Stranger than Fiction." *The University of Miami Inter-American Law Review* 18 (Winter, 1986-1987): 271-352.

Riggs, Ronald M. "The Grenada Intervention: A Legal Analysis." *Military Law Review* 1 (Summer 1985): 1-81.

Smart, P. St. J. "Revolutions, Constitutions and the Commonwealth: Grenada." *International and Comparative Law Quarterly* 35 (October 1986): 950-960.

Vagts, Detlev. "International Law Under Time Pressure: Grading the Grenada Take-Home Examination." *American Journal of International Law* 79 (January 1984): 169-172.

Verdross, Alfred. "Jus Dispositivum and Jus Cogens in International Law." *American Journal of International Law* 60 (1966): 55-63.

Waldcock, Claude H. M. "The Regulation of Force by Individual States in International Law." *Recueil des Cours* 81 (1952 - II): 455-515.

Waters, Maurice. "The Invasion of Grenada, 1983, and the Collapse of Legal Norms." *Journal of Peace Research* 23 (September 1986): 229-246.

____. "The Law and Politics of a U.S. Intervention: The Case of Grenada. *Peace & Change* 14 (January 1989): 65-105.

Wheeler, Laura K. "The Grenada Invasion: Expanding the Scope of Humanitarian Intervention." *Boston College International and Comparative Law Review* 8 (Summer 1985): 413-430.

X. ARTICLES IN EDITED VOLUMES

Ashby, Timothy. "The Reagan Years." In *The Caribbean After Grenada*, pp. 269-278. Edited by Scott B. MacDonald, Harald M. Sandstrom, and Paul B. Goodwin, Jr. New York: Praeger, 1988.

Cypher, Dorothea. "Urgent Fury: The U.S. Army in Grenada." In *American Intervention in Grenada: The Implications of Operation Urgent Fury*, pp. 99-108. Edited by Peter M. Dunn and Bruce W. Watson. Boulder, Colo.: Westview Press, 1985.

Fonteyne, J.B.L. "Forcible Self-Help by States to Protect Human Rights: Recent Views from the United Nations." In *Humanitarian Intervention and the United Nations*, pp. 197-221. Edited by Richard B. Lillich. Charlottesville: University of Virginia Press, 1973.

Hall, David K. "The Grenada Intervention." In *Selected Readings in Defense Economics and Decision Making*. Newport, Rhode Island: U.S. Naval War College, 1985.

Hayes, Margaret Daly. "Girding for the Long Run." In *Grenada and Soviet/Cuban Policy: Internal Crisis and U.S./OECS Intervention*, pp. 211-224. Edited by Jiri Valenta and Herbert Ellison. Boulder, Colo.: Westview Press, 1986.

Hopple, Gerald, and Cynthia Gilley. "Policy Without Intelligence." In *American Intervention in Grenada: The Implications of Operation Urgent Fury*, pp. 55-72. Edited by Peter M. Dunn and Bruce W. Watson. Boulder, Colo.: Westview Press, 1985.

Manigat, Leslie. "Grenada: Revolutionary Shockwave, Crisis, and Intervention." In *The Caribbean and World Politics: Cross Currents and Cleavages*, pp. 178-221. Edited by Jorge Jeine and Leslie Manigat. New York: Holmes & Meier, 1988.

Moore, John Norton. "The Role of Regional Arrangements in the Maintenance of World Order." In *The Future of the International Legal Order*. Vol. III. *Conflict Management*, pp. 122-164. Edited by Cyril E. Black and Richard A. Falk. Princeton: Princeton University Press, 1971.

_____. "Toward an Applied Theory for the Regulation of Intervention." In *Law and Civil War in the Modern World*, pp. 3-37. Edited by John Norton Moore. Baltimore: Johns Hopkins University Press, 1974.

Pastor, Robert. "Grenada and the American Foreign Policy Context." In *American Intervention in Grenada: The Implications of Operation Urgent Fury*, pp. 15-28. Edited by Peter M. Dunn and Bruce W. Watson. Boulder, Colo.: Westview Press, 1985.

_____. "The Invasion of Grenada: A Pre- and Post-Mortem." In *The Caribbean After Grenada*, pp. 87-108. Edited by Scott B. MacDonald, Harald M. Sandstrom, and Paul B. Goodwin, Jr. New York: Praeger, 1988.

Reisman, Michael, and Myres S. McDougal. "Humanitarian Intervention to Protect the Ibos." In *Humanitarian Intervention and the United Nations*, pp. 167-195. Edited by Richard B. Lillich. Charlottesville: University of Virginia Press, 1973.

Salamanca, Beth A. "Vehicle Bombs: Death on Wheels." In *Fighting Back: Winning the War Against Terrorism*, pp. 35-47. Edited by Neil C. Livingstone and Terrell E. Arnold. Lexington, Mass.: Lexington, 1986.

Uhlig, Frank, Jr. "Amphibious Aspects of the Grenada Episode." In *American Intervention in Grenada: The Implications of Operation Urgent Fury*, pp. 89-98. Edited by Peter M. Dunn and Bruce W. Watson. Boulder, Colo.: Westview Press, 1985.

Valenta, Jiri and Virginia Valenta. "Leninism and Grenada." In *Grenada and Soviet/Cuban Policy: Internal Crisis and U.S./OECS Intervention*, pp. 3-37. Edited by Jiri Valenta and Herbert J. Ellison. Boulder, Colo.: Westview Press, 1986.

Wiarda, Howard. "The Impact of Grenada in Central America." In *Grenada and Soviet/Cuban Policy: Internal Crisis and U.S./OECS Intervention*, pp. 105-122. Edited by Jiri Valenta and Herbert J. Ellison. Boulder, Colo.: Westview Press, 1986.

Zakheim, Dov. "The Grenada Operation and Superpower Relations: A Perspective from the Pentagon." In *Grenada and Soviet/Cuban Policy: Internal Crisis and U.S./OECS Intervention*, pp. 175-185. Edited by Jiri Valenta and Herbert J. Ellison. Boulder, Colo.: Westview Press, 1986.

XI. SIGNED PERIODICAL ARTICLES

Adams, William C. "The Public's Attitudes." *Public Opinion* 7 (February/March 1984): 53-55.

Adelman, Kenneth et al. "Where We Succeeded, Where We Failed: Lessons from Reagan Officials for the Next Conservative Presidency." *Policy Review*, no. 43 (Winter 1988), pp. 44-57.

Akehurst, Michael. "The Use of Force to Protect Nationals Abroad." *International Relations* 5 (May 1977): 3-23.

Ashley, Richard, and R.B.J. Walker. "Speaking the Language of Exile: Dissident Thought in International Studies." *International Studies Quarterly* 34 (September 1990): 259-268.

Beck, Robert J. "The 'McNeil Mission' and the Decision to Invade Grenada." *Naval War College Review* 44 (Spring 1991): 93-112.

Bishop, Maurice. "U.S. Preparing to Invade Grenada." El Salvador Solidarity Campaign, *El Salvador News Bulletin*, no. 10 (September 1981).

Bostdorff, Denise M. "The Presidency and Promoted Crisis." *Presidential Studies Quarterly* 21 (Fall 1991): 737-750.

Chayes, Abram. "Law and the Quarantine of Cuba." *Foreign Affairs* 41 (1962-63): 550-557.

Diederich, Bernard. "Interviewing George Louison: A PRG Minister Discusses the Killings." *Caribbean Review* 12 (Fall 1983): 17-18.

Haggard, Stephan, and Beth A. Simmons. "Theories of International Regimes." *International Organization* 41 (Summer 1987): 491-517.

Keohane, Robert. "International Institutions: Two Approaches." *International Studies Quarterly* 32 (December 1988): 379-396.

Kratochwil, Friedrich, and John Ruggie. "International Organization: A State of the Art on the Art of the State." *International Organization* 40 (Autumn 1986): 753-775.

Leiken, Robert S. "Eastern Winds in Latin America." *Foreign Policy*, no. 42 (Spring 1981), pp. 94-113.

Maingot, Anthony P. "Options for Grenada: The Need to be Cautious." *Caribbean Review* 12 (Fall 1983): 24-28.

Meron, Theodor. "Democracy and the Rule of Law." *World Affairs* 153 (Summer 1990): 23-27.

Motley, James Berry. "Grenada: Low Intensity Conflict and the Use of U.S. Military Power." *World Affairs* 16 (Winter 1983-1984): 221-238.

Owens, Mackubin Thomas. "Grenada, Nicaragua and International Law." *This World*, no. 9 (Fall 1984), pp. 3-14.

Renfrew, Nita A., and Peter Blauner. "Ollie's Army." *New York*, December 7, 1987, pp. 101-134.

Robinson, Michael Jay, and Maura Clancey. "Student Attitudes." *Public Opinion* 7 (February/March 1984): 52-53.

Wendt, Alexander. "Anarchy is What States Make of It: The Social Construction of Power Politics." *International Organization* 46 (Spring 1992): 391-425.

Index

About the Book and Author

Robert Beck's study focuses principally on two related questions. First, how did the Reagan administration decide to launch the invasion of Grenada? And second, what role did international law play in that decision? *The Grenada Invasion* draws on extensive interviews and correspondence with key participants—and on the recently published memoirs of those who participated in or witnessed the administration's deliberations—in order to render a new and more complete picture of Operation "Urgent Fury" decisionmaking. Beck concludes that international law did not determine policy, but that it acted briefly as a restraint and then as a justification for action.

Robert J. Beck is assistant professor in the Woodrow Wilson Department of Government and Foreign Affairs of the University of Virginia. He is coauthor of *International Law and the Use of Force: Beyond the U.N. Charter Paradigm* (1993).